G000272465

CORNISH STUDIES

Second Series

FOURTEEN

INSTITUTE OF CORNISH STUDIES

EDITOR'S NOTE

Cornish Studies (second series) exists to reflect current research conducted internationally in the inter-disciplinary field of Cornish Studies. It is edited by Professor Philip Payton, Director of the Institute of Cornish Studies at the University of Exeter, Cornwall Campus, and is published by University of Exeter Press. The opinions expressed in *Cornish Studies* are those of individual authors and are not necessarily those of the editor or publisher. The support of Cornwall County Council is gratefully acknowledged.

Cover illustration: 'Padstow Minstrels circa 1900', from the Padstow Archive. Reprinted courtesy of the Padstow Museum.

CORNISH STUDIES

Second Series

FOURTEEN

Edited by

Philip Payton

UNIVERSITY
of
EXETER
PRESS

First published in 2006 by
University of Exeter Press
Reed Hall, Streatham Drive
Exeter, Devon EX4 4QR
UK
www.exeterpress.co.uk

© Philip Payton 2006

British Library Cataloguing in Publication Data
A catalogue record for this book is
available from the British Library

ISBN 10: 0 85989 799 0
ISBN 13: 978 0 85989 799 0
ISSN: 1352-271X

Typeset in 10/12pt Times by Kestrel Data, Exeter

Printed and bound in Great Britain by
Short Run Press Ltd, Exeter

Contents

INTRODUCTION

One of the many roles of Cornish Studies as a discipline—and, therefore, of the series *Cornish Studies* itself—is to inform, influence and
assist those planners and policymakers charged with guiding Cornwall's
future. In the past, articles on subjects as disparate as tourism,
devolution, housing, in-migration, and the environment have proved
useful documents in the hands of such practitioners. The more general
elucidation of Cornwall's history, culture and identity in *Cornish
Studies* has also provided a substantial and authoritative corpus from
which those who are required to understand Cornwall and the Cornish
might draw.

The nature and future of the revived Cornish language is one of
the many themes that has been explored over time in the pages
of *Cornish Studies*, notably in Kenneth MacKinnon's seminal 'Cornish
at its Millennium: An Independent Study of the Language Undertaken
in 2000' in *Cornish Studies: Ten* (2002). As a direct result of the
Mackinnon report, furnished for the Government Office South West
and discussed in Mackinnon's important article in *Cornish Studies: Ten*,
the Cornish language now has a degree of 'official' recognition from
the British State. This, in turn, has prompted the creation of a language
strategy by Cornwall County Council, together with the allocation of
central government funding to support that strategy. There are now
opportunities for the development of Cornish—not least in schools and
in education generally—that simply did not exist before. But a major
obstacle to progress is the continuing lack of a single, standard written
form of the language, one of the many legacies of the essentially
amateur way the revival of Cornish was managed in the twentieth
century. Not surprisingly, the Cornish Language Partnership—a public
and voluntary partnership established to foster the development of
the language (which includes among others both Cornwall County
Council and the Institute of Cornish Studies)—has identified the need
to make significant progress towards a single, standard written form as

a prerequisite for any serious advances that might be made in bringing revived Cornish to a wider public.

In this edition of *Cornish Studies*, Bernard Deacon—a fluent Cornish-speaker and the Institute's representative on the Cornish Language Partnership—offers some important observations on the processes of standardization. To illuminate the Cornish situation, he draws upon comparative academic work on language standardization conducted elsewhere, providing insights that will no doubt inform the deliberations of the Cornish Language Partnership as it wrestles with what is inevitably a difficult and contentious issue. Briefly examining the background to the diversity that currently characterizes revived Cornish, Deacon discusses the failure of the revivalist movement thus far to establish a standard form, and argues that in many respects in its twentieth-century revival 'Cornish had many resemblances to invented languages such as Klingon': the hypothetical *Star Trek* construction. He explains the failure of both Unified and Common Cornish (Kernewek Kemmyn) to become standard forms, neither having emerged as a 'synecdoche': a dominant dialect.

Unified came close to this position, argues Deacon, but growing dissatisfaction in the 1980s led to the emergence of new dialects. Of these, Kernewek Kemmyn—based, like Unified, on medieval Cornish, but with a newly constructed pronunciation and spelling—was promoted by its adherents as the synecdoche apparent. However, not only did some Cornish speakers continue to use Unified but others were drawn to Unified Cornish Revised—an attempt to bring the revived language closer to the Tudor period—and still others were attracted by Modern (or Late) Cornish: based on the language as it was last spoken traditionally. All this was evidence of what academics had known already: that there is nothing inherent in a dialect—its vocabulary, grammar or aesthetic attractions—that in itself makes it fit to become a standard. Criticizing the apparent assumption of many revivalists that medieval versions of Cornish are somehow 'pure' or 'superior', Deacon points out that—with its newly-won 'official' status —the Cornish language has shifted from being the property of a tiny number of amateur linguists and into the public domain, where it is now an object of legitimate interest and ownership for everyone living in Cornwall. As Deacon concludes, this profound shift necessitates a return to the revivalist assumptions of the recent past, to re-examine them critically and to ask some fundamental questions about the purposes of the language revival and the role of Cornish in modern Cornish society. And this process should not be confined to the little band of amateur linguists but must reach out to the Cornish public at large: only then can the standardization of Cornish proceed effectively.

Meanwhile, academic work on the historic Cornish language continues apace, and in his article in this collection, Nicholas J.A. Williams alights on comparisons between Cornish and Breton, as evidenced in so-called '*i*-affection'. Professor Williams has emerged in the last decade or so as a foremost scholar of the Cornish language, culminating in the forthcoming publication of his critical edition with translation of *Bewnans Ke*—co-edited with Graham Thomas—the fifteenth-century Cornish-language miracle play discovered in 2000 among papers bequeathed to the National Library of Wales. Published by University of Exeter Press in conjunction with the National Library of Wales, this critical edition establishes a new standard in Cornish-language scholarship, and will be welcomed everywhere as a major contribution to our understanding of the Cornish language and its literature. In his article here, Williams looks in detail at *i*-affection—a phenomenon common in the Brythonic languages—a term which refers to the way in which a short or long *i* in a syllable fronts and raises the vowel in the preceding syllable. There are two types of *i*-affection, as Williams explains, 'final *i*-affection' and 'internal affection', both of which are found in historic Breton and Cornish. However, the phenomenon has largely disappeared from modern Breton, and Williams suggests that—although the evidence is perhaps fragmentary—the same was happening in the verbal system of LC (Late, or Modern Cornish), one indication among many of how the Cornish language was developing naturally beyond the medieval period and into the modern.

An interesting feature of recent debate about the Cornish language is the discussion concerning evidence for the existence (or otherwise) of a medieval 'Cornish Bible'. In his article in this present edition, Matthew Spriggs enters the ring, presenting 'Additional Thoughts on the Medieval "Cornish Bible"'. Already a distinguished archaeologist at the Australian National University, Professor Spriggs has also acquired an enviable international reputation as our leading scholar of the social history of the Cornish language, especially in its Late or Modern period. His 'additional thoughts' revisit Malte Tschirschky's refutation, voiced in *Cornish Studies: Eleven* (2003), of the 'evidence' presented by Charles Penglase to support his view that John Tregear must have had access to a Middle Cornish translation of the Bible when compiling his *Homilies* c.1555–58. Spriggs agrees that Penglase has not produced any corroborating evidence to give credence to his claims, but—as Spriggs observes—this does not mean that evidence cannot be found. Spriggs returns to such evidence to ensure the 'proper hearing' it deserves, using his customary forensic skills to sift through and evaluate a range of fascinating contemporary material, including that of the seventeenth- and eighteenth-century Cornish language enthusiasts. But having given that evidence its fair hearing, he concludes that none of it yet proves the existence of a medieval Cornish Bible. Optimistically, he adds '[l]ike Tschirschy, I too would also be delighted to be proved wrong . . . [t]he discovery of *Beunans Ke* and the reappearance of several other notable Cornish language works in recent years gives us hope that more may yet be found.' But, as Spriggs concludes, the likelihood of any new discovery being a medieval Cornish Bible 'would still seem slim'.

In a second contribution to this volume, Spriggs also deploys his impressive forensic abilities to address the identity of the 'Duchess of Cornwall' in Nicholas Boson's well-known seventeenth-century work *The Duchesse of Cornwall's progress to see the Land's end & to visit the mount*. Spriggs traces the several historical attempts to uncover the identity of the Duchess and to date the manuscript accurately, as well as to establish its authorship beyond doubt. In so doing he alights upon the key evidence unnoticed by earlier scholars, including Henry Jenner in 1924, a draft subscription proposal in Thomas Tonkin's hand—thought to date from 1739—for his *Archaeologia Cornu-Britan[n]ica*, a compendium of all that was then available in the Cornish language. Among the contents is the telling passage: 'Her Royal Highness the Dutchess of Cornwall's (supposed to be Lady Catherine Gordon, wife of Perkin Warbeck, in whose time it is thought to have been written) Progress to the Land's End, & the Triall of Harry Lader (or, Harry the Thief)'. As Spriggs remarks, it seems likely that this remarkable identification was a tradition imparted to Tonkin by the Bosons, by way of his correspondent William Gwavas, and that the person in question was indeed Lady Catherine Gordon. She was the wife of the pretender Perkin Warbeck, who landed near Land's End in September 1497, precipitating the second Cornish rebellion of that year. Perkin had already styled himself Prince of Wales—whose companion title was Duke of Cornwall—and so it follows that his wife would be 'Duchess of Cornwall'. Moreover, as Spriggs notes, that she should be so-called in a work written c. 1660 may well be evidence of a lingering survival in seventeenth-century Cornish folk-memory of the events of 1497, a further intimation of the particularist Cornish sentiment that characterized the period.

Gemma Goodman, in her contribution, moves the discussion of literature and identity from the early modern period to the twentieth century. Concerned with what she terms 'literary anthropology', Goodman concentrates on 'the possible meeting point between literature and anthropology' and its potential for tackling issues of Cornish identity—including the notoriously difficult, not to say controversial, questions of 'insider' and 'outsider' constructions of Cornwall and the Cornish. As she asks rhetorically: 'Who speaks for Cornwall? . . . [i]s there an authentic voice?'. She turns to the fiction of Edith Ellis— better known as Mrs Havelock Ellis, wife of the eminent psychologist —to begin discussion of such issues, focussing on two collections of Ellis' short stories: *My Cornish Neighbours* (1906) and *The Mine of Dreams* (1925). As Goodman observes, Ellis was an 'outsider' but, in contrast to many other outsider constructions of Cornwall of the period, she was interested principally in people rather than landscape. She was an outsider who had come to live in a Cornish community, and her story-telling dwelt upon the dynamics of the insider–outsider relationship, her fiction enlivened with more than a hint of auto-biographical insight.

Intriguingly, as Goodman points out, the narrator in the short stories develops from her initial position as a 'naïve outsider'—with pre-conceived and unrealistic notions of Cornish life—to a more nuanced, sometimes ambivalent and certainly privileged status where she becomes privy to the hitherto hidden inner workings of local society. Paradoxically, however, her position within the community is due to her being a 'superior' outsider, a wise and educated person whose opinion is sought constantly, and this prevents her full assimilation into Cornish life. Ultimately, the narrator decides to leave Cornwall: she does not 'belong'. But this not the end of the saga, for Ellis turns the insider-outsider relationship on its head when Mrs Pengilly—one of the erstwhile Cornish neighbours—is made to visit London, an event which opens up the social and cultural distance between the narrator (now domiciled in the capital) and her Cornish visitor. This, as Goodman notes, is emblematic of the wider inequality in power relationships from which Cornwall still suffers. But, she insists, the meeting point of insider and outsider representations has always been at the heart of 'how we look at and think about "difference" and [Cornish] identity': now as much as in the past. Despite the inherent inequalities, argues Goodman, there is much to be gained by trying to understand and learn from 'multiple constructions of Cornwall and Cornish identity', rather than merely retreating to 'the misperceived strength of homogeneity'. And the work of Edith Ellis, as 'literary anthropologist', helps point the way.

Briar Wood, in her article, also takes up the subject of twentieth-century Cornish literature, presenting us with a panoramic survey of twentieth-century Anglo-Cornish poetry written by women. She chooses the metaphor of the 'crowdy crawn', already deployed to good effect by the Cornish poets Brenda Wootton and Ann Trevenen Jenkin to evoke a multifaceted, eclectic, catch-all, odds-and-ends approach to poetry where different themes, moods and subject matters might all usefully rub shoulders together. A 'crowdy crawn', as Wood explains, is in Cornwall a traditional artefact, 'a framework covered in skin, a drum like receptacle in which to keep useful odds and ends, or a wooden hoop covered with sheep skin for taking up corn. Sometimes used as a tambourine.' As Wood argues, '[t]he multipurpose role of the instrument in domestic life, and in artistic and agricultural production can also apply to poetry.' Indeed, '[f]or women, the fact that the Crowdy Crawn can connote the need for multi-tasking and adeptness at it, makes it particularly appealing.'

Having set the stage, Wood continues with her own 'crowdy crawn', ranging across representations of women and by women in Anglo-Cornish poetry from the close of the nineteenth century until the beginning of the twenty-first. She searches for continuity and connections between tropes, language, history and themes in writing by women, and seeks to determine how representations have altered over the last century or so. Evidence is sought from writers as disparate as Ithell Colquhoun and Penelope Shuttle (in their works, for instance, Wood detects in common tinctures of 'grey', a harshness in Cornish land or seascapes), and like Gemma Goodman she sees merit in the multiple and often conflicting 'Cornwalls' portrayed by poets from sometimes radically different backgrounds. Amidst this diversity there are, for example, the revivalist poets—inspired variously by Celticism, Catholicism, Arthurianism, and linguistic and folkloric enthusiasms —but even here, despite the inevitable ideological commitment, there is a refreshing reflexivity, exemplified in Brenda Wootton's wry observation:

> For Richard Gendall's sake
> The Cornish language I must learn
> To freely speak, 'tis true.
> But English I must comprehend,
> To help me so to do.

Familiar names such as Anne Treneer, Gladys Hunkin, Frances Bellerby and Zofia Ilinska pepper Wood's survey. The 'insider–outsider' nexus is considered, there is discussion of the often metaphorical context of emigration in which so much of modern Cornish consciousness is located, and the place of Anglo-Cornish poetry by women in contemporary Cornish society is also examined. As Wood concludes: 'If poetry published in contemporary journals can give some indication of the future of Anglo-Cornish women's writing, then it suggests continuity and connection through the extension of established themes . . . there is certainly much to look forward to.'

The twentieth-century literary theme is further explored by Graham Busby and Patrick Laviolette in their article 'Narratives in the Net: Fiction and Cornish Tourism'. Specifically, their intention is to interrogate 'literary tourism'—or 'the hermeneutic and semiotic realization of place as a travel destination', to give it its full academic designation—through the deployment of a Web-based methodology designed to detect links between literature and tourism in Cornwall. Their hypothesis is, in essence, that we should expect there to be a strong relationship between literary representations of Cornwall by writers of fiction (such as Winston Graham and Daphne du Maurier) and decisions by their readers to visit Cornwall as a tourist destination. They sketch briefly the role of such literary figures—some 'outsider' (like John Betjeman) and a few 'insider' (such as 'Q')—in helping to construct contemporary representations of Cornwall as 'different'. This 'difference', of course, is part of the literary tourist allure that attracts visitors to Cornwall. As Busby and Laviolette note, the concept of literary tourism is not new. Scholars have identified at least half a dozen types of literary tourism, and Busby and Laviolette discuss these in summary, finding Cornish examples to illustrate each one.

Two twentieth-century authors predominate in the relationship between literature and tourism in Cornwall, Busby and Laviolette argue: Daphne du Maurier (1907–89) and Winston Graham (1910–2003, author of the *Poldark* novels). They chose the latter for their Web-based investigation, posting a simple message on an internet message board: 'Has anybody visited Cornwall specifically because of the *Poldark* books and television series?' Within days enthusiastic responses from individuals in Britain, America and Australia began to confirm what Busby and Laviolette had suspected. In all, there were 227 responses. They constitute, as the authors readily admit, a relatively small and self-selecting sample from which only tentative conclusions may be drawn. Nonetheless, the responses confirm Cornwall as a literary tourism destination *per se*. They also reveal a deep-seated loyalty to Cornwall, with tourists prepared to re-visit repeatedly, and show the extent to which visitors need to develop at least some topographical knowledge in their search for locations in 'Poldark country'. And as Busby and Laviolette also acknowledge, looking to the future, it is but a short step from the Web as a methodological tool to the Web of global hyperreality where 'increasingly interconnected narratives of identities in Cornwall' can be shared and developed by like-minded Poldark and other literary tourism enthusiasts.

Tourism is, for better or worse, a mainstay of the early twenty-first century Cornish economy. However, although—as Busby and

Laviolette and other contributors have remarked—there is a strong symbiotic relationship between tourism and contemporary constructions of Cornish 'difference', the place of the tourist industry in reformulating Cornish identity is only rarely acknowledged. This is in marked contrast to Cornwall's earlier mainstay, hard-rock mining, where the relationship between mining and Cornishness—at home and abroad in the Cornish diaspora—has often been made explicit. And yet, despite this oft-repeated link, there is all too often only a hazy understanding of the role played by Cornish mining in the wider history of British industrialization: this despite the recent publication of Allen Buckley's *The Story of Cornish Mining* (2005) and the announcement in May this year that the bid for World Heritage Site status for the Cornish mining landscape had been successful. Jim Lewis, in his article in this collection, echoes this general point and seeks to redress the balance, offering a detailed account of the Cornish copper mining industry between 1775 and 1830.

The impacts of war and peace dramatically affected those fortunes, as Lewis shows, and it was the arrival of substantial London capital in 1809 that saved Cornish copper from the worst ravages of the Napoleonic wars. However, the experiences of these London investors were not always happy, faced as they were by what they considered an inadequate accounting system and an unfamiliar Cornish business culture based on trust and an intricate network of connections and obligations. After 1815, however, with the arrival of peace, the London interests coalesced around the figure of John Taylor, whose modernizing agenda in the Cornish mines ushered in a period of sustained improvement in Cornish steam technology. But, as Taylor recognized, on the whole Cornish mining did not yield vast profits to its investors, with many mines kept going principally to support a local network of trade and commerce. Indeed, this was the expressed aim of many local interest groups, and helped to explain some of the mistrust and misunderstanding that existed between Cornish and London investors. As Lewis concludes, '[i]n terms of comparative regional industrialization, Cornwall is significant because it provides this example of a clash between outside capital and local vested interests operating within a mature and highly organized industry.' One consequence, as Lewis notes, was that after the peace of 1815 London capital was increasingly enticed to the new—or restored—metal mines of Latin America, while many of the labouring Cornish miners themselves 'took the opportunity to leave their unstable home industry and follow British capital to the ore fields of the New World in search of higher wages'.

Lewis also quotes a telling opinion published in the *West Briton* newspaper in December 1821: 'There are few persons resident in Cornwall who are not, either directly or indirectly, interested in the prosperity of the mines.' This reflected Cornwall's economic and employment dependency upon the mining industry but it also articulated the central place mining by then enjoyed in Cornish estimations of who they were and what Cornwall was about. Few then could have imagined the situation that would obtain by the turn of the next century, with copper all but obliterated and tin in considerable trouble; nor could they have foreseen that the baton of 'Cornish mining' to all intents and purposes would have passed by then to the china clay industry of mid-Cornwall. The dislocation—including wholesale emigration—that marked this dramatic transition ensured that trade unionism and a wider Labour movement would be slow to develop in Cornwall. But there were fits and starts and bursts of activity, and one of these was the 1913 clay-workers' strike, which lasted eleven weeks and involved some 5,000 men.

As Ronald Perry and Charles Thurlow acknowledge in their article on the subject, the 1913 clay-workers' strike has entered Cornish lore as an iconic event. The young A.L. Rowse, whose father was a clay-worker, recalled vividly the electric atmosphere of the time. In the strike's aftermath, as Garry Tregidga has shown in his recent (2006) book *Killerton, Camborne and Westminster: The Political Correspondence of Sir Francis and Lady Acland, 1910–29*, the legacy of industrial conflict had a profound effect on local attitudes and helped fuel the dramatic albeit fleeting rise of Cornish Labour in 1918. Much later, in the early 1970s, the BBC television drama 'Stocker's Copper' caught the flavour of popular remembrance of the strike in the clay country. The two central characters, a striking Cornish clay-worker and a Welsh policeman brought in as part of a contingent to 'break' the strike, develop a bond of shared values and traditions—hymn-singing, mining, Nonconformity, even a sense of Celtic fraternity—that is ultimately undone by greater powers who, as usual, divide and rule. Even today, as Garry Tregidga and Lucy Ellis have demonstrated, passions still run high in the china-clay country among the descendents of those involved in the strike.

However, Perry and Thurlow offer an alternative analysis to this conventional remembrance, with its romantic image of community solidarity in the face of crushing injustice. They draw a wider picture, noting that even in the clay country the strike was not solid, with perhaps half the workforce reluctant to join in. Moreover, the clay-workers of West and North Cornwall and West Devon took no part in the strike. More interesting still, mid-Devon ball clay workers—led by a different trade union—engaged in a strike of their own which led (unlike the Cornish strike) to a successful conclusion. Local economic conditions, rivalries between different unions, divisions within local religious and political groupings, and the important role of external 'interlopers' are all examined as Perry and Thurlow search for explanations for the Cornish experience. Poor organization and a lack of solidarity ensured that the workers were at a disadvantage compared to the employers, who acted effectively and in concert. The authors' wry conclusion is that: 'Perhaps the key reason why the Cornwall strike failed and the Devon strike succeeded was that in Cornwall employers responded to the traditional rallying cry "One and All" whereas the claymen did not. In Devon, ironically, the opposite was the case.'

Perry's and Thurlow's contribution is certain to renew the debate about the 1913 clay strike and the broader subject of Cornish labour history. Terry Chapman's article 'Nationalized Cornwall' is similarly innovative, and sets the experience of 'nationalization' in Cornwall against the wider background of policy and political change in Britain as a whole. Interestingly, he argues that while it was practical necessity that in Cornwall brought utilities such as gas and electricity under public ownership, the attempts to nationalize Cornish extractive industries and (later) Falmouth Docks owed much more to socialist ideological aspirations. Although, as Chapman agrees, Cornwall's pre-war socialists were not avid supporters of what they saw as 'centralist nationalization', there were those who advocated some form of public ownership. E.G. Retallack Hooper—a well-known Cornish-language revivalist—demanded just such a 'new economic system', while A.K. Hamilton Jenkin's booklet *The Nationalisation of West Country Minerals* made the case for State intervention in the Cornish extractive industry. At the beginning of the Second World War the worthies of the Cornish Tin Mining Advisory Committee (CTMAC) were suspicious of any kind of State involvement, warning that 'Cornishmen were prejudiced against outside interference', but at the war's end they were calling for public ownership of mineral rights, these to be administered in Cornwall by the CTMAC or its successor. As Chapman observes: 'This would be nationalization with a Cornish face, public ownership managed from within Cornwall.' For a time, indeed, it appeared that the china clay industry might well come under some form of State control, Harold Wilson chairing a conference on the issue in the late 1940s.

Chapman charts the ebb and flow of nationalization in Cornwall against the background of developments on the UK stage. The Conservative victory in 1951, for example, put an end to talk of nationalizing china clay. Thereafter, 'nationalization' became problematic for both the Conservatives and Labour, the Tories moving strongly towards State subsidies for key British industries during the Heath era, only to decisively abandon such an approach under Thatcher. Labour meanwhile, vacillated in its 'act of faith' commitment to nationalization—hitherto a cornerstone of socialist action—to see it abandoned eventually under New Labour. Falmouth Docks was briefly caught up in these policy shifts but by then, argues Chapman, the docks were probably too 'peripheral' to have benefited from State control. Today, in Cornwall—as elsewhere in the UK—nationalization has had its day. But, as Chapman intimates, this may not be the end of the story because '[i]n the energy sector . . . as short-term anxieties over rising prices and instability of supply compound those over longer-term environmental costs, both Cornwall and the UK as a whole face some tough choices.'

This concern for contemporary—and future—Cornwall reflects a wider determination within the Cornish Studies community to ensure that present-day Cornish issues are given due consideration. One issue that has caused much anxiety in recent years is the so-called 'Darkie Day' controversy at Padstow. 'Darkie Day', which takes place each year at Padstow on Boxing Day and New Year, has generally been a low-key event when compared to the world-famous Padstow May Day celebration, with its dramatic 'Obby 'Oss. Until recently, press interest was limited to a few lines in local newspapers, while such external observers who witnessed Darkie Day imagined—probably quite rightly —that the tradition was merely a latter-day survival of the Cornish 'guizing' custom where revellers disguised themselves (typically by blackening their faces) and engaged in informal music-making and street dancing. However, as Merv Davey explains in his careful analysis of the current situation, the event was suddenly cast in a new light when the late Bernie Grant MP (Labour) denounced Darkie Day as racist. Face blackening, an important part of Darkie Day 'guizing', was inherently offensive, he argued, while the term 'Darkie' and the apparent mimicking of black 'minstrels' were also unacceptable. Later, Diane Abbott MP (Labour) added her voice to the objections, alleging the wearing of 'Afro-wigs' and the use of the word 'nigger' by revellers. In 2004 the police attended the event on Boxing Day and collected video evidence for submission to the Crown Prosecution Service.

As Davey notes, the 'Padstow debate' (as he terms it) has polarized, critics claiming that the event is offensive to black people— and indeed all people with anti-racist sympathies and sensitivities—and defenders insisting that critics are simply misinformed about the nature of the event and the intention of its participants. There is also a sense among some of the event's supporters that they are the victims of metropolitan disdain for Cornish identity and culture. Davey picks his way through this minefield, including its legal implications, with considerable dexterity. He examines the 'guizing' tradition, of which Darkie Day is apparently a variant, and charts the development of the Padstow event in the twentieth century, including the acquisition of the 'minstrel' ambience with its particular repertoire of songs, distinctive clothing and method of blacking-up. Davey argues that these 'minstrel' features mirrored popular British culture in the mid-twentieth century (when the 'Black-and-White Minstrel Show' was prime time television), and that by 2005—when he was able to observe the event at close quarters—these elements had largely disappeared. Indeed, the name of the event had by then been changed to 'Mummers' Day'—a recognition by the participants that their erstwhile name was inappropriate—and Davey detected a genuine willingness to respond positively to suggestions, accommodating them where possible.

It is not clear whether 'blacking-up'—an act central to the 'guizing' tradition but also at the heart of the 'racist' allegations—will also be subject to such negotiation. But Davey is clear that '[t]he blackened faces are part of . . . early tradition and are a customary disguise rather than a deliberate depiction of black people'. He is persuaded that the Padstow Mummers, as they are now called, intend 'no harm or offence', and concludes that any campaign to discourage or ban the event would be unfortunate. He also draws a broader conclusion: 'The "Padstow debate" is part of a much wider debate about diversity in modern Britain and what happens when cultural expression in one group is found to be offensive by another.' As he remarks, '[f]or celebration of diversity to function effectively as a philosophy promoting a healthy society it must be seen to treat groups equally, and risks being discredited if it appears not to do this.'

Genuine distress seems to have been caused to both critics and supporters of what we now call Mummers' Day. Cornish culture deserves to be respected but so do the sensibilities of other groups. The role of the Cornish Studies practitioner, it might be argued, is to demonstrate the equal worth of Cornish culture in today's society and to ensure its proper consideration in academic and other circles. But surely it is also to contribute to the wider debate about diversity in modern Britain, helping informed observers—just as Davey has done—to understand the roots of potential conflict and to look for the means of amicable resolution.

Professor Philip Payton,
Director, Institute of Cornish Studies,
University of Exeter, Cornwall Campus,
Tremough, Penryn, Cornwall.

CORNISH OR KLINGON?
THE STANDARDIZATION OF THE
CORNISH LANGUAGE

Bernard Deacon

INTRODUCTION

There are estimated to be upwards of six thousand languages in the
world today, although a disturbingly high proportion of these are under
threat of extinction. All these languages have their histories. And then
there are those languages that have been invented over the last century
and a half. The 'fastest growing language in the galaxy' has been
claimed to be Klingon, invented for an alien race which was first heard
speaking it in *Star Trek: The Motion Picture* in 1979.[1] In 1984 Marc
Okrand, a linguist, invented its grammar, vocabulary and orthography.[2]
Since then Trekkies (*Star Trek* devotees) have enthusiastically
attempted to learn this language, to the extent that in 1999 over
six hundred people could claim to be speakers, while the Klingon
Language Institute had over one thousand members.[3] Klingon, the
product of a globalized American TV culture, would seem to be
hundreds of light years away from Cornish, a language with a long and
respectable history. But is it? In this brief review of the attempted
standardization of revived Cornish my argument is that, in its twentieth
century revival, Cornish had many resemblances to invented languages
such as Klingon.

Being a language fit for aliens, Klingon promoters deliberately
revel in its inhuman irregularities.[4] However, this is unusual for
deliberately invented languages.[5] The website of the Klingon Language
Institute is, significantly, hosted by the Logical Language Group.
Its language—Lojban—claims to possess an unambiguous grammar,
phonetic spelling and the 'unambiguous resolution of sounds into

words'. Unlike historic languages, with their messy irregularities and other human foibles, languages such as Lojban or the older Esperanto (which dates from 1887) are 'easy to learn'.[6] Those familiar with the dialects of revived Cornish will have heard similar claims.

VARIETIES OF REVIVED CORNISH

Historically, Cornish became a distinct language somewhere in the latter part of the first millennium when the dialect of the British language spoken in south western Britain began to diverge from that of the Welsh. The history of this language can then be traced to the death of its last speakers around 1800. What is written and spoken now is revived Cornish, a resuscitated version that has no unbroken chain back to the historical language. Indeed, at least one observer has argued that the gap between the historic language and revived Cornish is so wide that we should describe revived Cornish as 'pseudo-Cornish' or 'Cornic', in contrast to the traditional, authentic and 'genuine' historic language.[7] Significantly, this comment was made even before the increased pluralism that marked Cornish from the mid-1980s. Revived Cornish itself is usually dated from Henry Jenner's *Handbook of the Cornish Language*, published in 1904.

However, this is more a convenient starting point than an accurate date for the genesis of the language's resurrection. For that we would have to go back further, to the lessons written by Wladislaw Lach-Szyrma in the 1890s or to Jenner's own initial foray into language revival in the late 1870s, when he proposed, unsuccessfully, to form a society that would advise on the 'correct' spelling of the language. Now, more than a century later, there are somewhere between one hundred and two hundred relatively fluent speakers, the exact number being uncertain as no direct survey has ever been undertaken. The most recent guess, in 2000, often given the imprimatur of being 'official' due to its appearance in a report on the language sponsored by the Government Office South West, is only that—a guess, one that relied in turn on the estimates provided by the various revivalist groups.[8] These had very good reason to indulge in inflation of the truth in the context of a perceived struggle over resources.

Whereas we cannot be sure of the precise number of speakers, it is crystal clear that there is not one standard Cornish but three main varieties. A century or more of revivalism has produced a situation in which there are competing dialects that are unusually based on temporal rather than spatial differences, surely unique among languages. Users of Unified Cornish and Unified Cornish Revised base their spelling on the Tudor period and the mid-sixteenth century. The Common Cornish (Kernewek Kemmyn) school prefers a somewhat earlier period for its ideal pronunciation, around 1500, but in the process discards the historical spelling of Cornish. Finally, Modern Cornish enthusiasts aim to speak and write the Cornish of the later seventeenth or early eighteenth centuries, three generations or so before its eventual demise as a community language in the fishing ports of Penwith. A century and more of language revivalism has thus failed to produce a standard Cornish. But that is not the same as saying there has been no effort at standardization. For there has.

FAILED ATTEMPTS AT STANDARDIZATION
Standardization of languages occurs in two overlapping ways. First, there is a *de facto* process of standardization, as speech communities converge on a standard form. Second, we might identify a more *de jure* standardization, involving the explicit intervention of official state bodies, professional language planners and so forth. But in the case of Cornish we have had neither. The lack of a decent-sized speech community has made the first form of standardization difficult and the absence of official recognition before 2003 made the second one irrelevant. Instead, there has been an attempt at standardization led by amateur linguists and the voluntary enthusiasts of the language movement. This involved an effort in the twentieth century to devise a standard Cornish based on its late medieval form, one that involved two phases. The first phase was led by Robert Morton Nance who, rejecting Jenner's earlier tendency to favour later forms, in the 1920s 'unified' the spelling around the corpus of historic medieval literature, although this involved only one *genre*, that of religious drama. 'Unified Cornish' remained the proto-standard until the 1980s, when it came under scrutiny from two directions.

First, a group of revivalists re-discovered the prose writings of later Cornish and decided to build their Cornish on this more modern form, one closer both in time and appearance to the many traces of Cornish that had survived in the physical and cultural landscape around them. Second, another larger group was attracted to the work of Ken George who, echoing an emerging dissatisfaction with the Unified Cornish compromise (medieval spelling conventions but modern pronunciation) decided to seek to recover the 'exact' pronunciation of 1500 and radically adjust the spelling so that one grapheme (letter or group of letters) as far as possible reflected one phoneme (sound).[9] In doing this, it was claimed that Cornish would become easier. Attracted by the promise of an easier language to learn, the majority of the voluntary movement—but probably involving the active participation of a mere 50 or so people—adopted what later became called 'Common' Cornish (Kernewek Kemmyn). The supporters of this new version were able to seize the institutions of the revival in the mid-1980s, notably the Cornish Language Board. In doing this they cloaked themselves with a degree of legitimacy. But, critically, they failed to persuade all users of Cornish to adopt their system. Instead of confronting this problem directly, the leaders of the Common Cornish project relied on a 'survival of the fittest' strategy, ignoring the heretics and prosecuting their own form with extreme vigour, taking every opportunity to portray it as the equivalent of 'Cornish'. But, unfortunately for those who wished to make Common Cornish into the standard written form, the other forms not only survived but thrived. In doing so they drew in new speakers while producing their own teaching materials, books and other resources. Thus, while the first phase of standardization eventually succumbed under the weight of its own internal contradictions, the second phase of standardization also failed, an outcome made easier by the tiny speech community and the limited domains of spoken Cornish, thereby reducing pressures to conform.

Nonetheless, this failed standardization has interesting lessons if we apply to it the concepts involved in the study of language standardization. This is what I do in the rest of this article, relying heavily on Robert Millar's *Language, Nation and Power: An Intro-duction* and a few other works in order to provide a window onto the Cornish language.[10] By putting Cornish in a more comparative context we can begin to think less introspectively about the issues that surround its standardization, now that we are in the position when a *de jure* process has finally begun. This became a practical option once Cornish received official status through being recognized under the Council of Europe's Charter for Regional and Minority Languages.

DIALECTS AND SYNECDOCHES

In any language standardization process involving a living language, a dominant dialect will emerge, termed by Joseph a synecdoche.[11] This dialect will be codified and written consistently and will seek equality with other standardized languages. But what causes one dialect among several to be transformed or to transform itself into a standard language? Joseph points to internal and external motives. Internally, a language elite creates positions of power for itself by transforming its dialect into the standard. While self-aggrandisement may not form the explicit agenda of this elite, standardization in-evitably enhances the elite's profile. Thus 'a few users of the standard language accede to positions of authority which permit them to direct the future course of standardisation'.[12] Externally, comparison with other standard languages produces a perceived need to overcome a low esteem. The growth of nationalism in the nineteenth century, based on the idea that one nation equalled one language, was a powerful stimulus in triggering the drive to standardize languages and in doing so to purify them in order to differentiate them from their competitors. Joseph also points to the external motive of imperialism in pushing forward standardization of colonised languages, and in the Cornish case this takes the form of bureaucratization, as the involvement of state bodies increases external pressures for standardization.

Applying the concept of synecdoche to Cornish, Unified Cornish was clearly the synecdochic dialect of Cornish from the 1920s to the 1980s. It was believed by virtually all Cornish speakers to form a *de facto* standard. Its orthography and grammar had been codified and it had become the dialect used as symbol of formality and solemnity in Gorseth ceremonies and church services. To all intents and purposes this dialect was established as the equivalent of 'Cornish'. But the engineered standardization of Unified Cornish was unable to transform itself into an organic standardization. Although based on the corpus of a historic language, its genesis bore striking similarities with invented languages, in particular in the role of one key person—Robert Morton Nance—in its codification and dissemination. But growing interest in and knowledge of the actual historic language in the context of a failure to produce more than a trickle of speakers resulted in the loss of its synecdochic status in the 1980s.

In contrast Kernewek Kemmyn, or 'Common Cornish', Unified Cornish's late-medieval successor dialect, failed to establish itself as an unambiguous synecdoche. The Common Cornish project was an even more explicitly planned venture but, unlike Unified Cornish in the period before the 1970s, Common Cornish is not believed by all speakers of Cornish to be the best form of the language. It has also had to share the functional sphere—in Gorseth, church services, writing and the media—with the other dialects of Cornish. Twenty years after its introduction, the failure of the Common Cornish project to establish its dialect as the synecdoche was exposed by its inability to convince users of other dialects or many observers outside its immediate speech community that it should automatically become the standard written form when official status was obtained for Cornish in 2003.

Synecdochic dialects become standards through dissemination, through establishing their written form as that for the language as a whole. As we have seen, Unified Cornish had almost attained this situation in the 1970s. However, there needs to be a mass audience ready and willing to receive the standard as the only acceptable form. In the twentieth century that mass audience for Cornish just did not exist. The opportunity to establish Unified Cornish as the standard was thus missed. Now, in the twenty-first century and with the implicit support of the state, there is the possibility of imposing a standard through mass education. This, what Millar calls 'no alternative strategy', gives potential power to one dialect elite to impose its version on others. Advocates of Common Cornish saw the possibility of state subsidy and support for a long-term presence of Cornish in the education system as a lifeline, holding out the glittering prospect that their project might achieve standard status despite its inability to create a mass audience through voluntary efforts. For, as Millar points out, 'if the knowledge of a standardised form of any language remains in the hands of the language planning elite, it is unlikely that it can be treated as anything other than a complex game'.[13] However, in the Cornish case no dialect is tied to a living community of speakers in any real sense of a community using a Cornish dialect as its everyday means of communication.

CULTURE, NOT LINGUISTICS

Millar's work, based on comparative studies of a host of standardization cases, leads him to a conclusion that is fundamentally at odds with the cherished assumptions of the Cornish revival's amateur language planners. There is nothing inherent in a dialect—its vocabulary, grammar or aesthetic attractions—that makes it fit to become a standard. This naive but nonetheless almost universal belief within the Cornish language movement is clearly shown to be a chimera. In contrast 'societal and cultural patterns and pressures are at the heart of whether a given language variety will succeed as a standard or not'.[14] Standards that are associated with a strong or pervasive idea, whether cultural, political or religious, are more likely to succeed. One source from which a dialect may get its initial prestige is a 'given set of literary or cultural virtues'. In the case of Cornish, such literary virtues are traditionally supposed to revolve around the corpus of miracle and saints' plays from the fourteenth to early sixteenth centuries that form the bulk of its literature.[15] These have served as the core of an emerging 'Glasney myth'. Within this twentieth-century discourse, what is on the European scale quite a modest literature—confined to a single and very limiting *genre*—becomes a powerhouse of literary perfection. This myth conveniently locates the golden age of Cornish in its late medieval period, a time before the myriad corruptions of Protestantism, modernity and 'English' influence supposedly took effect. The inevitable developments of the language after its 'golden' or 'classical' age then become seen as simplifications or 'decay'.

All languages are prone to experience this hyper-conservatism as elements, usually among the middle classes, attempt to stifle the more dynamic everyday changes adopted by the language's users. Such attempts, whether by formal institutions such as the *Academie Francaise* or by less formal ones such as Radio Four listeners, normally these days face an uphill task in the face of a tide of Anglo-American linguistic change backed by the power of the global media-corporations. But they are also confounded by the stubborn insistence of those actually using the language to say *le weekend* or use *dreifio* instead of *gyrru*. But for Cornish the lack of such a community gives full rein to the schoolteacherly tendencies within the revivalist movement. Not content merely to fix vocabulary, the Common Cornish project went to the extremes of attempting to fix the sounds of the language on an ultimately hypothetical (as it can never be proven) phonemic system which it claims to detect was present in 1500. Deviations from this norm then also became a version of 'decay'.

CORPUS, STATUS AND ACQUISITION PLANNING

Such attitudes, ideological rather than scientific, and underpinned by taken-for-granted and unexamined cultural assumptions, lie behind the apparently technical process of language planning—in all languages and not just Cornish. Recently we have heard of corpus and status planning in Cornish, but this can usefully be extended to distinguish three activities within language planning—corpus planning, deciding what is the 'correct', 'pure' and 'best' basis for a language; status planning, enhancing the status of that language; and acquisition planning, encouraging a greater knowledge and use of it.[16] These processes do not simply appear one after the other, although there is a logical progression from corpus to status to acquisition planning. Instead they overlap, mutually informative rather than totally separate.[17]

In the Cornish context, corpus planning presents the trickiest problem because of the failure of the late medieval standardization project since the 1980s. Corpus planning itself involves three stages: selection, codification and elaboration. During the selection stage the problem is identified and norms are allocated. The problem for Cornish is simple. There is only a minute speech community, something that makes the argument that current speakers alone should decide on the standard written form a precarious one with disturbing implications for the future ownership of the language. For Cornish has significance in that it has played a deeply symbolic role as an indicator of Cornish 'difference' and a buttress for the Cornish identity since the second quarter of the nineteenth century; it is not significant as a spoken language. This central fact, though one that tends to be ignored by most revivalists, ensures that any standardization process has to tread carefully. Hitherto, the activities of the revival have proceeded in parallel with and in the main sealed off from the background role of the language as a symbol of Cornish identity. But when Cornish becomes a public language, inscribed in bureaucratic texts and disseminated in the schools, this cloistered position dissolves. Instantaneously, the form of written revived Cornish, up to this point of little interest or relevance to the mass of the population, becomes of great importance.

If there are two or more varieties or dialects of a language, during the selection stage decisions are made as to which is most acceptable in terms of vocabulary, structure and pronunciation. Yet the majority of Cornish revivalists have apparently already taken it for granted that the fifteenth century is the preferable basis for the language. This 'decision', stumbled into in the 1920s and reinforced by the anti-modernism of the early revivalists, lies like a log jam across the process of standardization. In any corpus planning for Cornish the rationale for basing the language on the fifteenth century will need to be seriously, explicitly and realistically re-examined. Only when we solve the huge issues around selection can we then move on to codification, the attempt to provide a prescriptive orthography, grammar and dictionary, reinforcing notions of 'correctness'. It is here that the coercive aspect of language planning becomes most obvious. Standardization is 'designed to control the language (and, implicitly, the behaviour) of a given populace'. However, on the other hand, faced with competition from a dominant language, standardization is also 'necessary for survival'.[18]

As was the case for selection, when codifying Cornish, the language revival worked within some deeply held assumptions that require careful examination. For example, the assumption that we need to (or can) identify the sounds of the Cornish of 1500 or thereabouts (or 1550 or 1700 come to that) and then studiously attempt to replicate them in a quest for some holy grail of authenticity appears to some as complete nonsense. In his excellent short paper, 'Thoughts on the Future of Cornish', Ashby Tabb has deconstructed this 'pipe dream' of recovering an old pronunciation, pointing out how real speech communities include a range of mutually intelligible vowel sounds.[19] The efforts of the amateur linguists who have colonized the Cornish language may well turn out in practice to be finely honed technical schemes but in the long run as effective as that misguided King Canute on his lonely beach.

The failed *de facto* late medieval standardization project of Unified and Common Cornish focussed more of their energies on codification rather than the more fundamental selection. But they also actively engaged in the third aspect of corpus planning, that of

elaboration. In this stage language planners pay heed to the relationship between their language and its neighbours, deciding what is
needed for a particular language in the wider world. Critically, this
stage involves a quest for 'purism', building and maintaining boundaries around a language.[20] I have already pointed out how the revived
Cornish movement generally and Common Cornish advocates in
particular have expended much energy avoiding the Englishness of
Cornish. They assert its separateness from that language, sometimes
going so far as to avoid historic Cornish spellings partly on the grounds
that the latter are over-influenced by English, and assiduously and
unscientifically differentiate between language developments (which
are acceptable) and 'English corruptions' (which are not).[21]

Such 'purism' is common to the process of standardization and has
its roots in nineteenth century nationalist ideologies and a xenophobic
distrust of external influence. This has been termed an 'external' type
of purism, co-existing with an 'internal' purism, where the language
planners look to fill the gaps in the language itself.[22] Medieval Cornish,
with a small vocabulary of around nine thousand headwords,[23] a total
the more modern Cornish material is unlikely to increase by more than
a thousand or two, is clearly in need of elaboration if it is to become a
language fit to compete in the modern world. Yet internal purism
also has its ideological dimensions. Millar points out how purism can
operate along temporal or social planes. Taking the latter first, social
purism can be elitist, proposing a 'proper' pronunciation, or ethnographic, for example involving a nostalgia for countryside virtues and a
concern to move away from urban decadence. In the English language
elitism is the strongest influence. And this is felt more strongly in
terms of pronunciation than vocabulary. Arguments over a 'received'
pronunciation and the discourses surrounding this remain strongly
elitist despite the de-bunking work of socio-linguists. This can be
observed most readily in Radio Four-land, speaking from (and largely
to) a Home-Counties mind-set.

Elitist purism can be combined with temporal purism, divided into
two kinds by Millar.[24] There is 'archaizing purism', looking to the past
and resuscitating the linguistic material of a golden age, involving an
exaggerated respect for past literary models and an excessive con-
servatism. And there is 'reformist' purism, 'cleansing the language of
foreign elements' and re-building it. These are not necessarily opposed
and may combine in any one process of purism, as is obvious from
a cursory examination of the Cornish standardization projects. Is it a
coincidence that Cornish dialects of all types have strong elements of
elitism in terms of 'correct' pronunciation, while the late medieval
project looks back to a 'golden age' of the religious plays and the

modern Cornish to a 'golden age' of earthy peasant speakers in west Penwith? Interestingly, these attitudes are ones shared with deeply ingrained views of the English language in England. The irony is that the purist drive of Cornish revivalists is intimately connected to assumptions uncritically borrowed wholesale from the superordinate language—English. A reverence for the past and archaizing purism stem ultimately from the influence of English. In a contradictory fashion, the rationale for this process is then, somewhat bizarrely, claimed to be the restoration of the distinctiveness of Cornish from English and the purging of foreign (English) elements. But this flows from wishful thinking. The more mundane reality is that not only was the Cornish language in both its medieval and more modern phases inevitably affected by English but that Cornish revivalists have also been deeply affected by English assumptions and attitudes.

CONCLUSION
This brief foray into some comparative work on language standardization reveals how the *de facto* standardization project around late medieval Cornish adopted aspects that are widely familiar from other languages. Furthermore, we can also begin to explain why where has been so much emphasis on issues of pronunciation rather than vocabulary and on the codification rather than the selection stage of corpus planning. More discussion is surely required about the assumptions of the selection stage, including revisiting the basic purposes of the language revival and the role of Cornish in modern Cornish society. More broadly, Millar concludes in his study that corpus planning is very attractive to both professional and amateur linguists, and this has certainly proved to be so in the case of Cornish. However, it is 'doomed to remain a hobby, unless the corpus planning is associated with outreach ventures connected to the native speakers of the language variety in question and, quite possibly, the members of an ethnic group who do not speak the ethnic group language, but would like to'.[25] This means that, in the absence of a pool of native speakers, it is essential that Cornish language planning engages with the wider community and does not remain restricted to the often blinkered visions of the linguists and their enthusiastic followers. In the role of key individuals, the resort to more 'rational' spelling systems and the primacy given to 'ease of learning', revived Cornish has clear similarities with invented languages. Yet Cornish is not Klingon (or Esperanto). It is a language with a long history linked to a living identity. Its future is inextricably linked to the vitality of that identity and its standardization, in order to succeed, will have to recognize and resolve the tensions and contradictions posed by its past.

NOTES AND REFERENCES

1. Klingon Language, en.wikipedia.org/wiki/Klingon_language (accessed 15 June 2006). See also the Klingon Language Institute (www.kli.org/).
2. Marc Okrand, *The Klingon Dictionary*, London, 1985.
3. www.swipnet.se/~W-12689/survey (accessed 15 June 2006).
4. BBC, www.bbc.co.uk/dna/h2g2/A4744860 (accessed 15 June 2006).
5. Languages such as Esperanto are given various descriptions, including artificial, constructed or international. Here, I prefer the term 'invented languages' for these.
6. Tutmondo Esperantista Tunulara Organizo, www.tejo.org.info/pri (accessed 15 June 2006).
7. Glanville Price, *The Languages of Britain*, London, 1984, p.134.
8. Kenneth MacKinnon, *An Independent Academic Study on Cornish*, Government Office South West, Bristol, 2000; see also Kenneth MacKinnon, 'Cornish at its Millennium: An Independent Study of the Language Undertaken in 2000', in Philip Payton (ed.), *Cornish Studies: Ten*, Exeter, 2002, pp. 266–82.
9. The rationale for this was set out in Ken George, *The Pronunciation and Spelling of Revived Cornish*, Torpoint, 1986.
10. Robert Millar, *Language, Nation and Power: An Introduction*, London, 2005.
11. John Joseph, *Eloquence and Power: The Rise of Language Standards and Standard Languages*, London, 1987, p. 2.
12. Joseph, 1987, pp. 43–6.
13. Millar, 2005, p. 71.
14. Millar, 2005, p. 88.
15. See Brian Murdoch, *Cornish Literature*, Cambridge, 1993.
16. Robert Cooper, *Language Planning and Social Change*, Cambridge, 1989.
17. Einar Haugen, 'The implementation of corpus planning: theory and practice', in J. Cobarrubias and J.A. Fishman (eds) *Progress in Language Planning: International Perspectives*, New York, 269–89.
18. Millar, 2005, p. 102.
19. Ashby Tabb, 'Thoughts on the future of Cornish', unpublished paper, 2005.
20. Millar, 2005, p. 103.
21. Bernard Deacon, 'Deconstructing *Kernewek Kemmyn*: A Critical Review of *Agan Yeth* 4', unpublished paper, 2005 (available from author). See also Neil Kennedy, 'Verbal Hygiene and Purism', unpublished paper, n.d.
22. George Thomas, *Linguistic Purism*, London.
23. Jon Mills, 'A Comparison of the Semantic Values of Middle Cornish *luf* and *dorn* with Modern English *hand* and *fist*', *Language Sciences* 18.1, 1996, pp. 71–86.
24. Millar, 2005, pp. 104–05.
25. Millar, 2005, p. 112.

I-AFFECTION IN BRETON AND CORNISH

N.J.A. Williams

WHAT IS *I*-AFFECTION?

I-affection is a widespread phenomenon in the Brythonic languages. The term refers to the way in which a short or long *i* in a syllable fronts and raises the vowel in the preceding syllable. There are two kinds of *i*-affection. The first, known as final *i*-affection, involves instances where the affecting *i* was in a final syllable now lost, e.g. Cornish *tew* 'is silent' < Proto-British **tawît*, Breton *sent* 'saints' < Late Latin **santî*. The other kind is known as internal affection. Here the affecting vowel is in a medial syllable and in consequence remains, e.g. Cornish *melin*, *melyn* 'mill' < Latin *molîna*, Cornish *Costentyn* < Latin *Constantînus*, Breton *terriff*, *terriñ* 'to break' < Proto-British **torrîma*.[1] One sometimes finds final and internal *i*-affection together, so-called 'double *i*-affection'. Take, for example, the Breton word *ebestel* 'apostles' < Latin *apostolî*. Here the final long *i* (subsequently lost) has raised *o* > *e* and then the newly affected vowel has raised *a* to *e* in the preceding syllable.

There are occasions where expected *i*-affection does not occur. Some instances are peculiar to one language or dialect. Compare, for example, Welsh *defnydd* 'matter' with *i*-affection but MB *daffnez* 'matter' without it, though both derive from Proto-British **damnijo*. Notice also that the contrary phenomenon of *a*-affection can also prevent *i*-affection. A good example is Welsh *Hafren* 'Severn' < Proto-British *Sabrinâ*. Here the final *â* had already lowered the short *i* in *Sabrinâ* to *e* before it could cause *i*-affection. Had the *i* in *Sabrinâ* been long, *i*-affection would have occurred, and the name would appear in Welsh as **Hefren* (LHEB: 576).

I-affection is phonetically similar to what in the Germanic languages is known as *i*-umlaut. *I*-umlaut is responsible for such alternations as German *Mann*, *Männer*, English *man*, *men*; German *Fuß*, *Füße*, English *foot*, *feet*, and in the verbal system, German *ich falle* 'I fall' but *er fällt* 'he falls'. *I*-umlaut is also the cause of less obvious oppositions, for example, English *fox* but *vixen*, *God* but *giddy*, originally 'possessed by a god', and *blood* but *bless*, originally 'to sprinkle with blood.' The fronting of vowels in anticipation of an *i* in the next syllable is very common in languages generally. In spoken French, for example, the word *joli* 'pretty' is not [ZOli] but [Zœli], where the first vowel is fronted to [œ] in anticipation of the following *i*.

I-AFFECTION IN THE MIDDLE BRETON VERB

In Breton *a* and *o* are changed to *e* by *i*-affection, *ou* becomes *eu* and *e* may also become *i*. The unaffected vowel is usually seen in the second person singular imperative, e.g. *car* 'love', *caf*, *kaf* 'find' and *lavar* 'say'. *I*-affection occurs in a variety of places in the verbal system. I will discuss briefly some parts of the Breton verb, where *i*-affection tends also to occur in the corresponding positions in Cornish.

The third person singular present indicative

In MB one finds such forms as *seu* 'stands' (stem *sav*), *queff* 'gets' (stem *kaf-*), *re* 'gives' (stem *ro-*). *I*-affection is very common in the third singular present-future in Welsh also, e.g. MW *seif* 'stands' (cf. MB *seu*), *keiff* (cf. MB *queff*), *eirch* 'asks' (stem *arch*), *keidw* 'keeps' (stem *cadw*), *pyrth* 'bears' (stem *porth*).[2]

I-affection in the third singular of the present can probably to be derived from an original conjunct desinence in *-ît*. Thus MB *seu* 'stands, rises' and Middle Welsh *seif* 'stands' are both reflexes of Proto-British *stam-ît*. *I*-affection is also normal in MB in the second person singular, and the first, second and third person plural of the present. Since, however, I am interested in the comparison with Cornish and these latter forms of the verb are poorly attested in MC and LC, I will not discuss them in either Breton or Cornish.

The third person singular of the i-preterite

In OB, but not in MB, one finds forms of the third singular of the preterite in *-is* with *i*-affection of the preceeding vowel, e.g. *guoteguis* 'silenced', *dichreuis* 'began' and *ecdiecncis* 'escaped', in which *i*-affection occurs (Fleuriot 1964: 308). Such forms are exactly comparable with similar MW preterites in *-is*, e.g. *trenghis* 'perished', *kedwis* 'kept', *delis* 'caught', *gelwis* 'called', *diengis* 'escaped', *enwis* 'named', *erchis* 'asked' and *seuis* 'stood', all with *i*-affection. Similar preterites are also common in MC, e.g. *leverys* 'said', *yrhys* 'asked', *sevys* 'stood', etc.

The ending *-is* (*-ys*) of the Breton, Welsh and Cornish third person singular derives from an earlier desinence **-iss* < **-îsti*. Alongside this ending, Brythonic also had an ending **-ass* < **asti*, which becomes *-as* in Welsh and Breton, giving such third person singular preterites as MB *credas* 'believed' and *clevas* 'heard'; MW *gwelas* 'saw' and *twyllas* 'deceived'. Preterites in *-as*, as we shall see, are also common in MC and LC also. The preterite ending in *-as*, lacking as it did a high front vowel, could not cause *i*-affection in any of the three Brythonic languages. We thus find MW *cafas*, MC *cafas* and MB *caffas*, all meaning 'got, found' and all with unaffected *a* in the root.

The verbal noun in -el
This regularly shows *i*-affection in MB: *meruel, mervell, mervel* 'to die' (stem *maru-*); *seuell, sevel* (stem *sau, sav*; cf. Welsh *sefyll*), *teuell, tevel, teuel* 'to be silent' (stem *tau, tav*), *fellel* 'to fail' (stem *fall*), and with dissimilation of the final consonant, *teurell* 'to throw' (stem *taul*) and *gueruel* 'to call' (stem *galu*). The suffix *-el* is believed to derive from Proto-British **-ilis* (WG: 393).

THE LOSS OF *I*-AFFECTION FROM MODERN BRETON
Modern Breton has largely dispensed with *i*-affection in the verbal system. As we have noted above, the present tense in MB commonly shows *i*-affection in the third person singular. *I*-affection also occurs in the other persons of the present, except the first person singular, which invariably exhibits the root vowel. Thus in MB one finds, for example, *leverez* 'thou sayest', *leveret* 'you say', *leveront* 'they say', all with double *i*-affection, but *lavaraff* 'I say', without it. The first person singular of the present without *i*-affection together with the second singular imperative (e.g. *lavar*) and the imperfect (e.g. *lavaren, -es, -e*, etc.) provided a basis for the analogical deletion of *i*-affection from much of the verbal system in ModB. *I*-affected forms do occur in the verbal system of ModB but they are the exception rather than the rule.[3]

In MB *i*-affection is regular in the third person singular of the present, but tends to be lost in ModB in this position. A striking example of such loss in ModB can be seen in the two versions of *Doctrin an Christenien*. The first text was published in 1622 and is written in MB; the second is in ModB and was published in 1677. The first sentence of the 18th lesson reads as follows in the two texts:

1622

M. Petra à dle vn guir Christen da ober bemdez pan **seu** *é guele?* 'M. What should a true Christian do each day when he rises from his bed?'

1677

Petra à dle ur guir Christen da ober dious ar mintin pa **sao***?* *'What should a true Christian do when he rises in the morning?' (DC: 50, 51).*

The MB has *pan seu* 'when he rises' (cf. Cornish *pan sef*) with *i*-affection, while the ModB text has *pa sao* without it.

As has been noted above, in MB *-as* has already replaced *-is* as the regular third person singular ending of the preterite. Because the desinence *-as* does not cause *i*-affection, *i*-affection is already absent from the most frequently used person of the MB preterite, though it is usual in the first and second persons. By the ModB period *i*-affection has in many verbs disappeared from the preterite entirely.

In ModB *i*-affection is still usual with verbal nouns ending in *-iñ* and *-el*, for example, *terriñ* 'to break' (stem *torr*), *pibiñ* 'to bake' (stem *pob*), *sevel* 'to stand' (stem *sav*), *mervel* 'to die' (stem *marv*), *envel* 'to name' (stem *anv*). Elsewhere *i*-affection has largely disappeared. Hemon, for example, says,

> The root of certain verbs sometimes changes under the influence of an ending. In this case, both regular and irregular forms coexist: **lavarout** 'say' gives **lavarit** and **livirit**, **lavarot** and **leverot**. **Karout** 'love' gives **karit** and **kirit**, **karot** and **kerot**. (BG: 61)

Kervella (124-25, § 206) is more radical still. He prints the entire paradigm of the verb *karout* 'to love' and the stem in every person of nine separate tenses is *kar-* throughout, affected forms *ker-* and *kir-* being wholly absent.

I-AFFECTION IN MIDDLE AND LATE CORNISH

In MC *a* becomes *e* by *i*-affection, *o* becomes *e* and *ow* becomes *ew*. It is not possible to say with any certainty that *e* becomes *y* in MC by *i*-affection, since it is by no means clear that the short vowels represented by <e> and <y>are distinct and separate phonemes. There are, moreover, other factors involved in some vowel alternations in Cornish. Historically *e* alternates with *o* in some verbs quite independently of *i*-affection: for example, the monosyllabic singular imperative *dog* 'carry' (W *dwg*) alternates with disyllabic forms, such as, the first person singular of the present, *degaf* (W *dygaf*). It is theoretically possible that the alternation between *o* in the monosyllables *colm* 'bind!' and *tor* 'break!' on the one hand, and *e* in the dissyllables *kelmys* 'bound' and *terrys* 'broken' on the other, are in Cornish of the same origin as the *o — e* alternation in *dog — degaf*. In other past participles, such as, *lethys* 'killed' and *gwenys* 'pierced', the vowel is the result of *i*-affection of *a*. It is reasonable , therefore, to assume that in *kelmys* and *terrys* the *e* is the result of *i*-affection of *o*.

From the sixteenth century onwards original *ew* in Cornish disyllables and polysyllables has a marked tendency to become *ow*. Thus *clewes* 'to hear' becomes *clowas* and *tewel* 'to throw' becomes *towel*. Tregear, for example, writes the past participle of *kewsel* 'to speak' as *kowses* and *kewses* within a few lines of each other (TH 1). In earlier MC the past participle of *tewlel* 'to throw, to intend' is *tewlys*, *teulys*:

> *y doull ganso o **tewlys** 'his plan was plotted by him' PA 7c*
> *yn trok horn y fyth **teulys** 'into a coffin of iron he will be*
>   thrown' RD 2166
> *the vn carn y fue **teulys** 'onto a pile he was thrown' RD 2333.*

In LC -*ys* of the past participle is often written with *e* or *a*, suggesting that the unstressed vowel has become schwa. The result of the two phonetic developments of stressed *ew* > *ow*, and the weakening of unstressed -*yz*, would lead us to expect to find *tewlys* written <towles> or <towlaz> z in the later language. This is exactly what we do find:

> *mabe cothe adam **towles** why a weall tha vysshew bras*
>   'Adam's elder son you see cast to great mischief' CW
>   1501–02
> *Leben pe reg Jesus clowaz tero Jowan **towlaz** tha bressen 'Now*
>   when Jesus heard that John had been thrown into prison'
>   RC 23: 189.

These forms are the result of spontaneous phonetic developments and have nothing to do with the analogical loss of *i*-affection. One could, nonetheless, argue that the regular development of *tewlys* > *towles*, *towlaz* assisted the analogical loss of *i*-affection elsewhere. The development *tewlys* > *towlaz* must incidentally also be borne in mind when discussing the two attested forms of the preterite, *kewsys* 'he spoke' and *cowsas* 'he spoke' (see below).

THE PRESENT-FUTURE

Lever 'says' > laver

I-affection is frequent in MC, though not universal, in the third person singular of the present-future. A good example of *i*-affection is provided by the form *lever*, the third person singular present-future of the verb *leverel* 'to say'. As can be seen from the following examples, *i*-affection is the rule in MC in this part of the verb:

> *del* **lever** *zyn an levar* 'as the Book tells us' PA 135d
> *A el me a* **leuer** *thy's* 'O angel, I tell thee' OM 736
> *a* **leuer** *y vos map dv* 'who says he is the son of God' PC 326
> *me a* **leuer** *an guyr thy's* 'I tell thee the truth' RD 64
> *Me a* **lever** *zyvgh mester* 'I tell you, master' BM 118
> *So me a* **levar** *thewgh why* 'But I tell you' TH 27
> *enoch me a* **levar** *thyes* 'Enoch, I tell thee' CW 2110.

The first person singular is *lavaraf* and the singular imperative is *lavar!* 'speak!' Forms like these began to influence the third person singular of the present-future so that it was analogically reshaped from *lever* to *lavar, laver*. The variant *lavar, laver* 'says' is first to be noted in Tregear's Homilies (*c.* 1555). It is not uncommon thereafter:

> *kepar dell* **lavar** *an Abostyll pedyr* 'as the apostle Peter says'
>   TH 3a
> *den veith ny* **lavar** 'no man says' SA 59
> *Pew a* **laver** 'Who will say?' SA 59
> *me a* **laver** *the gee* 'I tell thee' SA 62
> *Martesyn te a* **lavar** 'Perhaps thou wilt say' SA 62a
> *me a* **laver** *e bask e honyn* 'I say "his own passover"' SA 64a
> *why a* **lavar** *gwyre dremas* 'you speak true, good man' CW 588
> *eva me a* **lavar** *theis* 'Eve, I tell thee' CW 792
> *me a* **lavar** *theis an case* 'I will tell the the case' CW 903
> *me a* **lavar** *theis dibblance* 'I tell the plainly' CW 1839
> *ha me a* **lavar** *dhîz* 'and I will tell thee' BF: 17.

This is a well-attested and incontrovertible example of the analogical loss of *i*-affection.

kef, kyf 'finds, gets' > *caf*

We have already noted MB *queff* 'gets', MW *keiff*, ModW *caiff* 'gets'. The equivalent in MC is *kyf, kef*, which is widely attested:

a gef bos lour 'that will get enough fodder' OM 1060
ef a gyf yn araby 'he will find in Arabia' OM 1930
ena why a gyf asen 'there you will find an ass' PC 176
me a'n kyf by god ys blod 'I will find him by God's blood' RD
    543
ny gyf methek a'n sawya 'he will not find a doctor who will
    heal him' RD 1648
me an kyff lel 'I find it truly' BM 392
ena wy a gyff yn lel 'there you will find truly' BM 967
me as kyef pan vydnaf ve 'I get them when I want' CW 1457
ty a gyef in yet vdn eall 'thou wilt find an angel in the gate'
    CW 1753.

By the LC period this has apparently given way to a form **caf*. I know
of only one example, from the folk-tale 'Jowan Chy an Horth' recorded
by Lhuyd from Nicholas Boson at the end of the seventeenth century:

    ha enna ti an kâv 'and there thou wilt find him' BF: 17 (also
    AB: 257a).

If we had more LC, we would no doubt have more examples of *caf*
'gets, finds' without *i*-affection.

THE CORNISH PRETERITE IN -*YS*

Kewsys 'spoke' > cowsas

The -*ys* preterite *keusys, kewsys* with *i*-affection is common in MC.
Nonetheless from the earliest texts there is a slight tendency to replace
it with the -*as* preterite without *i*-affection. In *Pascon agan Arluth*, for
example, one finds both **A**. *kewsys* and **B**. *cowsas*, both meaning
'spoke':

    A.
    an ioull ze adam kewsys 'the devil spoke to Adam' PA 6c
    An ioul ze grist a gewsys 'The devil spoke to Christ' PA 14a
    ihesus a gewsys arta 'Christ spoke again' PA 34c
    Ihesus a gewsys arte 'Jesus spoke again' PA 74a
    Kayphas arta a gewsys 'Again Caiaphas spoke' PA 93a
    pylat a gewsys yn scon 'Pilate spoke at once' PA 101c
    Iudas scaryoth a gewsys 'Judas Iscariot spoke' PA 104a
    Han ezewon a gewsys 'And the Jews spoke' PA 105a
    hy a gewsys del ylly 'she spoke as she was able' PA 166a.

B.

an lauar crist pan **gowsas** 'when Christ spoke the word' PA 68a

orto Ihesus a **gowsas** 'to him Jesus spoke' PA 80d

pedyr arta a **gowsas** 'Peter spoke again' PA 84d

gurris ve yn y golon yn delma gul may **cowsas** 'it was put in his heart so to do, so that he spoke' PA 89bc

worth ihesus ef a **gowsas** 'to Jesus he spoke' PA 92a

pan **gowsas** *crist yn della* 'when Christ spoke thus' PA 94b

Pylat arte a **gowsas** 'Pilate spoke again' PA 126c

a watta ef a **gowsas** *agis mygtern* 'behold, he said, your king' PA 147c

ze stirya yw a **gowsas** *arluth prag y hysta vy* 'what he said is to be interpreted, Lord, why didst thou forsake me? PA 201c

Marrak arall a **gowsas** 'Another soldier spoke' PA 246a.

The unaffected form *cowsas* is the normal one in later Cornish:

Dew a **cowsas** *an ger* 'God spoke the word' SA 61a

y **cowses** *gans chardge pur greyf* 'he declared with a strong injunction' CW 1538

kyns lemyn sure a **gowzas** 'who declared spoke before now' CW 2422

Ha e **gowzas** 'And he spoke' RC 23: 179

Ha an dean a **gowzas** 'And the man spoke' RC 23: 179

Ha an arleth Deew a **gowzas** *tha an venen* 'And the Lord God spoke to the woman' RC 23: 179

Tha an venen e **cowzaz** 'To the woman he spoke' RC 23: 181

Ha tha Adam e a **gowzas** 'And to Adam he spoke' RC 23: 181

Deu a **Couzas** *an geryou ma* 'God spoke these words' BF: 41

Deiu **Cowsas** *Gerria ma* 'God spoke these words' BF: 55.

We have seen above that MC past participle *tewlys* appears as *towlaz* in LC. LC *cowsaz* 'spoke' might therefore be the regular phonetic development of MC *keusys*, *kewsys* with erstwhile *i*-affection, rather than a variant in -*as* without it. The change of *ew > ow* had not taken place by the time of the manuscript of PA, i.e. by the early fifteenth century at the latest. *Cowsas* in PA, therefore, is not a phonetic development of *kewsys*. It must rather be a different form of the preterite. If *cowsas* and *kewsys* 'spoke' co-existed in Middle Cornish, LC *cowsas*, *cowzas* can either be understood as continuing MC *cowsas* or, as is perhaps more likely, as representing the LC reflexes of both MC *kewsys* and *cowsas*. This latter view gets some corroboration from Tregear's spellings, *eff a gowses* TH 43, *eff a gowsys* TH 43, which are halfway between *kewsys* and *cowsas*. At all events, it seems likely that the prevalence of *cowsas* in the later language may have assisted the loss of *i*-affection in other preterites.

Tewlys 'threw' > *towlas*

The past participle of the MC verb *tewlel* 'to throw, to intend' has been mentioned above. The verb in MC has a preterite in -*ys*

> *ef as* **tewlys** *dre sor bras zen ezewon yn treze* 'he threw them in great anger in among the Jews' PA 103c
> *me re* **teulys** *dew grabel* 'I have thrown two grappling-hooks' RD 2271

By the later sixteenth century this has been replaced by a preterite in -*as*:

> *rag an wethvas a ruke offrennia ii mittes, hy a* **dowlas** *in offering a Dew moy agis y oll* 'for the widow offered two mites, she cast into the offering-box of God more than them all' SA 64.

The third person singular ending of the -*ys* preterite is always written <is> in SA, e.g. *ha'n hynwis e gois* 'and he called it his blood' SA 61a; *Ef a causis an geir* 'He spoke the word' SA 62; *me a leveris thees* 'I told thee' SA 62a; *Peder a leveris* 'Peter said' SA 63; *ef a ruk e corf ha leveris* 'he made his body and said' SA 64a and *An keth Austen ma a leveris* 'This same Augustine said' SA 66. The form **towlas* seen in *hy a dowlas* at SA 64 cannot, therefore, be a phonetic development of the preterite *tewlys* 'threw'. In this respect it differs from the LC past participle *towlaz* 'thrown' (see above), which could quite easily represent MC *tewlys*. The preterite **towlas* in SA must be an analogical replacement of an -*ys* preterite by an -*as* preterite, in which there is no trace of *i*-affection.

Sevys 'stood up, arose' > *savas*

In other verbs the loss of *i*-affection is more certain, for example in the preterite of *sevel* 'to stand'. The MC -*ys* preterite of the verb is *sevys*, which is well attested:

> *onan yn ban a* **sevys** 'one stood up' PA 81a
> *Ena pan* **sevys** *yn ban* 'Then when he stood up' PA 166a

En marrek na a **sevys** *oll yn ban y goweze* 'That soldier roused his companions completely' PA 245a

Ihesu crist . . . **sevys** *gallas ze gen le* 'Jesus Christ has risen, he has gone to another place' PA 255b-c

Del **sevys** *mab du ay veth* 'As the son of God rose from his grave' PA 259a

kepar del **sevys** *a'n beth* 'just as he rose from the grave' RD 666

ny **seuys** *nes* 'he did not rise at all' RD 1021.

In LC, however, one finds several examples of *savas* for *sevys*:

Ha e **savaz** *am'àn amez e uili* 'And he got up out his bed' BF: 18

ha mi a **savaz** *am'àn* 'and I got up' BF: 18

ne rege hi doaze ha **zavaz** *derez leba era an flô* 'until it came and stood over the place where the child was' RC 23: 196.

This is a clear instance of the loss of *i*-affection in the preterite.

Closely related to the verb *sevel* is the verb *drehevel* 'to raise, to rise'. This has a preterite in *-ys* with *i*-affection in MC, of which only one example is known to me:

Y ij luff y **trehevys** 'he raised his two hands' BM 4431

John Boson, however, in his version of the Apostles' Creed uses a form with *a* rather than *e* in the stressed syllable:

ha an trugga deth Eau **derauas** *arta durt an Marrow* 'and the third day he rose again from the dead' BF: 41.

Here also *i*-affection has been lost.

Leverys 'said' > *lavaras*
The third person singular of the preterite of the verb *leverel* 'to say' is *leverys* in MC. The form is very frequent and I cite here only a handful of examples:

Iudas fals a **leuerys** 'false Judas said' PA 36a

ha'n el thy'm a **leuerys** 'and the angel said to me' OM 844

ty re'n **leuerys** *iudas* 'thou hast said it, Judas' PC 759

an el thy'n a **leuerys** 'the angel told us' RD 1062

Y **leferys** *offeren* 'he said mass' BM 4419

*an tas a **leverys*** 'the Father said' TH 1

*ha ef a ruk e corf ha **leveris*** 'and he made his body and said'
SA 64a

*ha in delma y **leverys** an gyrryow ma* 'and thus he said these
words' CW 1374–75.

By the LC period the unstressed syllables have been reduced to schwa
but the stressed *e* < *a* by *i*-affection remains. We thus find such forms as
lavèraz BF: 19, *laveraz* BF: 51, 52 x 6, and *laveras* BF: 52. These are
examples of a purely phonetic development. Since the stressed vowel
is still *e*, *i*-affection remains. Not infrequently in LC, however, the
stressed vowel *e* has been analogically replaced by *a*, in the following
quotations for example:

*eue **levarraz** droua* 'he said that it was' BF: 25

*Deu a Couzas an geryou ma, ha **lavaras*** 'God spoke these
words, and said' BF: 41

*ha Deu **lavaras** dothans* 'and God said to them' BF: 53

*Ha Deu **lavaras**, Mero* 'And God said, Behold' BF: 53

*Deiu Cowsas Gerria ma—ha **lavaraz*** 'God spoke these
words—and said' BF: 55

*Ha e a **lavarraze*** 'And he said' RC 23: 174

*Ha an vennen a **lavarraz** tha an hagar-breeve* 'And the woman
said to the evil serpent' RC 23: 175

*Deew a **lavarraz*** 'God said' RC 23: 175

*Ha an hagar-breeve a **lavarraz** tha'n vennen* 'And the evil
serpent said to the woman' RC 23: 175

*Ha an arleth Deew a gerias tha Adam ha **lavarraz** thotha* 'And
the Lord God called to Adam and said to him' RC 23: 178

*Ha e **lavarraz*** 'And he said' RC 23: 178

*Ha an arleth Diew a **lavarras** tha an hagar-breeve* 'And the
Lord God said to the evil serpent' RC 23: 180

*Ha an tempter theath thotha ha **lavarraz*** 'And the tempter
came to him and said' RC 23: 186

*Buz e gwerebas ha **lavarraz*** 'But he answered and said' RC
23: 186

*Ha **lavarraz** thotha: mo thosta maab Deew* 'And said to him: if
thou art the son of God' RC 23: 187

*Chreest a **lavarraz** thotha* 'Christ said to him' RC 23: 187

*Ha **lavarraz** thotha: oll a rimah ve vedn ry theeze* 'And said to
him: all these I will give' RC 23: 188

*Ha en gye **lavarraz** thotha* 'And they said to him' RC 23: 195.

In these cases all trace of *e* by *i*-affection has been lost. *I*-affection has been analogically removed.

debrys 'ate' > debras > dabras

In the MC texts the verb *dybry*, *debry* 'to eat' has a preterite in *-ys* in the third person singular:

> *kemer tyyr spus a'n aval a **dybrys** adam the das* 'take three
> pips of the apple which thy father Adam ate' OM 823–24.

By the sixteenth century *dybrys* has been replaced by a preterite in *-as*.

> *hy a gemeras ran an frut hag an **debbras*** 'she took part of the
> fruit and ate it' TH 3a
> *hag eff a **thebbras*** 'and he ate' TH 3a
> *agan Savyour a **thebbras** an pascall one* 'our Saviour ate the
> paschal lamb' TH 52.

Nicholas Boson, recorded by Lhuyd, has *ha'n bara dzhei a **dhabraz*** 'and the bread they ate' BF: 19; cf. AB: 253a. Here **dabraz* is unmotivated, given that the unaffected stem is *deber* rather than **daber*. It seems that analogy with other verbs that demonstrate *e—a* alternation has produced the unwarranted form *dhabraz*. This can, nonetheless, be regarded as a further analogical loss of *i*-affection.

THE CORNISH VERBAL NOUN IN -EL

Sevel 'to arise' > saval

As has been noted above, the verbal noun suffix *-el* (*<*ilis*) causes *i*-affection of the preceding vowel. A good example is the verbal noun *sevel* 'to stand' (cf. *sevys* 'arose' discussed above). This is common in the MC texts, e.g. *sevel* OM 2575; *sevell* PA 240d; *seuel* OM 1348, 1407, 1690; *seuell* PA 22c, 22d. In the later MC texts the final syllable is often reduced to *-al*, *-all*, e.g. *sevall* CW 93, 1210, 1774. Nonetheless the root vowel here is still *e*, the reflex of *a* by *i*-affection. There is some evidence that in LC the root vowel was altered to *a* by analogy with the stem form *saf*. There are only two examples known to me:

> *Pe reg e **saval**, e comeraz an flô* 'When he got up, he took the
> child' RC 23: 198
> *îz **saval*** glossing *Seges, Standing corn* AB: 147c.

Though poorly attested, *saval* for *sevel* is a further example of the analogical loss of i-affection.

Leverel 'to say, to tell' > *lavaral*

The verbal noun *leverel*, *leferel* (cf. *lever* and *leverys* discussed above) is common in MC. By the sixteenth century the unstressed final syllable has weakened to the neutral vowel schwa and is written in a variety of ways: *leverall* SA 59 x 4, CW 1175; *leverol* BF: 31 x 3 and *laveral* BF: 15, 16. In all these cases the stressed syllable remains *e* < *a* by *i*-affection. On occasion in LC, however, one finds forms where the stressed syllable has been analogically changed from *e* > *a* (cf. *lavaras*, *lavaraz*, etc., of the preterite):

> *ha mee ved'n **lavarel** deese* 'and I will tell thee' BF: 16
> *ha me vedn **lavarel** dhîz* 'and I will tell thee' BF: 17
> *a reeg doaze teeze veer thor an Est tha Jerusalem, **Lavaral***
>   'wise men came from the East to Jerusalem, saying' RC 23:
>   194.

There is also a reduced form of the verbal noun, written *lawl*, *laule* or *laol*. This I take to be a reduction of *lavarel*, *lavaral*, possibly via the stages: **l'var'l* with loss of unstressed syllables, > **larl* with simplification of the impossible cluster **lv*, > *laul* by vocalization of the cluster *rl* > *ul*. The reduced form of the verbal noun is well attested:

> *pu reg **laule** theese?* 'who told thee?' RC 23: 179
> *a restah debre, thort an gwethan a reege a vee **laule** theeze a na*
>   *rosesta debre?* 'didst thou eat from the tree from which I
>   told thee: thou shouldst not eat?' RC 23: 179
> *thor an wethan a reege a vee **lawle** theeze chee na raage debre*
>   *anothe* 'from the tree I told thee, thou shalt not eat from it'
>   RC 23 : 182
> *Ha an arleth Doew reeg **lawle*** 'And the Lord God said' RC 23:
>   183
> *Thort an termin notha Jesus reeg dalla a boroga, ha tha **laale***
>   'From the time from which Jesus began to preach, and to
>   say' RC 23: 190
> *Ha e ez devannaz tha Bethalem, ha reeg **laule** thonz* 'And he
>   sent them to Bethlehem and said to them' RC 23: 196
> *cowsez gen Arleth neve der an prophet o **laule*** 'spoken by the
>   Lord of heaven by the prophet, saying' RC 23: 198–99
> *a ve cowzez gen Jerman an prophet, **laule*** 'that was spoken by
>   the prophet Jeremiah, saying' RC 23: 199

Kouza, **lâol** glossing *Dico . . . To say, to speak, to tell* AB: 54c
Dho dissembla, dha **lâol** *gou* glossing *Simulo . . . To feign, to counterfeit, &c.* AB: 150b–c
an peath eggee e **Lal** *tha ni da zeel* 'that which he tells us on Sunday' LAM: 228.

Although reduced in form, *lawle* should be considered a variant of *lavaral* and thus further evidence for the loss of *i*-affection in LC.

THE REPLACEMENT OF -*EL* AND -*Y* OF THE VERBAL NOUN
In ModB, as we have seen, the suffix -*el* of the verbal noun, which causes *i*-affection, is frequently replaced by a suffix which does not. Thus, for example, MB *leverel* becomes ModB *lavarout*. Something similar appears to occur in LC, where the two endings -*el* and -*y* of the verbal noun are on occasion replaced by -*a*. I have only a handful of examples:

Dho **honua** glossing *Appello . . . To Name or Call* AB [4]3a (MC *henwel*)
Dho **tulla** glossing *Perforo, To bore through* AB: 117c; *Tolla, Bore; Tellyz, Bored, perforated, &c.* AB: 248a (MC *telly*)
a **towlah** *rooze en mor* 'throwing a net into the sea' RC 23: 191; *ha lebben thera Ma* **toula** *tho gwellaz mar pel itna* 'and now I am intending to see as far in it' BF: 29 (MC *tewlel*).

Lhuyd's *Dho honua* 'to name' is curious, given that the expected unaffected stem would be *hanow*, rather than *honow. I assume that *honua* derives from *hanwa, where the labialized consonant cluster *nw* has lowered $a > o$. In this context one should note that Thomas Boson writes:

Naras **hanwall** *de Arlith Deu heb oatham, rag na vedn an Arlith gave do Neb ra E* **hanwelle** *heb oatham* 'Thou shalt not name thy Lord God in vain, for the Lord will not forgive anyone who names him in vain' BF: 41.

One might take the forms *hanwall, hanwelle* to be comparable with *saval* discussed above, i.e. with loss of *i*-affection even before -*el*. There is evidence, however, that MC internal *e* is on occasion lowered to *a* before *n*, e.g. *hana* x 2 (MC *henna*) 'that, this, he' glossing *Is* and *Iste* AB: 73b.[4] *Hanwall, hanwelle* may conceivably be examples of the analogical loss of *i*-affection. They may also be phonetic developments of *i*-affected *henwel* itself.

The replacement of *-el* by *-a* in *towla* < *tewlel* is mentioned above for the sake of completeness. It must be admitted that the stem would have been *towl-* even without the change of suffix from *-el* > *-a* (cf. *cowsys* < *kewsys* above).

Notice incidentally that Lhuyd cites *dho golli* (alongside *Kelli*) glossing *Perdo, . . . To lose, to destroy* AB: 117b and *loski* glossing *Uro . . . To burn, to parch* AB: 177c. In both cases the final *-i/-y* remains, but *i*-affection has been lost in the stem.

A further loss of *i*-affection occurs when instead a form in *-el* with *i*-affection the bare stem without *i*-affection is used as the verbal noun. The most obvious example is the common variant of the verbal noun *cows* 'to speak', which occurs alongside *kewsel, cowsel*:

> *heb **cows** ger y clamderis* 'without speaking a word she
>   fainted' PA 165d
> *rag **cous** orthyf ha talkye* 'to converse with me and to talk' OM
>   150
> *rak ef the **cous** whetlow gow* 'because he utters false stories'
>   PC 1392
> *pan eses ganso ov **covs*** 'when thou wast talking to him' BM
>   1051
> *hag inweth ow **cows** dre y apostylls* 'and also talking through
>   his apostles' TH 7a.

Cows 'to speak' also has a LC form in *-a*, seen for example in *Mêz **cowsa** nebaz an gwella* 'But to speak little is best' LAM: 246; ***Kouza*** glossing *Dico . . . To say, to speak* (AB: 54c) and in the famous sentence quoted by Carew, *Meea na vidna **cowza** sawzneck* 'I can speak no Saxonage' LAM: 272.

The only other example known to me of a verbal noun in *-el* replaced by the unaffected stem-form is cited by Lhuyd: *Dho **maru*** glossing *Intereo . . . To die, to fail or come to naught* AB: 72a. The more usual form is *merwel* with *i*-affection (cf. MB *meruel, mervell, mervel* cited above).

THE PAST PARTICIPLE

The past participle in MB and ModB ends in *-et*, and this does not cause *i*-affection. It is apparent from the OB personal names *Matganet, Matgganet, Daganed*, all containing the element *-ganet* 'born' (Fleuriot: 314) that *-et* without *i*-affection was already in place in the earliest recorded stages of the language.

In MC on the other hand the ending of the past participle is *-ys* (< **-îto*) and this has always caused *i*-affection.

ervys 'armed' (stem *arf*) PC 939, RD 351; *yrvys* PA 241d,
242b, 250c, OM 2141, 2170, 2204

gesys 'left' (stem *gas*) PA 182d, 184c, 233d, OM 1492, 1589,
1606, BM 1254, TH 40a x 4; *geses* TH 1; *gesis* SA 61; *gerys*
TH 25a

gevys 'forgiven' (stem *gaf*) PA 185c, TH 38a, 44; *gyfys* PC 529;
gefys RD 1102

gylwys 'called' (stem *galow*) PA 124a, OM 676, 952, BM 1,
TH 1a, 2a, 6, 7a; *gilwis* SA 64; *gelwys* BM 168, 512, 645

guenys 'pierced' (stem *gwan*) PC 2376, RD 2603; *gwenys* TH
15a, CW 1572

hynwys 'named' (stem *hanow*) PA 214a, 217a, 217d, TH 29;
henwys OM 1771, BM 2550, CW 375, TH 31a; *henwis* SA
66a x 2, CW 12; *henways* BM 2455

kechys 'caught' (stem *cach*) PC 2293; *kychys* RD 2596;
chechys PA 48d

kefys 'got' (stem *caf*) PA 98c, 246d, TH 6, CW 743; *keffys* PA
119c, 128d, RD 1901, TH 10a; *kyfys* PA 141b, TH 37; *kyffys*
TH 11; *kyffes* TH 1; *kevys* CW 1496, 1745, 1896, 2205

kenys 'sung' (stem *can*) PC 903[5]

kerys 'loved' (stem *car*) RD 1221, BM 187, 675, TH 26 x 2, 31,
31a; *keris* PA 214d, BM 288, 570; *kerrys* CW 1327

leddrys 'stolen' (stem *lader*) RD 354

lezys 'killed' (stem *lath*) PA 17d, 49d, 95b, 98b, 118a, 119b,
128c, 141c, 210d; *lethys* OM 596, RD 340, 428, 593, BM 881,
976, 1517; *lethis* TH 23

megys 'nourished' (stem *mag*) BM 3872, 3886, 3893, TH 41,
49; *megis* SA 63a.

Lhuyd makes clear that *-ys* is usually pronounced *-ez* or *-az* in LC.
Speaking of the past participle he says:

I am sensible that the Modern Pronunciation of the Cornish,
does not confirm the Termination of this Participle's being
always in *-yz*: For they generally end it in *ez*, Saying *Kreiez*,
Called; *Trehez*, Cut; *Miskemerez*, Mistaken; *Dylîez*,
Revenged; *Guerhez*, Sold, &c. and sometimes in *az*: As
Ledhaz, Slain; *Kyrtaz*, Delayed; *Guesgaz*, Worn; tho' not
seldom, also in *yz*: As *Devydhyz*, Quenched; *Devedhyz*,
Come; *Bidhyz*, Drowned; *Kelmyz*, Bound; *Huedhyz*, Swoln.
(AB: 248b)

We must assume that the vowel of the suffix -*ys* in LC was actually the neutral vowel schwa, which Lhuyd heard differently in different environments. It should be noted that in the LC past participle *i*-affection is usually present in those verbs that can have it. Here are a few examples:

> **engrez** 'angered' (stem *anger*) RC 23: 199
> **gerres** 'left' (< *gesys*; stem *gas*) LAM: 230
> **humbregez** 'led' (stem *humbrank, humbrag*) RC 23: 185
> **kevez** 'found' (stem *caf*) BF: 25, 27; *keevez* BF: 25
> **kellez, kelles** 'lost' (stem *coll*) BF: 46, 48; *Kellyz* glossing
>   *Perditus . . . lost, destroy'd, undone* AB: 117b
> **ketchys** 'taken' (stem *cach*) Borlase 395
> **Kelmyz** 'bound' (stem *colm*) AB: 248b
> **Ledhaz** 'killed' (stem *lath*) AB: 104c, 248b
> **Selliz** 'salted' (stem *sall*) AB: 143c
> **Tegez** 'choked' (stem *tag*) AB: 157c.

The two forms *ledhaz* and *Tegez* cited by Lhuyd are clearly LC, as can be seen from the reduced final syllable. Lhuyd in his Cornish grammar also also cites the following past participles with *i*-affection: *ervyz*, *yrvyz* 'armed' (stem *arf*); *gevyz, givyz* 'forgiven' (stem *gaf*); *guenyz, guinyz* 'pierced' (stem *gwan*); *megyz* 'bred' (stem *mag*) AB: 248a. It is not clear whether these are LC forms which he had actually heard or MC forms he had merely read in manuscript. Lhuyd's *Po marh ledryz* 'When a horse is stolen' AB: 249a, on the other hand, is clearly a contemporary phrase which Lhuyd heard in Cornwall. This patently contains the past participle *ledryz* 'stolen' (stem *lader*) with *i*-affection.

Although the past participle is the most favourable environment in LC for the persistence of *i*-affection, there are a number of LC examples of the past participle without *i*-affection, where it would be expected:

> *pan glowa an nowethys y vos* **lathys** 'when he hears the news
>   that he is killed' CW 1137
> *rag tho angye* **lathez** 'for they are killed' RC 23: 200
> *Po the'ns* **Salles** *da* 'when they are well salted' BF: 43
> *Path' ens* **salles** *dah* 'when they are well salted' BF: 44
> *na vedn an Tavaz ma beska boz* **kavas** *arta en us ni* 'that this
>   language will never be found again in our age' BF: 46
> **garres** *ew ni* 'left are we' BF: 59 (for **gasys*)
> *But* **Kòlhyz**, *Lost* AB: 248a.

In the LC past participle too, then, analogy has been at work and *i*-affection is beginning to be lost.

CONCLUSION

In ModB *i*-affection in the verbal system has been largely removed by analogy. Although the sources are fragmentary, there is good evidence that *i*-affection was similarly being deleted from the verbal system of LC. The analogical loss of *i*-affection in the Breton verb is one of the features which distinguish ModB from MB. ModB as a written language is generally held to have begun in 1659 with the publication of Julien Maunoir's grammar (Hardie 1948: 9). At this same period Cornish was confined to the far west of Cornwall and was rapidly disappearing. Although Cornish lingered on in Mount's Bay until *c. 1785, it had ceased to be a community language by the early eighteenth century. By the LC period, analogy had already begun to delete* *i*-affection from the verbal system. If Cornish, like Breton, had survived into the nineteenth and twentieth centuries, we can be sure that *i*-affection would largely have disappeared from the Cornish verb.

NOTES AND REFERENCES

A shorter version of this paper was given at the Tionól of the Celtic School of the Dublin Institute for Advanced Studies in November 2001.

1. The Welsh personal name *Tegid* is from Latin *Tacitus* by internal *i*-affection. Many years ago I suggested (BBCS 22 (1967), 236–8) that the name of the British king *Pygys* at BM 2463 might be a misreading for **Tygys* 'Tegid, Tacitus'. In view, however, of the sixth-century Cornish inscription containing the name RICATI < ?**Rigocati* (LHEB 456–7), *Pygys* might be better understood as a misreading for 8*Rygys*, the expected MC development of **Rigocatus*.
2. My MB examples are taken from HMSB and my MW examples from GMW.
3. 'Vowel affection tends to disappear in Modern Breton, or becomes irregular' HMSB: 177.
4. I have discussed this lowering of *e* before *n* in *Studia Celtica* 32 (1998), 143–6.
5. PC 902–4 reads as follows: *peder me a leuer thy 's/ kyns ys bos kullyek kenys/ terguyth y wregh ov naghe.* Previous commentators have taken 8*kullyek-kenys* to be a noun meaning 'cock-crow'. This cannot be correct. I take *kenys* to be a past participle used actively: 'Peter, I tell thee/ before the cock shall have crowed/ thou shalt deny me thrice.'

ABBREVIATIONS

AB	Edward Lhuyd, *Archæologia Britannica*, London, 1707, reprinted Shannon, 1971.
BBCS	*The Bulletin of the Board of Celtic Studies.*
BF	O.J. Padel, *The Cornish Writings of the Boson Family*, Redruth, 1975.
BG	Roparz Hemon, *Breton Grammar*, 10th edition, translated, adapted and revised by Michael Everson, Dublin, 1995.
BM	Whitley Stokes, *Beunans Meriasek: The Life of St Meriasek*, London, 1872.
CW	Whitley Stokes, 'Gwreans an Bys: the Creation of the World', *Transactions of the Philological Society*, 1864, Part IV.
DC	Roparz Hemon, *Doctrin An Christenien*, Dublin, 1977.
Fleuriot	Léon Fleuriot, *Le Vieux Breton: éléments d'une grammaire*, Paris, 1964.
GMW	D. Simon Evans, *A Grammar of Middle Welsh*, Dublin, 1964.
Hardie	D.W.F. Hardie, *A Handbook of Modern Breton (Armorican)*, Cardiff, 1948.
HMSB	Roparz Hemon, *A Historical Morphology and Syntax of Breton*, Dublin, 1984.
Kervella	*Yezhadur Bras ar Brezhoneg*, La Baule, 1947.
LAM	Alan M. Kent and Tim Saunders (eds), *Looking at the Mermaid: A Reader in Cornish Literature 900–1900*, London, 2000.
LC	Late Cornish.
LHEB	K.H. Jackson, *Language and History in Early Britain*, Edinburgh, 1953.
MB	Middle Breton.
ModB	Modern Breton.
MC	Middle Cornish.
OB	Old Breton.
OM	'Origo Mundi' in E. Norris, *Ancient Cornish Drama*, London 1859, Vol. I, pp. 1–219.
PA	Whitley Stokes, 'Pascon agan Arluth: The Passion of our Lord', *Transactions of the Philological Society*, 1860–1, Appendix, pp. 1–219.
PC	'Passion Domini Nostri Jhesus Christi', in E. Norris, *Ancient Cornish Drama*, London, 1859, Vol. I, pp. 221–479.
RC	*Revue Celtique.*
RD	'Resurrexio Domini Nostri Jhesu Christi' in E. Norris, *Ancient Cornish Drama*, London 1859, Vol. II, pp. 1–199.
SA	*Sacrament an Alter*, the last sermon in the Tregear manuscript, ff. 59–66a, pp. 38–43 in Bice's edition of TH.

TH   John Tregear, *Homelyes xiii in Cornysche*, British Library
Additional MS 46,397, quoted from Christopher Bice's
cyclostyled text (no place) 1969.

WG   J. Morris Jones, *A Welsh Grammar, Historical and Comparative*,
Oxford, 1913.

ADDITIONAL THOUGHTS ON THE MEDIEVAL 'CORNISH BIBLE'

Matthew Spriggs

INTRODUCTION

Malte Tschirschky presented a refutation in *Cornish Studies: Eleven* (2003) of Charles Penglase's evidence for the existence of a Medieval Cornish-language Bible. He argued that the internal evidence adduced by Penglase from the *Tregear Homilies* is not convincing enough to claim that John Tregear had access to a Middle Cornish translation of the Bible. Tschirschky points out that Penglase draws on no corroborating evidence to suggest the existence of such a Bible, and can find none himself, casting further doubt on the thesis. He also claims that a translation was considered briefly during the Reformation and this would not have been needed if there were an earlier extant version.[1]

It is true that Penglase presents no corroborating evidence, but this does not mean that such evidence cannot be found. It can, and some of it has been alluded to in print previously but unfairly dismissed. It is deserving of a proper hearing. I would also argue that Tschirschky's final contention against Penglase's thesis is questionable: there is in fact no evidence that a Cornish Bible translation was considered, even briefly, in the sixteenth century.

The earliest printed reference to the possible existence of a Medieval Cornish Bible can be found in the *Quarterly Review* of 1875 in an unsigned article entitled 'MS. Collections at Castle Horneck. 1720–1772'.[2] This refers to the manuscript collections of William Borlase (1696–1772), Vicar of Ludgvan and antiquary. In 1875 Castle Horneck, where the collections were held, was the residence of John Borlase (1829–1889), a great-great grandson of William. The author of the piece was clearly John's younger brother William Copeland Borlase (1848–1899), antiquary, later an MP and finally a disgraced bankrupt.[3] The manuscripts appear to have come into his possession, presumably by family agreement, at some time in the 1870s and were sold and dispersed with his other possessions in 1887.

The relevant passage in the *Quarterly Review* reads:

> and (which is perhaps more interesting than all) we hear in this collection of a *Cornish Bible*, translated (as it seems from the context) into *that language* by John de Trevisa, Fellow of Queen's College, Oxford, at the close of the 14th and commencement of the 15th century. Here is a subject for inquiry indeed: apart from its bibliographical value, this volume, if it exists, would restore to the philologist the entire Cornish tongue.[4]

FOWLER'S FRUITLESS SEARCH

John Trevisa (c. 1342–1402), Vicar of Berkeley, was of Cornish origin. He is known for his translations from Latin to English of some of the major reference works of the time, such as Higden's *Polychronicon*. His periods of residence at Queen's College, Oxford, overlapped with those of Wyclif and his associates, the first translators of the Bible into English. His association with this group and possible role in assisting with or translating the entire Bible into English have been discussed in print since 1482, but remain in dispute. Trevisa's modern biographer, David Fowler, is his latest champion in this regard, but others remains deeply unconvinced.[5] Fowler first drew attention to the above quoted passage about Trevisa being the translator of the Bible into Cornish in his article 'John Trevisa and the English Bible' in 1960, discussing his own unsuccessful search to locate the reference to Trevisa's Bible in William Borlase's manuscripts:

> The 'collection' referred to appears to be a part of what the writer earlier calls 'the Heraldic and Parochial collections of Dr Borlase,' which he distinguishes from the *Collectanea* (p. 369). I have not been able to locate these 'Heraldic and Parochial collections,' either at the Morrab Library (Penzance) or at the Museum of the Royal Institution of Cornwall. Mr C.W. Borlase Parker, of Penzance, who owns some of the Borlase papers, tells me that he does not recognise them as resembling any of the papers in his possession. I assume that the author of the article in the *Quarterly Review* saw a reference by Borlase to Trevisa's translation, similar to

the one in the *Collectanea* (see above, n. 24) and jumped
to the conclusion that it was a Cornish Bible, since Trevisa
was a Cornishman.[6]

Fowler returned to the topic in his 1995 book *The Life and Times of
John Trevisa, Medieval Scholar*. He recalled that his 1960 paper was
written: 'without having at that time laid eyes on the "Heraldic and
parochial collections" of Dr. Borlase. I have since found Borlase's
"Memorandums in Heraldry" (1740) in the Morrab Library, Penzance,
and it contains nothing to support the claims of the writer of the article
in the *Quarterly Review* for 1875.'[7]

WILLIAM COPELAND BORLASE EXONERATED
In fact, William Copeland Borlase was indeed reporting on what he
had seen in 1875, and it is Fowler who was misinformed. The reference
to 'Heraldic and parochial collections' was a general one, referring
to several different manuscripts. One of them was doubtless the
1740 manuscript on heraldry that Fowler examined, but the pertinent
reference is to Borlase's *Parochial Memorandums of Cornwall*, begun
in 1740 and now to be found in the British Library.[8] Under the entry
for the parish of Endellion we find this note:

> 17. NB: Mr Jam: Tregeare of Endellyon has Mt Calvary Corn:
> & Engl: by J[oh]n Keig[win]: & other fragm[en]ts of Corn:
> and some Ant[ien]t Evidence of Inquis : 12 of Eliz. And is
> promis'd a Corn[ish]: Bible translated by J Trevisa (formerly
> belonging to ye Chivertons . . . ibid. p.6 {+ a MS : of the/
> Saxon nobles/ from W 1st to Eliz/

This is further referred to in the text as 'Mr Tregeare's Letter'.[9]
The original of the letter can be found in Volume 5 of the Borlase
Letterbooks, indexed as item 16, from 'Mr Ja: Tregeare of Endellion &
its Manors etc, 118–125'[10]. Page 6 of the letter (page 123 of the
manuscript) reads:

> I have now by me a Cornish MSS and the English thereof/
> Titled Mount Calvary or the History of the passion Death
> and/ Resurrection of our Saviour Jesus Christ written as
> conjectu[re]d/ Some Centuries past, English'd by the late Mr
> Jo[h]n Keigwin,/ in the year 1682 and other Fragments of
> Cornish and Some/ Ancient Evidence in the English Tongue
> w[hi]ch, was by/ Survey & Inquest: 12 Eliz—and I think since
> none have been/ taken: I was (some time since) promis'd a

Cor[nish].—Bible Translated/ By our Country man J. Trevisa.
But can't come in to't yet, it did/ Belong to that ancient family
of Chiverton Extinct;

On the envelope side is written by Borlase 'Mr Tregeares Acc[oun]t/ of
Endellion/ May 1753'. There is no further evidence in Borlase's
correspondence that any progress was made by James Tregeare in
tracking down the Bible.

Rumours of a Cornish Bible, however, go back more than a
half-century before this. In a letter to the pioneer Celticist Edward
Lhuyd dated 20 February 1691/92 the antiquary John Aubrey told how
he had recently fallen into conversation with a young Cornish gentleman in a London coffee house:

> He acquaints me further that one Mr Keygwin in ye W[est] of
> Cornwall is a great master of ye Cornish/ tongue: he hath the
> greater part of ye Bible in Cornish Ms and also/ the History of
> ye Passion of our Saviour, entituled Mount Calvary,/ in
> Cornish verse [in the old Saxon character] as also is ye Bible]/
> writ by a Monke severall hundreds of years since: & he hath
> other/ MSS of w[hi]ch I shall have a Catalogue.[11]

That the Cornish scholar John Keigwin (1642–1716) certainly had
the second manuscript referred to is well-established. He had obtained
Mount Calvary, also known as the Passion Poem, from William Scawen
or from Scawen's estate. It ended up a few years later in the hands of
John Anstis and is now lodged in the British Library. The manuscript is
in a Court hand, presumably the 'Saxon character' referred to, and
is fifteenth-century in age although perhaps a copy of a fourteenth-
century original. The young Cornishman is identified by Aubrey in a
later letter of December that year as Prichford (or Richford, Rickford,
Prickford or even Bickford—the handwriting is hard to decipher). He
had certainly seen the Poem, and had sent a transcript to Cardinal
Howard in Rome. Aubrey again repeats the claim of a Cornish Bible in
Keigwin's possession in that further letter to Lhuyd.[12]

ALTERNATIVE INTERPRETATIONS
Does this prove the existence of a Medieval Cornish-language Bible? I
think not. Given the amount of documentation of Keigwin's Cornish
language materials by contemporary scholars it seems most unlikely
that a Cornish Bible would have escaped the attention of his associates
and pupils, such as William Scawen, John Anstis, the Boson family,
William Gwavas and Edward Lhuyd. Keigwin was the most celebrated

Cornish language scholar of his age.[13] He is most notable for his translations of all the then-available Cornish language texts: *The Passion Poem* in 1682, *The Creacion of the World* between 1691 and 1693, and the three dramas of the *Ordinalia* cycle, the translations of which were completed in 1695. John Anstis, who clearly knew Keigwin well, writing around 1693 in a passage which refers explicitly to Keigwin's translation efforts then underway was quite adamant that there were no other known Cornish language works.[14]

Assuming that the young Cornish gent had seen something in Keigwin's possession early in 1691 or before, it is possible that it was a transcript of *The Creacion of the World* that Anstis had provided to Keigwin in order for him to translate it into English. According to a transcription made by Lhuyd for Thomas Tonkin in 1703, this translation was requested by Jonathan Trelawny, at that time Bishop of Exeter, in 1691. Later information gives 1693 as the date of its completion.[15] But perhaps the most likely manuscript to be confused with a Cornish Bible would be a transcript of the Cornish language *Ordinalia* play cycle, including as it does a kind of summary of the Bible from the Creation to the Crucifixion. It is thus a condensation of both Testaments in Cornish verse and so might be colloquially considered to be equivalent to a Cornish Bible. Indeed, to someone not conversant with Cornish a transcript of the text without translation might well give the impression of being such, with its Latin section titles: *Ordinale de Origine Mundi*, *Passio Domini* and *Ordinale de Resurrexione Domini*.[16] Anstis had also provided this to Keigwin, seemingly again in 1691, and from his own interest rather than at Trelawny's request as claimed above. In a letter to Trelawny probably dated to December 1693, Anstis claimed that Keigwin had already finished translating the *Ordinalia*, but he appears in fact to have finally completed the task in 1695.[17]

Copies of either of the above works could have also led to the story retailed to James Tregeare of a Cornish Bible more than fifty years later. An alternative source for the confusion—if that is what it is—would be actual passages of scripture translated into Cornish during the initial attempts at language revival in the late seventeenth century, the most notable of which are the translations by William Rowe of Sancreed of Genesis III, Matthew II, 1–20 and Matthew IV.[18] Keigwin's own efforts were far more modest in this regard, consisting as far as we know only of Genesis I.

Given the power of the Church and the status of the language in the fourteenth century, any Cornish translation of the Bible would seem unlikely, and nor has it been attempted at any time until the modern language revival. The only probable context for any attempt at such a translation would have been as part of a self-conscious language revival movement such as got going initially towards to the end of the seventeenth century, and of which Keigwin was so vital a part.[19] There is no good evidence, however, that such a translation was attempted, beyond the few isolated chapters noted above.

A REFORMATION CORNISH BIBLE PROJECT?

Tschirschky offered as a further argument against the existence of a Cornish language Bible: that a Cornish translation was considered during the Reformation and would have been unnecessary if there was already one in existence. The sources he gives for this idea (Kent and Fudge) go back to Berresford Ellis' 1974 book *The Cornish Language and its Literature*, but the latter is merely paraphrasing Henry Jenner's earlier work. Neither Ellis nor Jenner actually suggested that such a Bible translation was contemplated in Tudor times, although Kent does indeed make this claim.[20] The claim centres on two texts. The first is among 'Articles drawn out by some certaine, and were exhibited to be admitted by authority, but not so admitted' in about 1560. Jenner suggests that this was drawn up by the extreme Protestant party within the Church. One of the Articles concerned 'A punishment for such as cannot say the catechisme'. In this is included, 'Item that it may be lawfull for such Welch or Cornish children as can speake no English to learn the Praemisses in the Welch tongue or Cornish language'.[21] This is hardly persuasive evidence for an attempt to have the Bible translated into Cornish, although it did occur at a time when there was certainly a move to have it translated into Welsh, shown by the Act for the latter translation being passed by Parliament in 1563. The second text is the basis for Alan Kent's claim that: 'The English writer Nicholas Udall argued that the Bible, Service and Prayer book should be available in Cornish'. This goes considerably beyond what his immediate source, Ellis, suggests.

The document referred to is usually attributed to Udall but it is now believed to have been penned by Devon layman Philip Nichols as an answer to the rebel demands at the time of the 1549 Prayer Book Rebellion in Devon and Cornwall.[22] It was, perhaps, written more to discourage further rebellious activities elsewhere in the realm than as a considered response. The passage in question is in answer to the eighth demand of the rebels, which was:

> Item we wil not receive the newe service because it is but lyke a Christmas game, but we wyll have oure olde service of Mattens, masse, Evensong and procession in Latten not in English, as it was before. And so we the Cornyshe men

(whereof certen of us understande no Englysh) utterly refuse thys newe Englysh.[23]

Nichols' response reads in part:

> If ye had understand no English and for that consideration had by the way of petition made humble request to the King's Majesty and his Council in this or some other like fourme. Where it hath please your most excellent Majesty by the authority of your high court of Parliament to sette forth unto your most loving and obedient subjects in the English tongue one uniform way of divine service to be used in all churches within this your highness' realme of Englande, So it is, most gracious sovereign that we the Cornishmen, being a portion of your most loving faithful and true obedient subjects, being also as much desirous to take thereby such ghostly consolation and edifying as others of your majesty's subjects do, and being no less hungry, prompt, glad, and ready to receive the light and truth of God's most holy word and ghospel than any other part of your Majesty's realm, most humbly beseech your Majesty that with such convenient speed as to your most excellent highness shall seem good we may by your grace's provision have the same fourme of divine service and communion derived and turned into our Cornish speech that goeth abroad among the rest of your most loving and obedient subjects in the other parts of this your realm of England, etc. If ye had (I say) made such an humble and godly request as this I doubt not but that the King, our sovereign lord's Majesty, would have tendered your request, and provided for the accomplishment of your desires.[24]

I see a suggestion here, largely rhetorical, that the new Prayer Book might be translated into Cornish. Again, this is hardly a call for translation of the Bible itself. Tschirschky's further objection to the existence of a Cornish Bible prior to the Reformation is thus unpersuasive, relying as it does on a somewhat exaggerated reading of what the primary sources actually state.

THE CHIVERTON CONNECTION

Does the apparent link with the Chiverton family give us any further clues as to how talk of a Cornish Bible could have been circulating in the mid-1700s? Assuming that it is the west Cornwall Chivertons that were referred to rather than the Quethiock branch in the East, the last male heir would have been William Chiverton (c. 1554–1628), who married Mary the widow of Walter Borlase (1539–1602) in 1604. They brought up her children by Borlase, including his heir John of Pendeen who was great-grandfather of William Borlase, the antiquary. Mary predeceased William Chiverton in 1614 and in his will he named her daughter Philippa as sole executrix. In 1628 Philippa was married to Nicholas Hickes and they moved into the Chiverton home at Kerris in Paul. Hickes died in 1632 and she then married John Gwavas, a barrister, who also predeceased her in 1641. His death prompted a legal battle between Philippa with her sons by Hickes and John's brother William Gwavas, which carried on beyond her death in 1675.[25]

If any Chiverton Cornish manuscripts had passed into Gwavas family hands we would certainly expect to have some notice of them, because William's grandson was William Gwavas (1676–1742), the noted Cornish language scholar.[26] Gwavas accumulated many Cornish language materials during his life and one wonders if it was rumour of one of these being the Cornish Bible that James Tregeare was chasing up? From Gwavas' collaboration and correspondence with Thomas Tonkin on the language we know that he had had access to the *Ordinalia* and other works transcribed and translated from the Cornish by John Keigwin, but there is no suggestion of a Bible being known to either Gwavas or Tonkin. William Gwavas' widow Elizabeth was buried in Paul in December 1752 and one wonders if James Tregeare's letter to William Borlase six months later was sent at a time when he was making enquiry of their two surviving daughters as to the possible existence of a Cornish Bible amongst their estate?

As well as Philippa, however, there had been other heirs of William Chiverton through the marriages of his sisters into the Arundell of Menadarva (Camborne) and Trewren of Trewardreva (Constantine) families.[27] Both lines seem to have died out, but Thomas Trewren (1693–c. 1745) the last male in the Trewren family married Mary, daughter of Stephen Usticke and his first wife Catherine (née Borlase) of Botallack in St Just in Penwith. Catherine was one of William Borlase's sisters. Stephen was one of that large clan of West Penwith Usticks that included the Reverend Henry Ustick (1720?–1769), who had married Mary Borlase, a distantly related niece of William.[28] Henry Ustick, Vicar of Breage, transcribed various Cornish language pieces for William, and if a Cornish Bible had come down in this line it is very likely that Borlase would have heard about it.

It does seem that William Borlase may have at some stage got hold of James Tregeare's copy of William Jordan's *Creation of the World* in Cornish, as what is surely this manuscript is now part of the Gatley manuscripts held by the Royal Institution of Cornwall. It once belonged to William Copeland Borlase and this suggests it was handed down from William Borlase himself and was part of the collections from Castle Horneck until Copeland Borlase's bankruptcy forced their dispersal by sale in 1887.[29] It is likely too that William made use of Tregeare's 'other Fragments of Cornish' because in the Cornish Vocabulary at the end of his *Antiquities Historical and Monumental of the County of Cornwall* he annotates some words with 'J.T.' as his source, referred to in the key to the vocabulary as 'J.T. Tregere Ms'.[30] While some have wanted to see this as a reference to further now lost works of the sixteenth century John Tregear, translator of Bishop Bonner's *Homilies* into Cornish, it seems more likely that it is Borlase's contemporary who is being acknowledged here.[31]

It is not clear to me at present which James Tregeare he is. The Crowan Tregeares, who had held land in Endellion among many other places, had died out in the male line by 1731. Another branch of the family lived in West Penwith and I suspect that James was one of this line. Further research is needed to provide a firm identification for him.[32]

CONCLUSION

What we do know is that his promised Trevisa Bible copy never eventuated. Even today, while the New Testament has recently been published in two competing forms of revived Cornish, the prospect of a full translation of the Old Testament seems still some way off even with modern technological advances aiding production.[33] As noted earlier, there is a lot of debate as to how involved John Trevisa was in producing the first English-language Bible in the fourteenth century. It was certainly a team effort. How much more daunting would have been the task of attempting to translate the Bible into Cornish, a language with relatively few speakers and with very few indeed who would have been literate in the language.

Like Tschirschky, I too would also be delighted to be proved wrong about its past existence by the discovery of a Medieval Cornish Bible translation. The discovery of *Beunans Ke* and the reappearance of several other notable Cornish language works in recent years gives us hope that more may yet be found, but the likelihood of one of these being a Medieval Cornish Bible would still seem slim.

NOTES AND REFERENCES

1. M.W. Tschirschky, 'The Medieval "Cornish Bible"', in Philip Payton (ed.), *Cornish Studies: Eleven*, Exeter, 2003, pp. 308–16; C. Penglase, 'La Bible en Moyen-Cornique', *Etudes Celtiques* 33, 1997, 233–43.
2. *Quarterly Review* 139, 1875, pp. 367–95.

3. This is made clear by a comparison with the book *The Descent, Name and Arms of Borlase of Borlase*, London, 1888, written by W.C. Borlase and containing entire passages exactly the same as in the *Quarterly Review* article; it is confirmed by his entry in G.C. Boase and W.P Courtney, *Bibliotheca Cornubiensis*, Vol. III, London, 1882, p. 1085, that attributes the article to him and notes that he was paid 30 guineas for writing it. A sketch of his life is provided by P.A.S. Pool, *William Borlase*, Truro, 1986, pp. 277–78, which treats in detail of the earlier William.

4. *Quarterly Review*, 1875, p. 393. The same passage occurs in Borlase, 1888, p. 189.

5. R. Waldron, 'Trevisa, John (b. c.1342, d. in or before 1402)', *Dictionary of National Biography*, Vol. 55, Oxford, 2004, pp. 353–54; D.C. Fowler, *The Life and Times of John Trevisa, Medieval Scholar*, Seattle, 1995, see especially pp. 213–34 for the Bible controversy.

6. D. Fowler, 'John Trevisa and the English Bible', *Modern Philology* 58, 1960, pp. 81–98. The quotation is from fn.26 on p. 86.

7. D.C. Fowler, 1995, p .232.

8. BL Egerton Ms. 2657.

9. Egerton 2657, fol. 121 (in pen '108').

10. Morrab Library, Penzance, Borlase Letterbooks, Volume 5.

11. Bodleian Ms. Ashmole 1814, fol. 96.

12. Bodleian Ms. Ashmole 1814, fol. 101r. For the life of the Cardinal see, A. White, 'Howard, Philip [name in religion Thomas] (1629–1694)', *Dictionary of National Biography*, Vol. 28, Oxford, 2004, pp. 409–12.

13. M. Spriggs, 'Keigwin, John (1642–1716)', *Dictionary of National Biography*, Vol. 31, Oxford, 2004, p. 39.

14. Bodleian Ms. Eng.b.2042, fol.130r.

15. Bodleian Ms. Corn.e.2, title page. The identification and date for this transcript come from my ongoing research into the identification of the various manuscript copies of the plays, based on Lhuyd's correspondence. This attribution is also given in T. Tonkin's Ms. *Archaeologia Cornu-Britannica* in the RIC, p. 193, where William Borlase later added in pencil 'finish'd 1693 re Mr Ustick's Copy'.

16. All known copies derive from Bodleian Ms. 791, which was donated to the Library by Jacob Button of Worcestershire in 1615. See A. Hawke, 'A Lost Manuscript of the Cornish Ordinalia?', *Cornish Studies* 7 (for 1979), 1980, pp. 45–60; also B. Murdoch, *Cornish Literature*, Cambridge, 1993, pp. 41–74. The first published version, with translation, was E. Norris, *The Ancient Cornish Drama*, 2 volumes, Oxford, 1859.

17. The Anstis letter is in Bodleian Ms. Eng.b.2042, fol.150r. A letter from Martin Keigwin, John's son, dated 22 October 1693 occurs in the same manuscript, fol.144r. It states that translation of the Ordinalia was still underway at that time. The 1695 date for completion is found at the end of a transcript of the Ordinalia translation in Bodleian Ms. Corn.e.2, a volume once belonging to Thomas Tonkin.

18. BL Add. Ms. 28,554, copied by the Rev. H. Ustick from a Ms. owned by William Rowe's brother Matthew. Transcripts were printed by R.M.

Nance in *Old Cornwall* II(11), 1936, pp. 32–36; II(12) 1936, pp. 25–27; III(1), 1937, pp. 41–44. Erroneous references are given for these in Murdoch, 1993, p. 156. The original manuscript from which Ustick copied was passed down in the Rowe family for several generations, ending up in Boston, Massachusetts, in 1908 where it was seen by J. Hambley Rowe in the possession of John Rowe Needham. The latter died in 1910 and the manuscript then disappeared. Efforts to trace its whereabouts have so far been unsuccessful. Before his death J.R. Needham privately printed an account of his family that discusses the manuscript in some detail: *Memoirs of the Kereve Family and also Select Works of the Same*, Boston, 1908.

19. For discussion of the early language revival movement see M. Spriggs, 'William Scawen (1600–1689)—A Neglected Cornish Patriot and Father of the Cornish Language Revival', in Philip Payton (ed.) *Cornish Studies: Thirteen*, Exeter, 2005, pp. 98–125. I take this opportunity to correct a missed line and a missed date in that article. In the middle of p. 113, para. 2, line 9, 'recording the work of Edward Lhuyd' should be changed to 'recording the language, recruiting them to a cause that was further greatly stimulated by the interest of Edward Lhuyd'; on the bottom line of p. 110 the dates for Sir Lewis Molesworth should read 1853–1912.

20. A.M. Kent, *The Literature of Cornwall: Continuity, Identity, Difference, 1000–2000*, Bristol, 2000, p. 51; C. Fudge, *The Life of Cornish*, Redruth, 1982, pp. 25–26; P. Berresford Ellis, *The Cornish Language and its Literature*, London 1974, pp. 62–4; H. Jenner, *A Handbook of the Cornish Language*, London, 1904, pp. 12–13.

21. Jenner, 1904, p. 13. The original is said to be Corpus Christi College, Cambridge, MSS. Synddalia cxxi, but Jenner was quoting from BL Egerton Ms. 2350, fol. 54.

22. This identification is noted in J. Youings, 'The South-Western Rebellion of 1549', *Southern History* 1, 1979, pp. 99–122, in fn. 43. For this information she references G. Scheurweghs, 'On an Answer to the Articles of the Rebels of Cornwall and Devonshire', *British Museum Quarterly* 8 (1933–34), pp. 24–25.

23. Quoted in A. Fletcher, *Tudor Rebellions*, 3rd Edition, London, 1983, p. 115.

24. N. Pocock (ed.) *Troubles Connected with the Prayer Book of 1549*, Camden Society, 1884, pp.141–93. The quotation is on pp. 171–72, transcribed from BL Royal Ms 18B.xi. Ellis, 1974, p. 218, fn. 26 erroneously refers to this publication as 'Poccoche 141 foll'.

25. See J.L. Vivian, *The Visitations of Cornwall*, Exeter, 1887, p. 87. The court cases can be found in a series of Chancery documents in the Public Record Office, which were abstracted in 1939 in connection with some legal proceedings. The abstracts are now in my possession.

26. For Gwavas' life see M. Spriggs, 'Gwavas, William (1676–1741/2)', *Dictionary of National Biography*, Vol. 24, Oxford, 2004, pp. 339–340.

27. Vivian, 1887, pp. 10, 515.

28. For these relationships see Pool, 1986, Tables 1 and 2. For details of

the Usticke family I am indebted to the genealogical research of Lois Saleeba.

29. This was a transcript made by John Moore in 1698 from John Keigwin's copy. Moore's transcript is now bound up with William Gwavas' common-place book in the Gatley Collection of manuscripts. It is recorded as being in William Copeland Borlase's library in 1882—see Boase and Courtney, 1882, p. 1250. It was bought by the bookseller Quaritch and then sold on to John Gatley in 1895 according to a receipt for 4 pounds attached to the volume dated 8/7/95. Gatley's children donated it to the Royal Institution of Cornwall in 1936, as recorded in the report of the 1936 Annual Meeting in *Journal of the Royal Institution of Cornwall* 25 (1–2), 1937–38, pp. 15, 21.

30. J. Borlase, *Antiquities Historical and Monumental of the County of Cornwall,* London, 2nd edition, 1769, p. 414.

31. R.M. Nance, 'More about the Tregear Manuscript', *Old Cornwall* V(1), 1951, pp. 21–27 raises the matter on p. 26, noting that in the manuscript draft of Borlase's Cornish vocabulary to *Antiquities Historical and Monumental* then said to be in the RIC, the fuller 'John Tregeare' is given as the source: 'Another John Tregear, or some other scrap of the clerk's Cornish, may be referred to'. It would seem more likely that this was a transcription error by Borlase for James Tregeare. The manuscript referred to by Nance is almost certainly that now in the Cornwall Record Office as DD/EN 2000. See also R.M. Nance, 'Something new in Cornish', *Journal of the Royal Institution of Cornwall* N.S. 1(2), 1952, pp. 119–21, where on p. 121 the claim is made more obliquely. It is repeated more strongly in Berresford Ellis, 1974, p. 66.

32. For the Crowan Tregeares see Vivian, 1887, pp. 469–70. For information on the West Penwith Tregeares I am grateful to the genealogical researches of Elizabeth Christian, who provided information from R.W. Williams, *Tregears Around the World*, Livonia (Michigan), 1981.

33. The first was *Testament Noweth*, translated by Nicholas Williams, Redruth, 2002, in Unified Cornish Revised (UCR). A version in Kemmyn Cornish (KK), *An Testament Nowydh* was published by the Cornish Language Board in 2004, and the website for the Kemmyn Bible Project, *An Bibel Kernewek*, reports that 11 books of the Old Testament have been published in KK and a further 12 are in preparation: http://www.bibelkernewek.com/ (accessed 7 June 2006).

WHO WAS THE DUCHESS OF CORNWALL IN NICHOLAS BOSON'S (*c.* 1660–70) 'THE DUCHESSE OF CORNWALL'S PROGRESSE TO SEE THE LAND'S END ...'?

Matthew Spriggs

INTRODUCTION

The Cornish-language writer and gentleman merchant Nicholas Boson (1624–1708) of Newlyn probably wrote *The Duchesse of Cornwall's progresse to see the Land's end & to visit the mount* sometime between 1660 and 1670. Unlike his other two known works, *Nebbaz Gerriau dro tho Carnoack* ('A few words about Cornish') and *Jowan Chy-an-Horth, py, An try foynt a skyans* ('John of Chyannor, Or, The three points of wisdom'), this was not predominantly in the Cornish language. It was largely in English with occasional passages in Cornish. Also unlike his other two known works it has not survived in its entirety but only as passages quoted by Edward Lhuyd (1659/60?–1709) and William Borlase (1696–1772), both of whom clearly had access to manuscripts of the whole work. Borlase had seen two manuscript versions of the piece, one of which seems to be the same as the version that Lhuyd had access to. Borlase's Cornish language manuscript was started in 1748 and he is the last scholar known to have studied a complete manuscript of the *Progresse*.[1] Oliver Padel has produced the definitive publication of what remains of the *Progresse* and of the other works by Nicholas and further members of the Boson family.[2] As we shall also see, the Cornish scholar Thomas Tonkin (1678–1741/42) once had plans to publish the *Progresse* in his monumental work *Archaeologia Cornu-Brita[n]nica*, but later abandoned the idea and indeed in the end never brought his own work to publication.

The *Progresse* was written for the amusement of Nicholas Boson's children,[3] and perhaps also—along with his other Cornish language works—as a way of teaching them the Cornish language and its history. Like those other writings it might have been inspired and encouraged by the efforts of William Scawen (1600–89) to revive the declining language by getting literate speakers to send him letters written in Cornish. No such letters have survived but Scawen's call for writings in Cornish is a plausible spur for Nicholas to have undertaken his three literary efforts, which are unique for this time period.[4]

Robert Morton Nance dates the original to about 1660–70, and this would fit with the age of Nicholas' children, who were born in 1653 (Nicholas), 1655 (John), 1659 (Mary), and 1661 (Benjamen).[5] In *Nebbaz Gerriau*, probably written soon after 1675, he is explicit that he wrote the *Progresse* 'for my children'.[6] He also notes that in that work 'about the thirtieth page I have given my Observation[s] of the Cornish Tongue, how it came to be divided amongst the Britains, Welsh & Cornis[h]' and later apologises for the fact that in the *Progresse* he entertains the theory that Cornwall was settled from Brittany rather than the other way around. The manuscript was at that time either with his children or destined to be so as he writes that it 'should hereafter be seen in the Hands of my Children'. This reference to part of the content of the *Progresse* not included in any of the surviving extracts suggests that there was a serious purpose to the work in instructing his children (and any other readers) in Cornish language history. As noted by A.K. Hamilton Jenkin, the *Progresse* is otherwise a summary of the folklore of West Penwith. Nance gives the most delightful and informed discussion of its content, while missing the Cornish language history reference cited above.[7]

In brief summary, the story seems to have been as follows: The Duchess, having prayed at Penzance Chapel, goes to further devotions at the Chapel at Carn Bre, where Harry the Hermit is present. A distant view from there of the Scilly Isles is admired. Michell the monk and the Dean of Buryan draw up a petition in Cornish against Harry to present to the Duchess, wherein they claim he is really a witch. The grounds are: that he raises storms to make the journey to the Scillies longer and more perilous because the local women will not pay him their tithe eggs, the tithe rightly belonging to the Dean of Buryan; that he sits in an inaccessible cliff-top chair for much of the day; and that he regularly sails forth from a cave called Toll Pedden Penwith on the shoulder-blade of a sheep, causing consternation among the local inhabitants who are forced to pierce all such shoulder-blades after eating to try to prevent this. The assembled party then sees a huge sea horse, a mermaid, a Triton and many dolphins out to sea. After this they proceed to Newlyn and on to St Michael's Mount.[8]

The manuscript then includes a disquisition on various local places of interest such as the rock called the Armed Knight at Land's End, which we are told the Duchess had admired, the 'Daunce mine' or stone circles of the Merry Maidens (near Lamorna) and Boscawen-Un, 'Castoll Trerine' or Castle Treen, and St Michael's Mount. It appears that the Duchess is being given all this information while at St Michael's Mount. There was also discussion of the meaning of the names of local gentry families, of various place-names in Penwith, and further historical details. The prophecy about Merlin's Rock near Mousehole is here recorded in Cornish, and there are also other local sayings referred to. Additional folklore elements include a passage on fairies and one on a remarkable cure at Madron Well. The Duchess is reported to have presented those accompanying her with a golden hurling ball engraved with an inscription in Cornish urging fair play. The outline of the above comes from Lhuyd's manuscript and little extra can be added from the excerpts given by Borlase. As already mentioned, in another of Nicholas Boson's works it is noted that there was also a passage presumably near the end of the manuscript where an outline of the history of the Cornish language and people was given, attributing their origins to Britanny.[9]

There is one question about the *Progresse* that has exercised scholars from Henry Jenner onwards and that has never to my mind been satisfactorily answered: who is the Duchess of Cornwall that is being referred to by Boson? It is here that I think some addition to previous discussions of the issue is warranted.

SEEKING THE DUCHESS

The first printed notice of the *Progresse* was a brief one by W. Copeland Borlase in 1866, although he did not quote any passages from it. This was a passing reference in a paper about William Borlase's Cornish language manuscript. The substance of this was repeated by Jenner in 1877, who also repeated Copeland Borlase's mistaken attribution of the *Progresse* to John Boson, Nicholas' second son.[10] Jenner gave it further attention in his 1913 paper on the Borlase Manuscript, and it is there that we first find printed discussion of the identity of the Duchess. Jenner writes:

> The last princess who had held the title of Duchess of Cornwall down to the time that the story was written (about 1700) was probably Catherine of Arragon, in right of her two successive husbands, Arthur Prince of Wales and Henry,

afterwards Henry VIII, unless it is true (which is disputed) that her daughter Mary, afterwards Queen, was created Princess of Wales and Duchess of Cornwall in her own right, dignities which she is said to have resigned on the birth of her half-brother Edward. As a 'hermit at Chapel Carn Brea' comes into the story, the scene is probably laid in pre-Reformation times.[11]

Catherine or Katherine of Aragon married Prince Arthur in 1501, but he died the following year. She was then contracted to the 11-year-old Prince Henry, who became Henry VIII in 1509 and formally married her in that year. It could therefore be argued that she was Duchess of Cornwall from 1501–09, suitably in the pre-Reformation period. Her daughter with Henry, the later Queen Mary I, was born in 1516 and her half-brother Edward in 1537. If Mary was in fact created Duchess of Cornwall in her own right, this would have taken place at some point between 1516 and 1537, but she would hardly have been in any position to make a courtly visit on her own to Cornwall given her age until near the end of that period, and there is no evidence she ever did so. As Henry's estrangement from Katherine grew, in 1525 Mary was sent away ostensibly to govern Wales in Henry's name. She was sometimes referred to as Princess of Wales during this period, but there is no evidence that she was formally invested with the title. Her mother was finally banished from Court in 1531 and Mary too had fallen from favour before that date. Technically, much of her putative time as Duchess of Cornwall—the companion title to Princess of Wales—would have been in the pre-Reformation period prior to 1534. Katherine of Aragon would seem a much more likely candidate for the *Progresse* than Mary in the circumstances, but there is also no record of any visit by her to Cornwall.[12]

A breakthrough in *Progresse* scholarship came when Hamilton Jenkin gave notice of the much more extensive passages from the work to be found in Ms. Carte 269 in the Bodleian Library, Oxford. Cornish scholars had not previously been aware of these extracts, which were found in a notebook of Edward Lhuyd, the pioneer Celtic linguist. He had doubtless obtained a copy of the work from Nicholas Boson himself during a visit to Cornwall in 1700. Hamilton Jenkin's paper was read before the Royal Institution of Cornwall in May 1924 and published the following year.[13] It contains a complete transcript of the passages found in Ms Carte 269, and it is at the end of these that Lhuyd identified the author as Nicholas Boson rather than John Boson as had been believed up to that time. As Hamilton Jenkin noted, this 'upsets all former theories . . . Not only does this prove that the Duchess of

Cornwall's Progress was written some forty years earlier than was formerly supposed, but it shows that the "Nebbaz Gerriau dro tho Carnoack" also must have been the work of Nicholas Boson, the father'.[14]

In a footnote on the same page, paraphrasing Jenner, Hamilton Jenkin wrote: 'Historically speaking Catherine of Arragon was the last Duchess of Cornwall previous to the writing of this romance.' The *Journal* editor, Henry Jenner, expanded upon this in square brackets immediately after this: 'Unless it is true that Princess Mary (afterwards Queen) was created Duchess of Cornwall in her own right, but resigned the dignity when her brother Edward was born in 1537. But this is disputed. This Duchess of the tale is evidently so in her own right, not as consort.—Editor.' The basis for Jenner's final assertion is not clear. All that the passages that remain of the *Progresse* make clear is that the Duchess was travelling alone, with no Duke in tow.

In trying to provide a date for when the action of the story is supposed to have taken place, Hamilton Jenkin noted (again presumably following Jenner) that reference to a monk and a hermit are 'introduced to give the flavour of antiquity'. But he also refers to a passage quoted by Lhuyd: 'The Government of the Island was not then establish'd in the honourable house of Godolphin until afterwards the Dukedom came to be united to the Crown.' In a footnote he writes: 'This sentence also is clearly intended to put back the time of the action. The Godolphins became Vice-Roys of Scilly in 1571.'[15] The Duchy and the Crown became united in 1547 with the accession of Prince Edward as Edward VI. The strong link between the Godolphin family and the Scilly Isles in fact goes back to Edward's reign, when Thomas Godolphin was appointed Captain of the Scilly Isles in 1549. This might allow the pushing back of the date for the Godolphin control of Scilly from 1571 to mid-century[16].

Nance did not chance an identification of the Duchess in his own 1924 discussion of the *Progresse*, but referenced and accepted Hamilton Jenkin's identification of the author as Nicholas rather than John Boson, as did Jenner, who also referred to Hamilton Jenkins' paper in 1929. In a 1951 paper on Cornish prophecies Nance would only say that Boson's 'duchess was imagined as one of pre-Reformation days'.[17]

The final original contribution to the discussion, and one that rejects any pre-Reformation date for the Duchess in favour of an almost contemporary reference, is by Peter Pool. Writing originally in 1975 he suggested that the tale 'probably derived its theme from the visit of Catharine of Braganza to Mount's Bay in 1662 when on her voyage from Portugal to marry Charles II'.[18] He was not, of course, claiming that she was ever Duchess of Cornwall, merely that her visit may have in part inspired Nicholas to write the *Progresse*.

THE DUCHESS FOUND?

In the absence of any new direct evidence, it would seem that this is as far as we can go, with various possible identifications being given and none overwhelmingly obvious as the most likely point of reference for the *Progresse*. Jenner, however, had in fact twice seen the manuscript that I would suggest provides the definitive identification for the Duchess. The first time was on 21 March 1873 when he read his initial paper on the Cornish language to the Philological Society in London.[19] Prince Louis Lucien Bonaparte, a noted linguist, then had the manuscript in his possession and briefly showed it to Jenner at that meeting. After Bonaparte's death in 1891, his widow deposited his manuscripts—mainly relating to the Basque language—in the Provincial Libraries in Bilbao, San Sebastian and Pamplona in the Basque country of Spain. There were two significant Cornish manuscripts in his collection and one of them ended up among the papers in Bilbao. It was first brought to the attention of the Royal Institution of Cornwall in 1909 and abortive efforts were made to acquire it for that body.

In 1924, as part of a holiday looking at the cathedrals of western France and the Pyrenees, Jenner made the arduous trip to Bilbao, leaving by train early in the morning so that he could return to San Sebastian that night, noting that 'Bilbao is a rather unsavoury sea-port and not an attractive place to stay at.' He eventually looked at the manuscript for three to four hours and considering his short period of observation he got an enormous amount out of it and published a very good précis of its contents.[20]

It, and its companion volume in San Sebastian,[21] originally belonged with the other papers of Thomas Tonkin (1678–1741/2), many of which are now in the Royal Institution of Cornwall. Bonaparte had purchased them from the Penzance bookseller Rodda, supposedly in 1860.[22] The 'Bilbao manuscript' consists largely of correspondence between Tonkin and William Gwavas (1676–1741/42) concerning the compilation of Tonkin's *Archaeologia Cornu-Britan[n]ica*, planned as a compendium of all that was then available in the Cornish language.[23] An essentially complete draft of the Cornish Dictionary that was to accompany that work is included with the letters and other miscellaneous documents in Bilbao. It had been sent to Gwavas for his additions and corrections and then returned to Tonkin. The 'Maker Manuscript' recently donated to the Royal Institution of Cornwall is the somewhat mutilated original of the *Archaeologia*, but does not include the Dictionary.[24] William Pryce, who owned the manuscript of the *Archaeologia* at one time, published a severely abridged version of the whole, including the Dictionary, under his own name in 1790. The 'Bilbao manuscript' is what allowed Bonaparte to unmask what he saw as Pryce's plagiarism of Tonkin and Gwavas in a paper he published in 1861.[25]

The vital clue, not surprisingly overlooked by Jenner in his 1924 foray, is to be found in a draft Subscription Proposal for the *Archaeologia* in Tonkin's hand and presumably dating to 1738 as it refers to publication 'by Lady Day next 1739'. Among the contents, and scored through to remove it, is the passage: 'Her Royal Highness the Dutchess of Cornwall's (supposed to be the Lady Catherine Gordon, wife to Perkin Warbeck, in whose time it is thought to have been written) Progress to the Land's End, & the Triall of Harry Lader (or, Harry the Thief)'.

The fact that it was subsequently excised from the list of contents suggests that in 1738 Tonkin may not have yet seen it. Perhaps he viewed a copy soon after writing the proposed contents and decided it was unsuitable in a publication on the Cornish language as it was mostly in English? Or perhaps he was simply unable to access a copy? Tonkin is clearly quoting a tradition about the *Progresse*, rather than engaging in informed speculation, as have all later writers starting with Jenner. Where would his information have come from? Presumably not directly from Nicholas Boson nor from Edward Lhuyd, both of whom knew that it was a recently-written piece rather than one dating back to Lady Katherine Gordon's visit to Cornwall in 1497. Tonkin corresponded with Lhuyd and almost certainly also knew Nicholas Boson in his later years. He would have also come across Nicholas' son John and cousin Thomas. But the major assistance in his efforts to put together the *Archaeologia* came from William Gwavas, who was closely connected with the Boson family. When Tonkin was seriously engaged with preparation of the *Archaeologia*, between about 1735 and 1739, Nicholas (died 1708), Thomas (died 1719) and John Boson (died 1730) had all passed on. William Gwavas was his main link back to them and this suggests that his information about the Duchess came from the Bosons, mediated through Gwavas, who may have become confused about the date of composition of the *Progresse*. In a Gwavas letter contained in the 'Bilbao Manuscript' he mentions assistance only from Thomas and John Boson, and Nicholas may have died before Gwavas' own interest in the language was aroused.[26]

The next question is whether there is anything in the life of Lady Katherine Gordon that might correspond, however roughly, to the events described in the *Progresse*? And there is. Perkin Warbeck, posing as Richard Plantagenet, one of the Princes in the Tower supposedly miraculously saved from secret execution, landed at Whitesand Bay near Land's End in September 1497 from Scotland via Ireland, encouraged by the outbreak earlier that year of the Flamank-An Gof Rebellion and the abortive Cornish march on London. His wife Katherine Gordon, who was of Scottish royal blood, accompanied him. He placed her in the safety of the sanctuary of St Buryan or at St Michael's Mount while he made his doomed attempt on the Throne, as the titular head of the second Cornish rebellion that year.[27] He had himself proclaimed Richard IV at Bodmin and marched off to the east where his attempt foundered in Somerset and he was subsequently captured.[28] It was at St Michael's Mount that Katherine surrendered some five weeks later to the King's representative.[29]

Perkin had declared that he was Richard, Duke of York, brother of the murdered Prince Edward, Prince of Wales who had been destined to become Edward V. In fact both had almost certainly perished at the hands of Richard III in 1483 soon after the death of their father Edward IV. Prince Edward had been declared Duke of Cornwall in 1471, and it could be argued that Perkin as his putative surviving younger brother and claimed-next in succession might have been able to claim the titles of Prince of Wales and Duke of Cornwall after his decease, if Perkin had been who he said he was and the legitimacy of Richard III and his heirs is dismissed! In a 1495 letter to his future wife, Katherine Gordon, Perkin styled himself Prince of Wales.[30] This was presumably to underline his case for being considered the legitimate royal heir, and implies that he would also have considered himself Duke of Cornwall, the companion title. While in Cornwall such an appeal to Cornish nationalist sentiment would have also been useful, although we have no contemporary evidence that he styled himself so.

The suggestion of a link between Boson's 'Duchesse' and Lady Katherine Gordon has in fact once been made in print, by Canon Thomas Taylor in his 1932 book about St Michael's Mount.[31] He wrote:

> It is possible that an echo of Warbeck's rebellion may be recognised in the fragmentary Cornish Manuscript entitled *The Duchess of Cornwall's Progress . . . Inter alia* there is found the following:

> 'Rag gun Arlothas da
> Ny en gweel gun moyha.'
> (For our most excellent Dutchesse Right
> Unto the utmost we will fight.)

The *Progress* is the supposed record of the Duchess of Cornwall's progress to see the Land's End and to visit St Michael's Mount.[32]

Taylor footnotes the Hamilton Jenkin paper and also references, following Hamilton Jenkin, the somewhat similar story to that of the *Progresse* given in Bottrell's 1873 *Traditions . . . of West Cornwall* as 'A Queen's visit to Baranhual'.[33] Neither of these sources, however, mentions Lady Katherine as being either the Duchess or the Queen referred to. It was the Reverend Lach-Szyrma who first made the connection between the Bottrell story and Lady Katherine Gordon in 1878.[34] This was in a discussion on the history of St Michael's Mount that Taylor most certainly would have read in preparing his own book on the subject. One must conclude that Taylor then made the further connection, presumably drawing on the quotation suggesting that Cornishmen would have to fight to defend the Duchess.[35]

A folk memory that Perkin Warbeck had in fact styled himself as Duke of Cornwall may well have been around in the 1660s in West Cornwall, given its history of rebelliousness.[36] It would have been consonant with this pride in Cornish distinctiveness that such an unlikely heroine as Katherine Gordon as Duchess of Cornwall could have been chosen by Nicholas Boson. Some memory of her movements between Land's End, St Buryan and the Mount may also have been preserved in popular story into the 1660s. Katherine is certainly the only one of our pre-Reformation candidates who had a direct association with West Penwith. The story that Nicholas called one of his own daughters Katherine is a modern myth, promulgated by Nance and repeated most recently by Beresford Ellis.[37] But Nicholas' son John Boson certainly called his own daughter Katherin[e] when she was born in 1672. It would be nice to imagine that her name came from a remembered childhood story that itself grew out of a confused folk memory of rebellion nearly two centuries before.[38]

NOTES AND REFERENCES

1. The Rev. Henry Ustick (1720–69), in whose hand is the only extant manuscript of *Nebbaz Gerriau*, dating to 1750, interpolated in that copy where it refers to the *Progresse*: 'This MSS. is at present in the Hands of Mr. Rob. Davy of Ludgvan'. See Padel, 1975, p. 29. Thereafter the trail goes cold. The likely route by which the manuscript reached Davy was via Nicholas Boson's son and heir, John Boson (1655–1730). In John's 1728 will, Cornwall Record Office AP/B/3320, his friend 'Robert Davey of Ludgvan, gent' is one of the four executors. He either acquired it after John Boson's death, or after the death of John's principal beneficiary, his sister Mary Boson of Penzance, who died in 1738 (information in the

Madron parish registers, Cornwall Record Office). Sir Humphrey Davy was a scion of this Ludgvan family: G.C. Boase and W.P Courtney, *Bibliographia Cornubiensis*, Vol. III, London, 1882, p. 1152, entry on Robert Davy.

2. O. Padel, *The Cornish Writings of the Boson Family*, Redruth, 1975.

3. The identification of Nicholas as author is given at the end of Lhuyd's partial transcript (Bodleian Ms. Carte 269 fols. 40–45), where Lhuyd wrote in Welsh: 'Alhan o chwedl o waith Mr. Nicholas Boson o Newlyn, yn ei ievienktyd', which Padel translates as 'Out of a story of Mr Nicholas Boson of Newlyn's work, in his youth'. See Padel, 1975, p. 8. The Borlase Manuscript is Cornwall Record Office, Dd Enys 2000. As is discussed later, until 1925 the *Progresse* was believed to have been written by John Boson. For a short biography of Nicholas, John and other members of the Boson family see M. Spriggs, 'The Boson Family', *Oxford Dictionary of National Biography*, Vol. 6, 2004, pp. 713–14.

4. For Scawen's life and attempts at Cornish language revival see M. Spriggs, 'William Scawen (1600–89)—A Neglected Cornish Patriot and Father of the Cornish Language Revival', in P. Payton (ed.) *Cornish Studies: Thirteen*, Exeter, 2005, pp. 98–125, and references therein. The discussion of Scawen's letter-writing campaign is on pp. 107–8.

5. R.M. Nance, 'Folk-lore Recorded in the Cornish Language', Royal Cornwall Polytechnic Society 91st Annual Report, N.S. V (part II), 1924, pp. 124–45. The dating is discussed on page 141. For Boson family dates see the Paul Parish Registers, Cornwall Record Office. Nance, 1924, p. 141 erroneously lists Nicholas' children as 'John, Thomas and Katherine, the two former of whom have left written proof in verse and prose that they learnt Cornish'. John (1655–1730) was indeed Nicholas' son. Katherin[e], baptised 1672, was in fact a grand-daughter of the Nicholas in question, being one of four children of his son Nicholas. The Thomas mentioned here is clearly Thomas Boson (1635–1719) who was the elder Nicholas' cousin. C. Henderson later corrected Nance's errors while introducing some of his own—see his footnote on p. 30 of 'Nicholas Boson and Richard Angwyn', *Old Cornwall* II (2), 1931, pp. 29–32. Padel, 1975, p. 5 references the various uncertainties over these relationships. P.A.S. Pool, *The Death of Cornish*, Penzance, 1982 [orig. 1975], p. 12, fn. 21 only further confuses the matter. See Spriggs, 2004, 713–14 for a hopefully definitive statement.

6. Padel, 1975, p. 28. Theoretically *Nebbaz Gerriau* could have been written any time between 1675 and Nicholas' death in 1708. The 1675 date is given by the death of Richard Angwyn in that year, mentioned in the text as 'the greatest & the eldest of the late Professors of our Cornish Tongue'—see Padel, 1975, p. 26. For Angwyn's death see Henderson, 1931, p. 32. Of the *Progresse*, Boson notes in *Nebbaz Gerriau* (Padel, 1975, p. 28) that it was written 'some years past'. Nance suggested a date of around 1700, but there is no reason why it could not have been written up to 25 years earlier: R.M. Nance, 'Nicholas Boson's "Nebbaz Gerriau Dro Tho Carnoack"', *Journal of the Royal Institution of Cornwall* XXIII (2), 1930,

pp. 327–54. As Boson's listing of where Cornish was spoken at the time of writing is somewhat more geographically extensive than Lhuyd's list compiled in 1700, this suggests to me that it reflects the situation one or two decades prior to Lhuyd's visit. For a discussion of this see M. Spriggs, 'The Reverend Joseph Sherwood: A Cornish Language Will-'O-the-Wisp', in P. Payton (ed.) *Cornish Studies: Six*, Exeter, 1998, pp. 46–61, especially pp. 53–6.

7. A.K. Hamilton Jenkin, 'Lhuyd Manuscripts in the Bodleian Library. 1. The Duchess of Cornwall's Progress', *Journal of the Royal Institution of Cornwall* 21(4), 1925, pp. 401–13; Nance, 1924, pp. 124–45.

8. The summary is taken from Padel, 1975. The 'Daunce mine' identification as the Merry Maidens and Boscawen-Un, and 'Castoll Trerine' as Castle Treen is given by Hamilton-Jenkin, 1925, footnotes on p. 408. He also gives further useful elucidation of obscure points at various points in his paper.

9. Padel, 1975, pp. 26–31.

10. W.C. Borlase, 'Cornish Proverbs and Rhymes', *Journal of the Royal Institution of Cornwall* V, 1866, pp. 7–17. Reference to authorship of the *Progresse* is on p. 12; H. Jenner, 'The History and Literature of the Ancient Cornish Language', *Journal of the British Archaeological Association*, XXXIII, 1877, pp. 137–57. Reference to authorship is on p. 154. Also following Copeland Borlase, authorship was attributed to John Boson in G.C. Boase and W.P. Courtney, *Bibliotheca Cornubiensis*, Vol. 1, London, 1874, p. 38, and this was further repeated in H. Jenner, *Handbook of the Cornish Language*, London, 1904, p. 33. Jenner notes there that the *Progresse* consisted originally of at least thirty pages, based on Nicholas Boson's (he thought John Boson's) *Nebbaz Gerriau*, as discussed earlier.

11. H. Jenner, 'Descriptions of Cornish Manuscripts—1. The Borlase Manuscript'. *Journal of the Royal Institution of Cornwall* 19(2), 1913, pp. 162–76. The quotation is on pages 170–1.

12. These various dates are readily available in many texts. The source used here is A.H.D Acland and C. Ransome, *Handbook in Outline of the Political History of England to 1913 Chronologically arranged*, London, 1913. See also, C.S.I. Davies and J. Edwards, 'Katherine (1485–1536)', *Oxford Dictionary of National Biography*, Vol. 30, 2004, pp. 892–901; A Weikel, 'Mary I (1516–1558)', *Oxford Dictionary of National Biography*, Vol. 37, pp. 111–24.

13. Hamilton Jenkin, 1925, pp. 401–13.

14. Hamilton Jenkin, 1925, p. 404.

15. All these quotations are from Hamilton Jenkin, 1925, p. 406.

16. Information here comes from Acland and Ransome, 1913; H. Jenner, 'The Dukes and Earls of Cornwall', *Royal Cornwall Polytechnic Society 87th Annual Report*, 1920, pp. 207–23; A.L. Rowse, *Tudor Cornwall*, London, 1941, pp. 384–5; J. Chynoweth, *Tudor Cornwall*, Port Stroud, 2004, p. 143; J.P.D. Cooper, 'Sir William Godolphin', *Oxford Dictionary of National Biography*, Vol. 22, 2004, pp. 597–9.

17. Nance, 1924, pp. 140–145; H. Jenner, 'Some Miscellaneous Scraps of Cornish', *Royal Cornwall Polytechnic Society 96th Annual Report*, N.S. VI (Part III), 1929, pp. 238–55, especially p. 245; R.M. Nance, 'Cornish prophecies', *Old Cornwall* IV (12), 1951, pp. 443–53. The quotation comes from p. 448.

18. P.A.S. Pool, 1982, p.13.

19. Jenner's paper was subsequently published: H. Jenner, 'The Cornish Language', *Transactions of the Philological Society*, 1873–74, pp. 165–85. The date of his oral presentation of it is given in D.R. Williams (ed.) *Henry and Katherine Jenner: a celebration of Cornwall's culture, language and identity*, London, 2004, p. 28.

20. H. Jenner, 'The Cornish Manuscript in the Provincial Library at Bilbao in Spain', *Journal of the Royal Institution of Cornwall*, XXI (4), 1925, pp. 421–37. The quotation about Bilbao is on p. 423. The manuscript is Biblioteca de la Diputacion Foral de Bizkaia, Bilbao, Ms Bnv-69. As Jenner noted, the initial 'discovery' of the manuscript in Bilbao was by the Basque specialist Edward S. Dodgson. See Dodgson's own accounts: 'Manuscritos Celticos en Bilbao' and 'Los Manuscritos Celticos en la Biblioteca de la Diputacion de Vizcaya', *Boletin de la Real Academia de la Historia* 54, Madrid, 1909, pp. 256–7 and 338–40.

21. T. Tonkin, *The first Book of Mr Carew's survey of Cornwall, with large notes and additions*, 1733. Diputacion Foral de Guipuzcoa, San Sebastian, Ms. FDG m/s B-11. This is Tonkin Manuscript D in William Borlase's list, and was previously believed to be lost: see H.L. Douch, 'Thomas Tonkin, An Appreciation of a Neglected Historian, *Journal of the Royal Institution of Cornwall*, N.S. IV(2), 1962, pp. 145–80, especially p. 168.

22. Jenner, 1925, pp. 425, 436. The date of purchase given by Jenner must be wrong as Edwin Norris refers to the manuscript being in Bonaparte's possession in his 1859 publication, *The Ancient Cornish Drama*, Vol. II, Oxford, p. 471. Norris writes that Bonaparte had 'purchased [it] a few years ago from the descendants of Mr Scawen'. The statement is confused, perhaps he believed Bonaparte had acquired it from relatives of Tonkin rather than Scawen, but it does show that the purchase date was before 1860.

23. For Tonkin's life see Douch, 1962, pp. 145–80, and P.B. Ellis, 'Thomas Tonkin', *Oxford Dictionary of National Biography*, Vol. 54, 2004, pp. 969–70 (the latter is not wholly accurate in its details). For Gwavas see M. Spriggs, 'William Gwavas', *Oxford Dictionary of National Biography*, Vol. 24, 2004, pp. 339–40.

24. This manuscript was generously donated to the Royal Institution of Cornwall in 1999 by Deryk and Gussie Maker. I am currently preparing a paper on this newly-found Tonkin manuscript and its place in Cornish language history.

25. W. Pryce, *Archaeologia Cornu-Britannica*, Sherborne, 1790. Bonaparte and Norris were clearly outraged at what they considered to be Pryce's plagiarism, while Jago and Jenner were much less exercised; the latter pointing out that Pryce did, at least to an extent, acknowledge his sources.

See Prince L.L. Bonaparte, 'Cornish Literature', *Cambrian Journal*, 1861 (reprinted as a 4 pp. pamphlet); Norris, 1859, Vol. II, p. 471; F.W.P. Jago, *An English-Cornish Dictionary*, London, 1887, p. viii; Jenner, 1925, p. 435.

26. Mention of the assistance of Thomas and John Boson is in a letter by Gwavas dated 18 March 1731[/2] in the 'Bilbao Manuscript', fol. 30r. He also acknowledges the assistance of Mr John Keigwin of Mousehole, Mr [James] Jenkins of Alverton in Penzance, Mr Oliver Pendar of Newlyn, John Odger 'at the Lizard', and 'severall antient persons in Paul, St Just, St Kevern, etc/ Both men and women that could talke in the Moderne Cornish'. A draft or copy of the same letter can be found in British Library Add. Ms. 28,554, fol. 20r. This latter manuscript also contains letters to Gwavas from John Boson dated 1709, 1711 and 1720, one from Gwavas to John Boson dated 1711, an interchange of letters between Oliver Pendar and Gwavas dating to 1711, and further parts of the Gwavas-Tonkin correspondence of 1735–6, as well as the Creed in Cornish by Thomas Boson, dated 1710, also a hurling ball inscription by him, and verses on the death of John Keigwin (1642–1716) by John Boson. These suggest that Gwavas' serious interest in the Cornish language may have begun shortly after Nicholas Boson's death.

27. See I. Arthurson, *The Perkin Warbeck Conspiracy 1491–1499*, Port Stroud, 1994, particularly pp. 181–92.

28. See P. Payton, '"a . . . concealed envy against the English": A Note on the Aftermath of the 1497 Rebellions in Cornwall', in P. Payton (ed.) *Cornish Studies: One*, Exeter, 1993, pp. 4–13, and his *The Making of Modern Cornwall*, Redruth, 1992, Chapter 3, for the background to and the aftermath of the two rebellions.

29. Arthurson, 1994, p. 182. The story of Lady Katherine surrendering at the Mount is given in R. Carew, *The Survey of Cornwall*, London, 1602, fol. 155v (facsimile, *Devon and Cornwall Record Society*, Vol. 47, 2004, ed. J. Chynoweth, N. Orme and A. Walsham). The source for this information was presumably from Polydore Vergil: see *The Anglica Historia of Polydore Vergil AD 1485–1537* (ed. D. Hay), *Camden Series* LXXIV, London, 1950, pp. 108–109, the relevant passage being first published in 1534.

30. Arthurson, 1994, p. 123.

31. T. Taylor, *St Michael's Mount*, Cambridge, 1932, pp. 133–43.

32. Taylor, 1932, p. 141.

33. See Hamilton Jenkin, 1925, footnote on p. 404. 'A Queen's Visit to Baranhual' is in W. Bottrell, *Traditions and Hearthside Stories of West Cornwall, Second Series*, Penzance, 1873, pp. 67–72. It is the story of a Queen landing at Mousehole, in order to view the Land's End and the Logan Rock. The local population believe that she is also coming to view St Buryan Church and assemble there, but instead she wishes to visit the Pendar family who lived at Baranhual, en route to the Logan Rock, as she remembers that they are 'staunch friends to the royal cause' (p. 68). She gets drunk with old Dame Pendar and the visit to the Church, and indeed the other local landmarks, is abandoned. Baranhual is presumably

Burnewhall in St Buryan, first mentioned as a dwelling in the St Buryan Charter and in another source of 1319: see P.A.S. Pool, *The Place-Names of West Penwith*, Penzance, 1973, p. 42.

34. W.S. Lach-Szyrma, *A Short History of Penzance, S. Michael's Mount, S. Ives, and the Land's End District*, Truro and London, 1878, footnote p. 98: 'Can the Cornish legend of the Queen seen at Burnuhall be any tradition of Lady Katherine, who would be of course called the Queen of England by her retainers? She was young and very pretty. See Mr. Botterill's [*sic*, cf. Taylor's 'Botterell's'] "Traditions and Hearthside Stories of West Cornwall," pp. 67–73.'

35. No further clue is given by Taylor's earlier work, *The Celtic Christianity of Cornwall*, London, 1916, where he also refers to the *Progresse* on pp. 133–4, based on information provided by Henry Jenner. This earlier work discusses Harry the Hermit but hazards no guess as to the identity of the Duchess.

36. This history is dealt with in detail in M. Stoyle, *West Britons: Cornish Identities and the Early Modern British State*, Exeter, 2002; see also his 'Cornish Rebellions, 1497–1648, *History Today* 47 (5), 1997, 23–5, and 'Re-discovering Difference: The Recent Historiography of Early Modern Cornwall', in P. Payton (ed.) *Cornish Studies: Ten*, Exeter, 202, pp. 104–15.

37. Nance, 1924, p. 141; P.B. Ellis, *The Cornish Language and its Literature*, London, 1974, p. 89.

38. I would like to thank Joanna Mattingly and Mark Stoyle for comments on an earlier draft of this paper, and Charlotte MacKenzie for bibliographic assistance.

THE LITERARY ANTHROPOLOGY OF MRS HAVELOCK ELLIS: AN EXPLORATION OF THE INSIDER AND OUTSIDER CATEGORIES

Gemma Goodman

WHO IS AN INSIDER? WHO IS AN OUTSIDER?

Identity is established and maintained through the imposition of boundaries. To call oneself 'Cornish' is to state a common bond with people who also use the term to identify themselves, even if that term is personally modified for each person through individual inter-pretation and experience. What that identity consists of, the nature of identity, is that which we can and must continually discuss. However, the act alone of identifying oneself as 'Cornish' is also the act of claiming membership to a group. It is a way of categorizing oneself or other people. That group is established through the perception of commonality between members but it is equally maintained through perception of difference when compared to other groups or individuals. A boundary is, therefore, in place around the category 'Cornish' and people are judged to be on the inside or the outside of that boundary. The boundary can be drawn in relation to cultural, political and spatial concepts. To talk of boundaries is not necessarily reductive for they are not necessarily rigid. Who is judged to be an 'insider'? Who is judged to be an 'outsider'? How do these judgements take place and what are their effects? Is it possible to cross this boundary?

Debates surrounding insider and outsider categories are directly relevant to the representation and construction of Cornwall and of the Cornish. What is the position of artists who construct Cornwall and the Cornish? Who speaks for Cornwall? Who has or should have the authority to speak for Cornwall? Is there an authentic voice? Such questions, while pertinent to literary texts about Cornwall, are also central to debates within the field of anthropology and, more recently, discussions have focused on the possible meeting point between literature and anthropology.

Edith Ellis' fiction about Cornwall is ripe material through which to discuss these anthropologically-centred debates for the texts posit and sometimes answer many of the questions posed above. Edith Ellis is relatively unknown today. If she is known at all it is as the wife of eminent psychologist Havelock Ellis, rather than as an author in her own right. Isaac Goldberg's biography of 1926 entitled 'Havelock Ellis' dedicates a chapter to Edith Ellis but little has been written since concerning her literary output. Born in 1861 she was the author of novels, plays, and collections of essays published between 1898 and 1925. She died in 1916. This paper will concentrate on two collections of short stories: *My Cornish Neighbours* (1906) and *The Mine of Dreams* (1925).[1]

When I first came across the works of Mrs Havelock Ellis I found myself hoping she was Cornish. This was before reading the texts in any detail and I suppose I had in my mind that the primary focus of Cornish literary studies, at the moment at least, should be to rediscover and write about Cornish writers. From Westminster to railway companies to visiting writers, those who are not Cornish continually construct Cornwall. Perhaps a natural reaction, as Cornish scholars, to such control from 'outside' is to attempt to take control by perpetuating constructions that originate from the 'inside'. From study of Ellis' work it is clear that one cannot take the categories 'insider', 'outsider', 'native', or 'visitor' for granted. Her work explores and problematizes these concepts. A discussion rather than acceptance of such categories is therefore warranted.

Immediately clear even from a title such as *My Cornish Neighbours* is that, as a 'Cornish' writer, Ellis focuses on Cornish people rather than landscape. For long the Cornish landscape, rather than the Cornish people, has been the focus of texts by visiting writers. For example, both *An Unsentimental Journey Through Cornwall* by Dinah Craik, published in 1884, and *Goldengrove Unleaving* by Jill Paton Walsh, published in 1997, use Cornwall as a backdrop for non-Cornish characters.[2] The Cornish population may feature but often as an aside to the main non-Cornish characters. This trend has continued into the film industry which often uses Cornwall to tell stories where the main characters are not Cornish, as in 'Blue Juice', or where the landscape is used to represent imaginary places as in Trevor Nunn's film adaptation of 'Twelfth Night'.[3] Ellis' intention is not to harvest the beauty of Cornwall merely as canvas for storytelling purposes. Goldberg in reference to *Seaweed*, Ellis's novel set in Cornwall, asserts that 'among these ingenuous villagers Mrs Ellis found . . . the self same problems that attracted her in London'.[4] Phyllis Bentley would champion Ellis' writing if its focus is, as Goldberg attests, ubiquitous problems or concepts. Bentley in her book *The English Regional Novel* published in 1941 argues that the function of regional literature must be to delineate universalisms rather than illuminate the periphery.[5] The periphery can be a mouthpiece, therefore, as long as it does not speak for itself. Bentley restricts literature from the periphery by imposing a specific function for it to perform. Ellis, as a 'visiting writer' is doing something very different. Rather than impose universal themes onto Cornish characters, Ellis allows them to speak from their own experience. While a writer of fiction her work is positioned at the point where fiction and reality meet and, as a writer Ellis makes forays into the realm of anthropology. Her work is produced at the conjunction of literature and anthropology. Havelock Ellis notes at the beginning of his wife's posthumously published short story collection *The Mine of Dreams* that 'at times they present real people . . . sometimes they were suggested by real incidents, and once or twice . . . they record a real incident almost unchanged'.[6] While the later stories delve more into the realm of imagination, it is the earlier sketches (as Havelock Ellis calls them) that are the focus of this article.

THE NAÏVE OUTSIDER: OBSERVING BUT NOT SEEING

In the preceding paragraphs I have referred to Edith Ellis both as a 'Cornish' writer and as a 'visiting writer'. The inverted commas have been used because, although not of Cornish birth, she is not easy to categorize. Her body of work explores the insider, the outsider and their interaction with each other and such work questions the integrity of such categories. In a high proportion of the short stories Ellis uses a first person narrator. We never learn her name and it is possible Ellis wants us to think this character analogous with the author. For the purposes of this paper, however, I will refer to the narrator and the author separately. As an outsider come to live among a Cornish community, the narrator sets up a fruitful dynamic through which to explore the insider–outsider relationship.

Ellis opens both *My Cornish Neighbours* and *The Mine of Dreams* with the same short story, published under different titles ('Trenwin' becomes 'Wheal Dream' in the later collection). It is important that this story opens both collections because it poses many of the questions with which the texts as a whole are concerned. The narrator has recently arrived from London to live in Trenwin/Wheal Dream. She is conversing with a local farm owner by the name of Mrs Pengilly. The story hinges on the disparity in the women's perspectives. The narrator is the naïve outsider. She comes to live in Cornwall having previously formed an imaginative construction of Cornwall. Prior holiday visits have led her to think 'the whole place is ideal and the people kind and charming in every way'. Mrs Pengilly counters this assertion and its idealism with an insightful reply. She says 'There's good and bad and medium here as elsewhere'.[7] Mrs Pengilly tells the narrator about the lives of her neighbours, including the violent relationship between Tobias Penberthy and his wife Sally. The narrator responds with, 'what an interesting place to live in![8] The narrator thinks the weather is 'like heaven' while Mrs Pengilly's daughter-in-law 'don't know what to be at first' because such weather 'shows up the cobwebs and dirt'. The narrator 'thought farming . . . the healthiest and pleasantest pastime in the world'. Mrs Pengilly, incredulous, replies, 'Pastime! . . . It's just as much pastime, my dear, as a treadmill'.[9] It is the clash of these two perspectives which sign-posts the narrator's naiveté. The narrator's overly romantic imaginative construction clouds her ability to observe her new surroundings and absorb Mrs Pengilly's discerning commentary on local life. She has come to Cornwall in holiday mode, worrying only if the weather will be fine and paying no attention to the realities of everyday life. The idealistic construction in her mind overpowers the realities put before her by Mrs Pengilly. Despite the reality with which she is faced, her false construction of Cornwall remains intact.

At this point it seems unlikely that the narrator has the skills to delineate the lives of her Cornish neighbours. Not only is she the outsider in this community, she filters the reality before her through a preconceived, imaginatively fostered interpretation of Cornwall. In addition, her position as outsider will potentially be ingrained by the attitude of the local populace. Mrs Pengilly tells her that 'we 'ates new notions, and . . . most strangers too, for our motto be "one and all"'.[10] A blinded observer, then, and a society that excludes rather than welcomes the outsider. However, even though outsiders are not normally welcomed, Mrs Pengilly warms to the narrator and tells her 'you'll get to know us by and by'.[11] Mrs Pengilly has already brought the narrator into her confidence and the inner circle of gossip that is the currency of the local community. The gossip about Tobias and Sally's relationship is filtered through Jane Ann Trevaskis, Martha Hicks, Nancy Curnow, Charlotte Pengilly and then Mrs Pengilly, yet the narrator, and then the reader, is part of this chain and privy to the information fervently passed between neighbours. While the narrator is drawn into this conglomeration of women, Mrs Pengilly excludes

Tobias, the subject of the gossip. She warns the narrator not to take
Tobias on as a labourer as soon as he is out of earshot.[12] Through Mrs
Pengilly the narrator has been given access to knowledge internal to
this Cornish community and vital for her storytelling project.

Mrs Pengilly too has a penchant for storytelling. Not only does she
revel in relating gossip to the newcomer she is aware such material is
book-worthy. She says, 'If I was in the scribblin' line I could write a
book on my neighbours, and I needn't be troubled to make up nothin'
at all, for it's better nor play-actin' what goes on in this village at
times'.[13] Two potential storytellers are presented to the reader. One is
a naïve outsider, the other a knowledgeable insider.

This opening story poses questions that are central to *My Cornish
Neighbours* and *The Mine of Dreams*. The narrator just arrived from
London, has yet to adjust to her new surroundings; to realise that
her previous conception of Cornwall was, to some extent, fabricated
and unrealistic. While making this clear the text suggests the possibility
of progress for the narrator from outsider to insider, yet it never
guarantees its actuality. The text also questions the authenticity of the
outside observer by presenting Mrs Pengilly as a potential storyteller
already with access to and already part of the Cornish community.

'THE IMPOSSIBLE NECESSITY OF BECOMING INDIGENOUS'[14]

The title to this section is a quote from Terry Goldie's paper 'The
Representation of the Indigene'. Although Goldie is discussing
the relationship in Australia between the indigenous and the white
population, this quote is equally applicable to the quest of the literary
anthropologist. An outsider cannot comment on a community if they
remain firmly ensconced on its boundaries, hence the necessity of
becoming indigenous. Yet, if we are to believe Goldie, indigenization
of the outsider is impossible. I would like to look at this premise in
relation to Ellis' two collections of short stories.

As the short stories unfold, the narrator progresses from her
original position as naïve outsider. Her unrealistic constructions of
Cornish life are replaced with facts, knowledge of customs and
knowledge of local people based on face-to-face interaction. Each
story featuring the narrator serves to augment her knowledge of the
community in which she is living. 'Useless Tools' from *My Cornish
Neighbours* is a good example. Through Martha Hicks the narrator
learns of the local attitude towards the police. The narrator has lost her
watch and considers reporting it to the local constabulary. Martha
responds with, 'they'm useless tools hereabouts'.[15] The police are a
relatively new concept to this Cornish community, having been in place

for no more than 15 years. The attitude towards foreigners that Mrs Pengilly mentions in 'Trenwin' is here seen in action. The community distrust the policemen, even if of local birth, because their orders are from 'uplong'.[16] The uniform is representative of the extent to which the local community is controlled by outside forces. The actions of the policeman serve to compound the threat the local community perceive them to pose for they threaten unwritten and long accepted 'rights' the locals feel they have. For example, Matthew Trevaskis is fined 'for lettin' his bullocks wander in the lane they'd been allowed to go in for years'.[17] Such a threat to their everyday life brings the locals together in both excluding the police from their community and enacting revenge. The policeman who sought to fine Matthew Trevaskis is repeatedly thrown in the sea to teach him a lesson. Exclusion by the whole community severely weakens the power of the law and the unofficial system of law remains intact. Martha finishes the tale by telling the narrator 'A big reward do allus go further wi' the like o' we than police or the law.'[18]

'Useless Tools', one of the later stories in *My Cornish Neighbours*, shows the extent to which this community is willing to open up to the narrator. Martha gives her access backstage, behind the scenes. She is seeing how this community works and the group identity the locals possess. The narrator is accessing the light-hearted, frivolous anecdotes about this community 'Sally's Foot' where she is told about Sally's embarrassing visit to the doctor to see about her swollen foot (Sally only thinks to wash one foot in preparation for her visit and is mortified when the doctor asks to see both). However, she is also privy to the bare bones of this society, the unwritten laws that govern it, the threads that keep it together; the mechanisms by which the community functions. That the community is usually hostile to outsiders serves to highlight the privileged position the narrator has been allowed to adopt.

The narrator, then, undergoes a process whereby she abandons her imaginative constructions of Cornwall and situates herself within a Cornish community. Mrs Pengilly was right when she told the narrator she would come to know her neighbours, for the journey she undergoes from the moment of her arrival is one of acquiring knowledge and understanding of this community. However, this is not to say that becoming a member of a Cornish community is the same as becoming Cornish. The narrator is no longer simply an outsider but, at the same time, she is not an insider. Rather the categories of insider and outsider are not rigid. It is not the case that the narrator can step over the boundary between outsider and insider but neither is it the case that she is unable to develop from her original position as outsider. Phillip

Crang sees a region 'as a process being constantly constructed and reconstructed through the times and spaces of everyday practices'.[19] I think the way the outsider relates to the insider is also a process that is constantly constructed and reconstructed. At the point of interaction between an insider and an outsider the boundary between the two is constantly undergoing a process of shift and change according to that specific relationship. Whereas the actions of the policeman serve to re-inscribe the division between outsiders and insiders, the narrator's relationship with her neighbours causes the boundary to shift and merge and reform constantly.

The narrator comes to occupy a specific position within this Cornish community as a sage to whom many of the community come for advice and guidance. In 'Dogs' the retired sailor, after having met the narrator for only a few minutes, says 'You look kind, and as if you could understand things. I wonder would you take it amiss if I ask you for a piece of advice?'[20] 'The Idealist' is about a man obsessed with death. He is ostracised by the community but the narrator is fascinated by him and enters into a long conversation with him. It results in her appreciating the talent he has to see the soul departing at the moment of death. Nathaniel, who had previously spoken to no one about his experiences, tells all to the narrator.[21] This happens throughout the short stories and the narrator is constantly asked for advice.

This is how the narrator finds her place in the community. She enjoys the fact that her opinions matter and, at the same time, this position gives her access to her neighbours thoughts, fears and dreams. They open up to her. However, this role, while giving her access, also elevates her within the community. She is seen to be superior because she is educated and intelligent. The locals flock to her for advice because they believe her capable of a wise answer. Her position within the community is based on her difference from the Cornish inhabitants. They believe her to be wise because she has knowledge of places other than Cornwall. Therefore, despite the access this role allows, it also prevents her from being fully assimilated into the Cornish community. The point at which the narrator, an outsider, meets with the insider therefore, while allowing considerable access in one respect, maintains her identity as an outsider in another by drawing attention to her difference.

Despite the narrator's success in establishing a position within this Cornish community, she ultimately leaves Cornwall and returns to London. *My Cornish Neighbours* and *The Mine of Dreams* both close with the story entitled 'One and All' which documents the narrator's departure. It is fitting that this story should close both collections for it brings the narrator's life in Cornwall to a close and sees her return to

London. The Cornish motto 'One and All', previously cited by Mrs Pengilly and others as the example of their general enmity towards strangers, is an apt title for this story. It is clear the narrator's departure is due to the hostility exercised towards her by members of the community. The stories featured in both collections focus on cordial relations with the local population. It is a surprise, therefore, when Mrs Pengilly says the narrator has 'had to battle so freely wi' elements and nuisances of all sorts'.[22] At this point the reader is aware the stories have been a selective delineation of the narrator's experience. As readers we have been denied access to less salubrious aspects of the outsider-insider interaction. We can use our imaginations to fill in the gaps that now appear in the text, guided partly by Mrs Pengilly's comments. She denies the actions of some locals are necessarily malicious, rather a knee-jerk response to any outsider who comes amongst them. She says 'We've been reared to look on all up longs as natural foes, and though we all likes you, my dear, still it 'ave been a matter of principle with some, and wishing you no harm neither, just to show they could frustrate you in any undertaking.'[23] The attitude towards outsiders is ingrained and unlikely to be overturned by the narrator's brief time living in this community. Rather than criticize the reaction of some of her neighbours to the narrator, Mrs Pengilly accepts it as natural and simply asks the narrator does not 'take it to heart'.[24]

While the parting is sad for both the narrator and her friends within the community, the departure marks a definite end. There are no plans to return and the narrator wonders if she will ever desire to return. This implies that, despite the friends she has made, she does not belong. It seems that the animosity of some of the community has prevented her from making a lasting home in Cornwall. The introduction of the narrator, an outsider, into this community, distorted the boundaries between insider and outsider, forcing a shift and reconfiguration of these boundaries based on the specific way in which she related to and interacted with the Cornish community. The narrator's return to London results in the re-instigation of the boundary between outsider and insider because the interaction between insider and outsider, the specific relationship between the narrator and this community is terminated.

It is at the point of the narrator's departure that her role as literary anthropologist is most evident. Until 'One and All', the last story in both collections, the reader is unaware the narrator will return to live permanently in London. On her visit to London in 'Mrs Pengilly in London' the narrator, like Mrs Pengilly, longs to return to Cornwall. The narrator tells Mrs Pengilly, who is about to return home, that she will 'hurry through her work' in order to return to Cornwall 'as soon as possible'.[25] The story closes therefore by aligning the narrator with Mrs Pengilly as one who feels they belong in Cornwall rather than London. The reader is lead to believe she is making her home in Cornwall while rejecting the London way of life. Kirin Narayan in 'How Native is the "Native" Anthropologist' says 'those who are anthropologists in the usual sense of the word are thought to study Others whose alien cultural worlds they must painstakingly come to know'.[26] The narrator does just that, she comes to know the intricate workings of this Cornish community but, like the anthropologist, the final result is always a departure from that alien culture.

For the narrator, knowledge is the currency of exchange between her and the Cornish community. She answers their queries in return for access to their world. Even while immersed in this community, she retains a separateness that enables her to record observations and comment on the world around her. Whether or not this position lends credence to what the narrator has to say, will be discussed later. However, the text does not answer whether knowledge was the only thing the narrator wanted from this community. If this was the case her mission has been a success for she returns to London armed with the knowledge she set out to gain. If her desire was to live amongst the Cornish community and become an insider in the sense of becoming Cornish she has failed. It is possible to find evidence for both intentions through the text. 'Mrs Pengilly in London' posits the possibility that the narrator wants more than information; that she wants to belong. Whereas her elevated position as sage to the village and her understanding but not use of dialect suggest the narrator maintains a distance from her subject matter. By not revealing the narrator's intentions the ambiguity of the text keeps alive the possibility that to become indigenous is impossible.

At the centre of this text, therefore, hangs a question about Cornish ethnicity and identity. Is it impossible for the outsider to become indigenous? As the paragraphs above show, the text is far from answering this question and fosters further questions, rather than providing answers. This question is part of a wider debate concerned with how we define Cornishness. Where are the parameters? Margery Fee in her article 'Who can write as other?' says that 'If we simply conclude that if one feels Maori [or Cornish] one is, we fall into a new set of problems.'[27] At the opposite end of the scale would be a definition of Cornishness that relies solely on place of birth and parentage, and in between these two extremes are those born in Cornwall to non-Cornish parents and those born to Cornish parents in countries all over the world. I am inclined to question the problems that Fee sees arising from the conclusion that anyone can feel Cornish if they wish. In any case, it is not exactly something you can police. Cornish 'difference' has been a reality for centuries and persists in a post-modern world of globalization and mass communication. Although the Cornish are still discriminated against and although we do still have to fight to be heard in political, literary and other fields we can still take confidence from the persistence of Cornish 'difference' and identity, and know that it will not dissolve if those of non-Cornish birth claim kinship.

THE INSIDER AS OUTSIDER: MRS PENGILLY IN LONDON
Whether a person is an indigene or alien depends on the geographical location of that person. Mrs Pengilly an insider in Cornwall becomes an outsider when she visits London. The narrator decides to return briefly to London to take care of some business. Mrs Pengilly, upon invitation to join her, takes up the opportunity to fulfil a long-held dream of visiting the metropolis. London features prominently in both short-story collections, not as the oppressive seat of government but rather as a distant, magical place. Just as the narrator constructs a Cornwall in her imagination Mrs Pengilly and others have created a fictional London. Mrs Pengilly's imaginative construct of London, however, crumbles the moment she steps off the train. She is faced with a London that confounds and frightens her. The energy of this story is generated from the clash between rural Cornwall and urban London. Mrs Pengilly and her daughter are caught-up in a collision of worlds.

Ellis is not blind to the comic potential of two unwitting Cornish women thrust into alien urbanity. When Mrs Pengilly steps onto the platform she declares to the narrator that her and Charlotte (her daughter) 'have been almost murdered I' the full light o' day' because they didn't like the look of the man who sat opposite them.[28] Mrs Pengilly's primary ambition while in London is to see the 'statues' yet, without the narrator to act as guide, she mistakes some street actors for the real thing. The comedy is based on their lack of knowledge about the world around them but it is light-hearted rather than mean spirited.

The narrator, at home in the world that confounds Mrs Pengilly, finds her charges tiresome and embarrassing. We see a different side to the narrator than has been previously evident. In Cornwall she is elevated by the locals to the position of sage. It is a profitable role in terms of the information she receives but it is also a role she enjoys. In London, however, the narrator assumes a position of superiority over Mrs Pengilly and her daughter. She mocks their ignorance and is embarrassed to be seen in public with them. That which is normal for the narrator is highly unusual for Mrs Pengilly. Therefore, Mrs Pengilly is prone to notice and, given her propensity for speech, comment upon her surroundings. From the omnibus she studies the people going about their everyday lives and exclaims 'they all seem as if they were hurryin' to a deathbed or a confinement'. The narrator implores Mrs Pengilly to 'speak softly, as people can hear all we say'.[29] The narrator's attitude towards Mrs Pengilly contrasts with the way she was received by Mrs Pengilly in Cornwall. In 'Trewin'/'Wheal Dream' the narrator's ignorance of her surroundings is glossed over by Mrs Pengilly who is sure that she will come to know the people and the place in which she has come to live.

The difference between the two women is that the narrator adapts herself to her surroundings. After her initial ignorance in the opening story she sets out to learn about the Cornish community. She lets people talk and drinks in the knowledge that is available to her. As the stories progress she comes to learn why things happen, what is cherished by the community, what is detested, who is respected, who is feared or hated, how the community functions and the rules and rights by which it abides. Although the narrator attempts, to some extent, to imbue Mrs Pengilly with such knowledge of London she is unable to filter the information into a pattern of understanding and the world with which she is faced remains incomprehensible and alien.

Although Mrs Pengilly is unable to understand London her visit leads to greater understanding and appreciation of Cornwall. The physical distance from her life in Cornwall produces a new perspective. That which before was taken for granted is seen with a new eye, an eye that has also seen the streets of London. Her observations are only possible through contrast with an alien environment and, therefore, previous to this visit, such a perspective was unavailable to her. Ultimately, Mrs Pengilly comes to appreciate the only life she has ever known. She sees people 'livin' all their lives i' clouds o' furnace smoke' when she is surrounded by 'blue sea and green fields'.[30] She knows her farm work is hard and tiring but sees starving Londoners and thinks of Jacob 'tired, of course, but full o' flesh meat and contentment'.[31] Trinh T. Minh-Ha says 'The moment the insider steps out from the inside, she is no longer a mere insider (and vice versa). She necessarily looks in from the outside while also looking out from the inside. Like the outsider, she steps back and records what never occurs to her . . . as being worth or in need of recording.'[32] Through her visit to London therefore, Mrs Pengilly comes to occupy common ground with the narrator. She is able to look at Cornwall from a similar perspective to that of the outsider. I had previously conceived of this position that Mrs Pengilly now occupies, in terms of loss, the loss of being able to accept your environment at face value. Mrs Pengilly has the same concern for she says: 'I can't believe I shall ever put on my big apron again to make butter with a peaceful mind.'[33] Ultimately, however, despite the tribulations of becoming an outsider in London, Mrs Pengilly gains a perspective on her own world, where she is an insider, that enriches the experience of that world. When she returns to Cornwall she tells her son Jacob '"I'm home . . . Nothin' else matters. I keeps wanderin' round the house, almost swallowin' the very sunbeams as catch and kiss atween thy room and Charlotte's".'[34] Her son, made miserable by the monotony of life in Cornwall, dreams, as she once did, of visiting London. Despite her recent experiences she is happy for him to go, thinking it possible her son will find what she found in the hustle and bustle of London: a newfound respect for what she has always had.

THE APPROPRIATION OF DIALECT

Ellis is a non-Cornish writer who uses Cornish dialect in her short stories. Her use of dialect is delicate and has the effect of creating the melodic tone of Cornish speech for her characters. Ellis' rendition of dialect in her work differs from other representations of dialect. Take, for example, Clemo's dialect tales where almost every word is altered in order to represent the Cornish characters' way of speaking:

> Maid's in some stew . . . squaalin' oal last ebenin' an' ebben spok' to mawther fer two days.[35]

In contrast, Ellis' representation of Cornish dialect focuses its attention on conveying that way of speech by altering far fewer words.

> She'm a female of tremenjous speerit, but she've never had no comfortable outlet for it, and that's allus, as you knaw, a danger wi' our sex.'[36]

Ellis does not achieve the flow between words that we see in the Clemo extract where the words are softened to enable the sentence to tumble to a close. However, I do think her style of re-creating the Cornish way of speaking captures the tone in which she would have heard her Cornish Neighbours converse. In addition to words like 'allus' and 'knaw', which give the sentence it's tone, Ellis also has a handle on dialect words such as 'whisht' an example which she regularly uses in the text:

> She's some whisht, sure enough![37]

This extract comes from the short story entitled 'Sally's Foot'. In having Nancy Christopher say 'some whisht' Ellis shows that, not only does she know the tone of speech and the meaning of dialect words but she also understands how these words are used within a sentence. Rather than saying 'She's whisht' she says 'She's some whisht' a way of saying very ill or melancholy in Cornish dialect.

In his introduction to *The Mine of Dreams*, Havelock Ellis informs us that the majority of the short stories in *My Cornish Neighbours* were originally published in the London evening newspaper *The Echo*.[38] It seems, therefore, that to begin with at least, the target audience was city dwellers rather than the Cornish themselves. With this in mind I think it fair to say that Ellis's use of dialect caters to a non-Cornish audience without sacrificing the integrity of the text. Ellis does not break off from the speech of the Cornish characters in order to explain words that may be unfamiliar to her audience but she also renders dialect in such a way as to make it accessible to a non-Cornish audience. The representation of dialect is simple, she does not labour the text with literary constructions of speech that may be off-putting to a non-Cornish reader but she allows that reader to gain a flavour of the tone and syntax of Cornish dialect.

I began this article by saying that to call oneself 'Cornish' is to claim membership to a group. Dialect can be a badge of membership to that group, a way of distinguishing insiders from outsiders. Dialect, on the page or in face-to-face conversation is a component of identity that is tangible. It can be a way for insiders to exclude outsiders. The use of dialect in *My Cornish Neighbours* and *The Mine of Dreams* interacts with and mediates between the categories insiders and outsider.

In *My Cornish Neighbours* and *The Mine of Dreams* the narrator's voice is distinguished from the many Cornish voices by the absence of accent or dialect. It serves to highlight her position as outsider and this is no more so the case than in the opening short story of both collections. Here Mrs Pengilly's speech is contrasted with that of the narrator. Ellis achieves this contrast by creating an audible clash between Cornish speech and the Queen's English. Mrs Pengilly's lilting and melodic tone grates against the narrator's prim speech. For example, when Matthew Trevaskis appears he addresses the narrator with 'Gran'day'. The narrator's reply is 'Yes . . . it's like heaven.'[39] The two styles of speech almost grind against each other. The clash between styles of speech is repeated throughout the story and indeed in any story where the narrator speaks to a Cornish character. This has the effect of continually signalling the narrator as outsider and the dialect speaking character as insider.

The same is true when Mrs Pengilly visits London. Like the narrator in Cornwall, her way of speech identifies her as someone outside of her everyday environment. Dialect after all is fundamentally tied to place, to geographical location, in a way that other components of identity are not. Anyone can claim to feel Cornish or identify themselves as Cornish—even people who have never even visited Cornwall but dialect and accent signal that a person has lived and belongs in a particular place. The clash of worlds in which Mrs Pengilly is caught while in London is signalled by the clash between forms of speech. This is evident on the omnibus when Mrs Pengilly vocalizes her confusion at the alien world before her. She notices a line of 'sandwich men' a phenomenon she has not previously encountered. Therefore she is ignorant of their purpose and exclaims 'if they do it for their health, it don't seem to cure 'em, for they all look whisht, don't they?' It is not only what she says that identifies her as an outsider; it is the words she uses that underlines this position. Mrs Pengilly, used only to the Cornish environment to which she belongs, does not recognize that her speech is at variance with the speech of those around her. To the narrator, however, this is explicit and uncomfortable. The narrator tells the reader that she replied to Mrs Pengilly's comment about them being 'whisht' by explaining the sandwich men probably hadn't eaten for some time.[40] The narrator directly quotes Mrs Pengilly's use of the term 'whisht' putting it in inverted commas. She does not translate it for the audience but she highlights the word as if aware of its inappropriate use in London. By highlighting the clash in forms of speech the narrator posits herself as an insider and Mrs Pengilly as an outsider. She makes it clear that she is not using dialect in this situation. The narrator is aware of the power of speech to label or position a person in relation to the categories of insider and outsider while Mrs Pengilly is oblivious to the connotations attached to speech.

The clash between forms of speech continues throughout the short stories in both collections for at no point, despite what is stated above, does the narrator adopt Cornish speech. Her way of speaking is not modified in any way by her interaction with those who speak in Cornish dialect. However, as the first person narrator of a number of the short stories, she directly quotes the speech of the Cornish characters to the reader. Therefore, although the narrator does not speak in dialect, she is claiming a thorough knowledge of this form of speech to the extent that she can faithfully recreate the speech for her audience. It has been made clear above that dialect underlines the positions of insiders and outsiders and their interaction with each other. With regards to the narrator, even though when speaking her outsider status is underlined by the absence of dialect, her understanding of dialect demonstrated through the ability to accurately record her Cornish neighbours is indicative of the way she has forced a shift in the boundary between outsider and insider categories. The narrator occupies a middle ground between the two categories. She is not simply an outsider, she is not simply an insider.

DIALECT AND THE AUTHENTIC VOICE

It is the author, of course, and not just the narrator, who is making a claim to insider knowledge through the use of dialect. As a non-Cornish writer come to live among and write about the Cornish population, use of dialect is a way of demonstrating an intimate knowledge of that community. It is a visible way of showing the reader the extent of the author's knowledge and ability to record and comment upon Cornwall. It is a claim to authenticity. There is nothing particularly unusual about an outsider appropriating local dialect in their literature. K.D.M. Snell states that, in Britain, 'fictional representation of rural speech . . . is often relayed by outsiders'.[41] In relation to Cornwall the re-appropriation of dialect by outsiders could be seen as part of a wider system of control of the way in which Cornwall is represented and constructed by outsiders through literature and other mediums. A non-literary example would be the marketing strategy of the Great Western Railway in the early twentieth century to construct Cornwall as an exotic and exciting holiday destination under the slogan 'The Cornish Riviera'. Although this construction of Cornwall is aimed at a non-Cornish audience it cannot be stopped from seeping into the local Cornish culture. After all, this construction of Cornwall is successful marketing strategy because it is attractive and exciting. We have a situation, therefore, where not only are the dominant constructions of Cornwall being created by outsiders but the local population is inculcated in re-inscribing and so perpetuating such constructions.

In terms of dialect, therefore, the voice of the indigenous population is at best filtered through outsiders. This is exactly what we have in Ellis's texts. She is not a native literary anthropologist, and the Cornish characters that feature in the short stories are filtered through an outsider in the form of the narrator. Gareth Griffiths, in his essay 'The Myth of Authenticity,' says 'the act of constructing the speech of the already silenced may metaphorically, at least, be perceived as an act best characterised . . . by the metaphor of violence, however "liberal" in intention'.[42] There are many who would characterize the Cornish as silenced. If we were to agree with Griffiths then, Ellis' recreation of Cornish dialect as an outsider is an act of violence towards that indigenous population even if her aim is to faithfully recreate Cornish dialect and to provide a medium through which to give the Cornish a voice.

For many ethnic groups in the past, it seems the method of

countering the violence described by Griffiths has been to claim to have the authentic voice. To claim to have the authentic voice is to claim that an entire ethnic group speaks with one voice and consequently, therefore, is one essential subject. Stuart Hall discusses this trend in relation to the 'black' experience in Britain and Gareth Griffith in relation to Australian Aborigines.[43] Hall and Griffith both see the authentic voice and the essential subject as ultimately damaging to the ethnic group employing such methods in opposition to oppression. It is possible to see why ethnic groups would think the authentic voice to be an effective strategy against oppressive forces for to claim to have the authentic voice is a way for an ethnic group to take control over its own representation. It not only gives an ethnic group the opportunity to speak and be heard but it also lends credence to what they have to say in relation to the outsider. It is a chance to rebalance the scales.

Despite these potential advantages, however, Griffith and Hall are right to argue against an authentic voice and an essential subject. To argue for an authentic Cornish voice is, at the same time, to oppress or ignore other Cornish voices and label them inauthentic. Privileging the dominant voice, likely to be white and male, would mean that insiders would be part of disseminating and maintaining an oppression equivalent to that which the Cornish have been, and remain subject. Rather than one voice, there needs to be many Cornish voices, perspectives, experiences and many analyses of these perspectives, voices and experiences. Whether the claims to an authentic voice come from outsider or insider they are debilitating to Cornish Studies. I am reminded of the many voices present in Ellis' stories. Although it has only been possible here to discuss a few of the voices within Ellis' short stories, both collections contain many more voices. Although they are voices filtered through the mind of an outsider, they are many and, I think they are worth listening to and discussing. Ellis' recreation of the Cornish voice through her representation of dialect in the text is not an act of violence if the Cornish are also able to speak for themselves and if they are able to analyse and re-appropriate the constructions of outsiders. Ultimately Ellis' work is worth consideration and discussion and it can be given a productive position within Cornish studies, as can the constructions by other outside writers when its presence does not preclude or suppress other voices, perspectives, texts, and constructions out there to be tapped and talked about. Ellis' is one more voice I want to add to the mix. It is necessary to keep adding and adding and adding these voices, these voices that would never have been the authentic Cornish voice: the more the better.

Stuart Hall makes this argument in relation to the essential black subject. He sees the shift from the essential subject to multiple subjects in black cultural politics as 'the passing away of what at one time seemed to be a necessary fiction'. There have been times in the past where for the indigenous Cornish also the essential subject and the authentic voice have also been seen to be a 'necessary fiction' but, I think, more often created from the outside, imposed and accepted than germinated from within. There is no doubt that multiplicity is the way forward, yet Hall is aware of further difficulties. He says:

> This does not make it any easier to conceive of how a politics can be constructed which works with and through difference, which is able to build those forms of solidarity and identi-fication which make common struggle possible but without suppressing the real heterogeneity of interests and identity, and which can effectively draw the political boundary lines without which political contestation is impossible, without fixing those boundary lines for eternity.[44]

Directly relevant also to Cornish Studies, the question remains how to fight for and recognize many voices while claiming to belong together as one group, discernable from others by a long and continued recognition of difference. Looking for an answer to this centrally important question should be through exploring the multiple voices out there and the multiple constructions of Cornwall and Cornish identity, rather than turning to the misperceived strength of homogeneity.

CONCLUSION

I wanted to do two things in this article. Firstly, I wanted to talk about Edith Ellis as she has not been discussed in some time. Secondly, I wanted, through the work of Edith Ellis, to discuss and explore the categories of outsider and insider and their relationship to each other. Given the fact that, generally, Cornwall comes off worse in its relationship with outside forces—as critical analyses by observers such as John Angarrack have argued—it is perhaps difficult to imagine an aspect of the relationship between insiders and outsiders that is productive rather than detrimental to Cornish identity. Ellis's stories are an exploration of that meeting between insider and outsider at the level of people rather than the political power play of institutions and government. She was writing at a time when the tourist industry was in its infancy, when the meeting of insider and outsider was less frequent than we are used to in the twenty-first century. Today, the Cornish economy is significantly reliant on the influx of outsiders as soon as the sun begins to shine, and post-modern society facilitates constant contact between one geographical location and another. That said, given the perpetuation of Cornish 'difference' and the strong sense of identity the Cornish possess, that meeting point between insider and outsider is still key to how we look at and think about 'difference' and identity.

Edith Ellis has written other texts, such as *Kit's Woman*, which are located in Cornwall and are concerned with Cornish people and the Cornish way of life. There is much more that needs to be written both about her and about her work. In the information available about her life it was interesting to learn that, when away from Cornwall and in London society, she wrote in Cornish dialect. This was a writer for whom Cornwall was more than a holiday destination, a writer determined to become more than simply an outsider in Cornish society. From her position as a literary anthropologist who painstakingly came to know about Cornwall and the Cornish, she can tell us much about ourselves.

NOTES AND REFERENCES

1. Mrs Havelock Ellis, *My Cornish Neighbours*, London, 1906. *The Mine of Dreams*, London, 1925.
2. 'Goldengrove Unleaving' was previously published as two separate stories in the 1970s. Jill Paton Walsh, *Goldengrove Unleaving*, London, 1997; Dinah Craik, *An Unsentimental Journey Through Cornwall*, London, 1884; reprinted Penzance, 1988.
3. Trevor Nunn, film adaptation of 'Twelfth Night', Renaissance Films, 1996.
4. Isaac Goldberg, *Havelock Ellis: A Biographical and Critical Study*, London, 1926, p. 270.
5. Phyllis Bentley, *The English Regional Novel*, London, 1941.
6. Havelock Ellis, introduction to, Mrs Havelock Ellis, *The Mine of Dreams*, London, 1925, p. xvii.
7. *My Cornish Neighbours*, p. 8.
8. Ibid., p. 11.
9. Ibid., pp. 14–15.
10. Ibid., p. 8.
11. Ibid., p. 14.
12. Ibid., pp. 9–12.
13. Ibid., p. 14.
14. Terry Goldie, 'The Representation of the Indigene', in Bill Ashcroft, Gareth Griffiths and Helen Tiffin (eds), *The Post-Colonial Studies Reader*, London, 1995, pp. 232–6 (p. 234).
15. *My Cornish Neighbours,* p. 165.
16. Ibid., p. 166.
17. Ibid., p. 166.
18. Ibid., p. 169.
19. Phillip Crang, 'Regional Imaginations: An Afterword', in Ella Westland

(ed.), *Cornwall: The Cultural Construction of Place*, Penzance, 1997, p. 159.

20. *My Cornish Neighbours*, p. 28.
21. *The Mine of Dreams*, pp. 38–59.
22. *My Cornish Neighbours*, p. 194.
23. Ibid., p. 194.
24. Ibid., p. 195.
25. Ibid., p. 141.
26. Kirin Narayan, 'How Native is the "Native" Anthropologist', in *American Anthropologist*, vol. 95, New Series, 1993, pp. 671–86 (p. 671).
27. Margery Fee, 'Who Can Write as Other', in Bill Ashcroft, Gareth Griffiths and Helen Tiffin (eds), *The Post-Colonial Studies Reader*, London, 1995, pp. 242–5 (p. 244).
28. *My Cornish Neighbours*, p. 123.
29. Ibid., p. 130.
30. Ibid., p.130.
31. Ibid., p. 131.
32. Trinh T Minh-Ha, 'No Master Territories' in Bill Ashcroft, Gareth Griffiths and Helen Tiffin (eds), *The Post-Colonial Studies Reader*, London, 1995, pp. 215–18) (p. 217).
33. *My Cornish Neighbours*, p. 140.
34. Ibid., p. 185.
35. Jack Clemo, *The Bouncing Hills*, p. 39.
36. *My Cornish Neighbours*, p. 11.
37. Ibid., p. 17.
38. Havelock Ellis, introduction to, Mrs Havelock Ellis, *The Mine of Dreams*, London, 1925, p. xviii.
39. *My Cornish Neighbours*, p. 14.
40. Ibid., p. 131.
41. K.D.M. Snell, *The Regional Novel in Britain and Ireland 1800–1990*, Cambridge, 1998, p. 33.
42. Gareth Griffiths, 'The Myth of Authenticity', in Bill Ashcroft, Gareth Griffiths and Helen Tiffin (eds), *The Post-Colonial Studies Reader*, London, 1995, pp. 223–7 (p. 239).
43. Gareth Griffiths 'The Myth of Authenticity'; Stuart Hall, 'New Ethnicities'; in Bill Ashcroft, Gareth Griffiths and Helen Tiffin (eds), *The Post-Colonial Studies Reader*, London, 1995, pp. 223–7 (Hall); pp. 237–41 (Griffiths).
44. New Ethnicities', p. 225.

'THE WORDS ARE THERE BEFORE US': A READING OF TWENTIETH-CENTURY ANGLO-CORNISH POEMS WRITTEN BY WOMEN

Briar Wood

We take a clean and empty page
We aim to play it cool
The words are there before us
And we will call the rule
'Crowdy Crawn'[1]

CROWDY CRAWN OF POETRY

The comparison between Crowdy Crawn, 'a framework covered in skin, a drum like receptacle in which to keep useful odds and ends, or a wooden hoop covered with sheep skin used for taking up corn. Sometimes used as a tambourine,[2] and a collection of poetry is posited by Ann Trevenen Jenkin and Brenda Wootton, both poets whose writing has been located in twentieth-century Cornwall. The multipurpose roles of the instrument in domestic life, and in artistic and agricultural production can also apply to poetry. For women, the fact that the Crowdy Crawn can connote the need for multi-tasking—and adeptness at it—makes it particularly appealing.

As her daughter Sue Luscombe pointed out in the Introduction to *Pantomime Stew*, Brenda Wootton's vernacular 'portry' emerged from everyday life and speech. The language is a communal one—that of 'pantomime stew', described by Luscombe as 'the big enamel pot on top of the primus in the village hall, filled to the brim with something of everything, to keep everyone going long enough to finish that day's

rehearsal.'[3] It is also a communal language of 'Rubudullya'—
'nonsense'[4]—and of Crowdy Crawn. 'Crowdy' evokes etymologically
the crowd/crowdys fiddle or violin, referenced by Morton Nance as
having both Middle-English and Cornish sources. As a 'framework
covered in skin' the crowdy crawn can be read as a metaphor for the
human body. The continuity of the customs associated with Crowdy
Crawn through industrialization, migration and modernity can signify
ongoing connections across generations and historical changes. Sound
links the 'crowdy crawn' to English language 'crowd' and 'crown', so
suggesting perhaps song and poetry as populist practices.

Brenda Wootton's 'Crowdy Crawn' poem was written, her
daughter and editor Sue Luscombe explained, in 1974 'when Brenda
turned professional as a singer with Robert Bartlett, as the duo
'Crowdy Crawn'.[5] It explored a mix of anxiety and exhilaration about
public presentation through images that are domestic and geographical,
personal and communal. Wootton sang in a crowdy crawn of language:
Anglo-Cornish, Cornu-English, Cornish. She wrote narratives, comic,
tragic and mixed, family and local history, personal lyrics and nature
poems, poems about travel. Her 'Downlong' poem describes directions
in Cornu-English from a position centered in her Newlyn world:

> From where I lived in Newlyn Town, 'uplong' was the
> Gurnick and Gwavas Estate (top of Paul Hill), 'downlong'
> was Street an Nowen and the fish market, 'inlong' was
> Penzance, 'overlong' was the cliff, the quarry and 'Skilly Gap'
> and 'outlong' was Mousehole. It depended from where you
> started I suppose.[6]

Often deliberately breaking the rules of high culture, in which the
intellectual argument takes precedence over rhyme and rhythm,
the irreverence of Wootton's doggerel was designed to foreground the
concerns and humour of Cornish working culture, and to balance
argument with entertainment and wordplay. Humour is a part of
respect and understanding, rather than reverence, as the poem for 'My
Grandad Ellery–Leatherass', demonstrates:

> And me, my hair now just like that, I looked a real 'go-getter',
> Git high-heeled shoes with fancy straps and a naughty tight
>   white sweater!
> There's me, parading through St Just, a proper Newlyn
>   charmer,
> When stepping right in front of me, this git big red-faced
>   farmer!

'I don't know who 'ee are, my cock, when I seen 'ee pass,
You must be some relation t'all, to dear old Leatherass!'
Well, I was shocked, for in my mind, was the fat, bald man in
   bed!
And then I thought of the farmer's face, and of the things he'd
   said –
He'd meant it as a compliment! He loved my grandad dear!
The man who could charm horses and who'd never tasted
   beer!'[7]

Ann Trevenen Jenkin's Crowdy Crawn section in her poetry collection of 1997, *Gwel Kernow: A Cornish View*, offers a view on Cornish education and history, concluding with a poem on Myghal Josef An Gof, a Cornish blacksmith who, as a martyred participant in the 1497 protests against the taxes of Henry VII, has become a symbol of Cornish nationalism. Her most outspokenly feminist poem is included in this section; it is a demand for the Gorseth to be more welcoming to women: 'Vote for a female Grand Bard/Let's all elect her today.'[8] Jenkin herself was in fact elected the first woman Grand Bard from 1997–2000.

COMPARATIVE POETICS
The focus in this article is on representations of women and by women in Anglo-Cornish poetry, with some reference to Cornu-English and Cornish poetry. Poetry from the turn of the nineteenth century to the present is the main concern, though some reference to writing from before this period will be made.[9] It engages the question of whether there is some continuity and connection between tropes, language, history and themes in writing by women. How have representations shifted over the century, to the present? How does the treatment by women writers of language, themes and tropes differ from male authored writing? What do poets in Anglo-Cornish have in common with each other and how do they differ? How is their work connected to women from other places and can there be said to be a distinctive set of connections between Anglo-Cornish women poets?

The original working title was 'The Glamour of the Grey', taken from a poem in the 'Cornwall' sequence by Katharine Lee Jenner entitled 'On the Cliff', published in 1926 in *Songs of the Stars and the Sea* under the name Mrs Henry Jenner. Alan Kent has commented on recurrent themes in Katharine Lee Jenner's work, including 'the colour grey which forms the metaphorical basis of many of her poems'.[10] The greyness is connected to Cornish land, sky and seascape which 'is not only redolent of the mystery plays and holy wells of an idealised, fully operational Cornu-Celtic-Catholic culture, but of Catholic struggle and suffering'.[11] This title and the poem's symbolism drew perhaps too closely on a Catholic vocabulary to satisfy everyone of its wide applicability to Anglo-Cornish women's writing, yet its reference to an indefinable location, identity and belief, while evoking land, sea, saints and the human struggle in-between are recurrent factors in so much of Anglo-Cornish women's writing that it can be read as opening out into an infinite array of poetic references rather than confining or closing down the discourses about the 'Cornwall' of the title. It also gestures towards the internationalism of Cornish culture, while retaining condensed signifiers that reference the country/county's history, culture and concerns.

The etymology of 'glamour' in the OED is listed as 'early 18th cent. (originally Scots in the sense 'enchantment, magic'): alteration of GRAMMAR'. Although *grammar* itself was not used in this sense, the Latin word *grammatica* (from which it derives) was often used in the Middle Ages to mean 'scholarship, learning', including 'the occult practices popularly associated with learning'.[12] Added to more contemporary usage of the term as 'the attractive or exciting quality that makes certain people or things seem appealing or special . . . beauty or charm that is sexually attractive', the origins of the word when applied to Cornwall suggest a fantasy of place as erotic and real, a place of life and learning, to which and in which women can find a multiplicity of connections.

The title of another landmark collection, Ithell Colquhoun's 1973 *Grimoire of the Entangled Thicket*, drew attention to the linguistic, cultural and historical connections between grammar, poetry as spell, witchcraft as repressed/women's knowledge and Cornu-Celtic folklore. The sound of the word 'Grimoire' evokes 'gris' as grey and grim, a harshness that could refer to land/sea/sky, a backdrop on which humanity, vegetation and fauna flourish, depicted in the collection in black and white drawings. The sequence opens with a quotation in which Gwion drinks from Keridwen's cauldron and is able to forsee the future in Taliessin's 'The Battle of the Trees'.[13] Elaborating on the working title of Graves's *The White Goddess* which was 'The Roebuck in the Thicket' and its subtitle 'a historical grammar of poetic myth', Colquhoun's poems unpack that version of the White Goddess that had become such an ambivalent force in Graves' personal mythology— the powerful muse demanding sacrifice etc. into the locatedness of a Cornish studio, a natural world, an ecological system connected to ancient beliefs, yet plural in its paganism, less monolithic than *The* White Goddess (or *The* black goddess acknowledged later in his writing), recognizing the coherence and adaptability of composite cultural, historical, mythological and religious ideas, a bricolage of beliefs. Colquhoun herself describes this connection in *The Living Stones*: 'Even to-day "grammar" retains some of the power that made the "grimoire" magical.'[14]

Penelope Shuttle's poems too contain touches of grey, as in 'Travelling':

> I climb the hodden-gray hills
> From the harbour I hear the hoarse
> tender warning of the fog horn[15]

Similarly, in 'At Perranporth, March, 1976':

> No ships, no sunset,
> only the white cloud and the grey sea
> twined together to make evening.[16]

There is less emphasis here on the mystical than in Jenner's poetry, although magic is often glimpsed in the midst of everyday life. In her essay 'Women, Symbolism and the Coast of Cornwall' Judith Hubback suggests of Cornwall as a site of literary production that 'the unspoilt stretches of its coast mirror, with the interaction of sea and land, the receptivity and the potentialities of women's psyches'.[17] In her admittedly subjective reading, women writers like Virginia Woolf and Daphne du Maurier evoke the 'is-ness of the sea', 'woman's attunement to the flux and fall of the sea's tides' and the derring do-ness of 'plots and people' respectively.[18] Her own novel traces a local history in which 'man-woman patterns change greatly'.[19] And so they do in fiction, while poetry shares the long standing signifiers she writes of in which the beach can be interpreted as a middle ground while the sea, since it ebbs and flows, signifies movement towards and away from others, and life changes such as menstruation, pregnancy and menopause. In Penelope Shuttle's 'Maritimes' (suggesting Mary/mare/ maris) from *The Child-Stealer*, her first collection, the house/womb is imagined as the sea's plenitude: 'I go into the ocean, and rock there,/ just as my child turns/on the waterwheel of me/fed on the salt and blood of me.'[20]

Some reference to the many recent observations about Cornish culture and history will provide a theoretical framework in which to read poetic texts. A number of commentators have remarked, in various ways, on the convergence of the signification of women, feminization and Cornishness. Hayden observed that 'it would appear that the Cornish suffer similar material disadvantages to the female populations of many societies because they are a minority group with little political influence'.[21] Such comments need to be considered in a context where the marginalization of Cornish history has, according to Vernon, 'remained deeply unsettling to the national imaginary'. Discussing the well-known railway poster 'See your Own Country First', alongside guide books, sightseeing and the tourist gaze, Thomas points to 'the elision of Cornwall and the female'[22] and approaches a recognition of some separation between nature and culture, rather than the collapse of these separate elements into a female figure that promotes the tourist gaze.

Bernard Deacon has warned against 'homogenizing the oppressed group and underplaying differences among that group.'[23] His discussion of critical approaches to Cornish Studies—'From "Cornish Studies" to "Critical Cornish Studies": Reflections on Methodology'— in *Cornish Studies: Twelve* (2003) distinguishes Cornish Studies from feminism; this article reads poetry as an intersection of a plurality of discourses. Deacon identifies the significance of the multi-valency of signs; thus within

> the tourist discourse of Cornwall, the sign 'Celtic' becomes
> a moment attached to 'romance', 'tradition', 'King Arthur',
> 'standing stones', 'jewellery' and so on. But within a discourse
> of Cornish nationalism, 'Celtic' may resonate rather
> differently, articulating with 'rebellion', 'internationalism' and
> 'language' amongst other moments.[24]

To extend Deacon's example, as close readings of the poetic texts will show, this overview might be disrupted, confirmed or modified by queer and gendered interpretations. Conditions of production, publication, ideology and social conditions shape both texts and responses to them; they help to cultivate, as Deacon puts it, 'a sensitivity towards differing "Cornwalls".'[25]

As Deacon's discussion indicates, Celticism has been interpreted in many ways; Jenner's connections were with what has been described as the Celtic right. While Catholic Cornwall played a vital role in the politics of nationalist revival, Cornish Methodism is frequently understood to have been a dominant influence on the formation of characteristic elements of Cornish nationalist imaginings and representations. Kayleigh Milden argued in '"Are You Church or Chapel?" Perceptions of patial and Spiritual Identity within Cornish Methodism'[26] that the elements comprising an identification with Cornish Methodism are not always cohesive (being contradictory to many concepts of Celticism), although it has been a dynamic force in

narratives of nationalism and 'continues to be a multi-layered movement'. While fictional works by women negotiating Cornish Methodist
beliefs, such as Salome Hocking, are well established, the poetry
tends towards generalizing images. In Helen Dunmore's poems about
Wesley, Christian order, belief and control are disrupted by the past,
Gothic elements, sexuality, earth and skyscape, a multiplicity of
resistances. 'Preaching at Gwennap' focuses on the geography, while
the marginal historical detail and repetition of the title as a refrain puts
human faith in a context where it cannot be dominant. In fact the
perspective, in a refusal and diminishment of a masculinized Christian
history, is that of a bored and uncomprehending horse left 'standing
for hours'.[27] 'On circuit from Heptonstall Chapel' (Heptonstall evoking
a history of women's writing by connections with the Brontes and
Sylvia Plath) works this theme even more closely as it focalizes through
'The mare with her short legs heavily mud-caked'[28] in an ironic
commentary on the opening quotation from Samuel Wesley, John's
father, about the ability of his wife to bear suffering without complaint. The chapel 'facing all ways on its slabbed upland' becomes an
enduring monument to a way of life in which women were expected
to silently bear the burden of men, children and God, but whose
labour and the need to commemorate it yet communicates with women
in contemporary times. It is possible to read, even in the twentieth-
century poetry acknowledging the exclusion or management of women,
a legacy of Methodism in Cornwall that Philip Payton has described as
a contradictory (sometimes conservative) but often broadening and
modernizing influence on Cornish life:

> In general, Cornish Methodism exhibited a strongly
> egalitarian strand, reflecting the potential for socio-economic
> mobility and the relative lack of class consciousness in
> nineteenth-century Cornwall. Its theology, stressing concern
> for the needy and the equality of men before God, matched
> the political ideology of Cornish Liberalism.[29]

A HISTORY OF ANGLO-CORNISH WOMEN'S WRITING
W.H. Kearley Wright's *West-Country Poets* (1896) does contain a large
number of poems by women but they are way outnumbered by those
by men, and sometimes patronizingly referenced. Annie E. Argall, for
example has written some 'gems':

> Which, although eloquent, are rather short sermons in verse
> than poems. Most of her pieces have been written as she has
> lain in bed suffering from hip disease, from which she is now

happily recovering. Her patience, resignation, and sweetness of disposition are remarkable, and, considering her age, her poems exhibit great promise.[30]

Obviously in Kearley Wright's view, a paragon of all the virtues of a Victorian young lady, Annie E. Argall is no less marginalized than Mary Margaret Davis,[31] whose 'little volume of 'Poems on Various Subjects' 'are of no particular merit; but she appears to have lived all her life in her native island, her opportunities for inspiration were few and far between'. Why St Mary's in the Scilly Isles should have been any less inspiring than anywhere else is not quite clear, although even in Brenda Wootton's verse the Scillies are made to stand in for the very edge of modernity. Kearley Wright surpasses himself in excitement about Miss Lina Howell, a young lady from Truro represented by 'Canzonet', a poem about flowers calling out to Marguerite, a Nereid in waiting:

> She is a writer of graceful and musical verses, with a pleasant fancy, a poetic knowledge of flowers, although a very varied range of moods. Her verses have a wild-rose odour. She also paints pictures well, and seems to have a refined and artistic nature. Her father is a well-known travelling draper.[32]

The occupation of fathers and husbands is frequently mentioned in the biographies, while that of mothers is not. In fact the poem by Mary Margaret Davis from the Scillies about whom the editor is so dismissive 'Abstracts of a Sermon on the Nature and Duties of Kissing' is skilled, playful and ironic, deliberately constructed to mock the pomposity of sermons that would lecture against kissing as an indicator of the tenderness of human contact.

> The soother of life's daily woes—
> The poetry of dull cold prose—
>   What marvel it has stood
> The test of fashion, taste, and time,
> Of every nation, age, and clime,
>   The vicious and the good?[33]

Maria Gurney's poem 'Blue-Stockings Over the Border', anonymously published in *Blackwood's Magazine* in April 1828, also exemplified women's skill in writing poems that challenged male dominance through a combination of comedy, charm and irony as she warned the learned men of Oxford and Cambridge to beware the boundary-crossers. The poem describes this new kind of woman from the industrialized West Country as fearless when confronted with science and modernity, and it mimics the language of Biblical prophesy:

> Stand to your posts, ye adepts in astronomy,
>   A comet they'll see whilst your glass ye arrange, –
> Find out some fault in Dame Nature's economy –
>   Spots in the moon, which betokens a change.
>   Quake, ye geologists!
>   Tremble, conchologists!
> Put retorts in crucibles, chemists, in order!
>   Beware, antiquarians,
>   They're disciplinarians,
> These *talented* Blues who are passing the Border![34]

Further, she presages, such women will not be quiet because they have 'discover'd perpetual motion;/Attach'd to *their tongues*, t'will be henceforth their own'. The elaborate rhyme and stanza scheme is entirely appropriate to the poem's thematic concern in praise of educated women not afraid to use and even show off their erudition.

Close readings of Cornish local history provide a nuanced view of structures of gendering and their positioning across representations of location and time. Vernon has described the way a primitivism projected onto Cornwall after the industrial era has been, in turn, internalized, contrasted with tropes of Englishness and redirected by Cornish nationalism. Kent, in the Introduction to *Voices From West Barbary* picks up on the nomenclature that compared Cornwall with North Africa; it indicates that a comparison of representations across postcolonial paradigms must now be negotiated. Alan Kent has also pointed out that in terms of literary history, the *Ordinalia* presents 'a wide range of Cornish women',[35] a reading compatible with a need to recognize Cornish diversity of faith, class and occupation. Jenny Hamlet's 'Mazey Day' villanelle in *Poetry Cornwall*: No. 11, with its lullaby-like repetitions celebrates the feast of St John with a Madonna mother breast-feeding 'a brown child'[36] amidst the bustle of the crowd, possibly gesturing towards ethnic diversity.

In terms of recent history, Kennedy and Kingcombe describe an ongoing rejection of externally imposed images, such as 'the Poldark complex', and they describe an alternative Cornish embrace of 'eclectisicm' that is 'part of an outward-looking localism and creative impulses. The result is an imaginative DIY sub-culture driven by response to change and Cornish or "pan-Celtic" identifications'.[37] Alan

Kent described the 'post-Revival' writing of 1940–80, as that in which
writers were 'exploring the sense of difference amongst themselves,
and a wider Cornish difference from Post-war England'. It is also clear
that as social mobility became more prevalent, Cornwall increasingly
had 'a wider multiplicity of cultural expression';[38] the post-war period
was one of 'redefinition and imagining of Cornish identity'.[39]
Contemporary Cornishness combines this local 'eclecticism' with global
connections. Brenda Wootton's poem 'Celtic Genes' negotiates the
serious and comic borders of the debate about genealogy and Cornish
history. It begins by making fun of the outsider as expert:

> Did you see that there professor chap—last Wednesday, on
> the box?
> He'd been dabbling with our Cornish genes—t'was some old
> thing, my cocks!
> Seems he's been doing some research and goodness knows
> what else,
> And come up with this daft idea that Cornishmen aren't
> Celts!!
>
> To be a Celt or not to be—well I don't mind one bit . . .
> If he'd said I wad'n Cornish—well! I'd have had a bloomin
> fit![40]

The poem goes on to point out that the origins of Arthur, now
mythologized as a Cornish leader, are unknown, that it is Cornish 'to
turn the other cheek' although winning in rugby at Twickenham gives
widespread pleasure, that the landscape of Cornwall is varied, and that
the people of Cornwall are 'a motley crew' like 'the English, the
French and Spanish too'. Whatever men thought, Brenda Wootton as
Cornish woman asserted the right to a mixed and varied heritage. Read
as a dismissal of race as an indicator of identity, the poem is consistent
with a shift from the dominance of the discourses of race that informed
Henry Jenner's ideas about Cornishness, to more contemporary
models of how national and local characteristics signify. The conclusion
of the poem is ambiguously serious and a comic reversal, the sexual
innuendo hinting at the fact that the professor should 'leave our genes
alone'. A professor could, of course, be a woman and/or be Cornish in
the ways that Wootton implies, as well as a representative of the
history of scientific developments in which Cornwall has played a
significant part. Identity, Wootton's poem suggests, is not just a matter
of science and history, but it is also lived emotion, identification,
locatedness in Cornwall and commitment.

Voices From West Barbary: An anthology of Anglo-Cornish poetry 1549–1928, edited by Alan Kent, includes two poems by Margaret Ann Courtney (1834–1920) a folklorist and author of *Cornish Feasts and Folklore* (1870). Both 'A Picture' and 'The White Ladie' indicate skill with versification and language. 'A Picture' is a Shakespearian sonnet describing a shorescape in generalized terms, traversed at the volta (turn) by:

Two women home returning wearily
From mussel-picking; wet with sea and spray,
Bare-legged, with creel on back plodding their way.
Men gazing seaward, leaning on a wall,
Sweet summer twilight brooding over all.[41]

The labouring women and watching, waiting men creates an image that could be compared in its placing of working people in plein air, to the Newlyn school of painting. 'The White Ladie' is a familiar enough folk ballad figure of the belle dame sans merci, signifier of class exploitation, for whom no man is good enough and who betrays local men to a press ganging captain. Its five line rhyming stanzas are unhurried but compact, and the repetition, like that in other Anglo-Cornish poems with similar structure and rhyme sequence (for example, Hawker's 'The Fatal Ship'[42] and Ilinska's 'Ruan Lanihorne')[43] serves to heighten the suspense while establishing the inexorability of its themes.

Remarkable too are the nine poems by Katharine Lee Jenner from her 1926 collection *Songs of the Stars and the Sea*. In his reading '"Song of our Motherland": Making Meaning of the Life and Work of Katharine Lee Jenner 1853–1936', Alan Kent has written of the collection's reference to 'Arthuriana and Grail-lore', 'the Civil War and Saints' as repeated tropes of a romanticized past, while 'The Exile' is perceived to be the 'one poem that makes a concession to modernity'.[44] Attuned as it is to romanticism and a mythic past, the collection demonstrates a visionary awareness of feminine images and is directed towards hearing and speaking of women's concerns. In an internationalist moment, infused with the ambiguities of colonialism, it is dedicated to Her Highness the Ranee Margaret of Sarawak. The opening sequence, which refers to the star cluster of the Pleiades and therefore the seven sisters of Greek mythology, begins with a poem 'The Song' structured as a series of questions:

> To what rhythm ring the stars of Heaven?
>   Is it too sublime
> For our ears of dust to catch its chime?
>   Do Pleiades give answer to deep Orion's chant?[45]

An abstract reading might be: can meaning be read into a universe of signs? Does gendering bring meaning to art? Is women's art—the chora/chorus of Pleiades/sisters—a response to masculinity, Orion, Arcturus? The poem provided its own answer by suggesting that we can see 'God's celestial spheres' but not their music, which is that of angels; 'our music' is found on earth:

> Our ear upon the ground
> We catch our mother's note,
>   The sob, the sigh, the strain,
> The holding in of forces,
>   The bursting forth with pain
> Of life from hidden sources,
>   The ceaseless change of form,
> The unity of aim
>   In blending multiform,
> Which all things here proclaim.

Read as a prayer/poem of worship to the Virgin Mary as the Immaculate Conception and Stella Maris, these verses merge spiritual matters with an involvement in practical concerns of Cornish daily life, so often dictated by the sea. Marina Warner wrote of representations of the Virgin:

> Within the imagery of these planets and constellations, the Virgin's association with the sea must never be forgotten, for in a different age the night sky's principal practical function was navigation. Mary's astral character gives her, in medical legend, hegemony over tempests, not only as the star that leads sailors to safety, but even more directly as a goddess with powers to still the wind and calm the waves.[46]

Earth, as the third poem in the sequence elaborates, is imagined to be female. In an image that fuses Christian and Cornish signifiers the poet responds to her own question about whether earth's sins make her an unseen spot in the universe with the description of a heavenly body that must 'shine through Heaven's inmost space/For from her clay is shown/The mystic body of Christ in every place.' Sea and moon are imagined as feminine too.

The greyness suggests an in-between state, an identity positioned at the edge of insider/outsider status; the long poem 'Cornwall' begins with a description of a 'mystic land'. 'On the Cliff' describes humanity in the closing lines:

> For the dead is the deep black velvet of the night;
> For us set in between, the glitter of the grey.[47]

'The Exile' takes as its theme the alienation of the London migrant. This positioning in turn disrupts the homely representation of a land that could be Cornwall, but is signified in terms that empty it of any specific reference:

> There is wailing of the west wind on the land,
>   There is lapping of the water on the beach,
> There is sighing of the rushes in the sand,
>   There is breaking of the breakers out of reach,
> In the land that is mine own, the land of moor and down –
>   But I only hear the clanging roar of London Town.[48]

Similarly 'O Mystic Land' evokes a homeland unspecific enough to be both Cornish and Catholic:

> On every vale and hill
>   Are holy names, which still
> Can stir men's hearts and thrill
>   With love of holy deeds,
> By Saints and Martyrs done,
>   Who won their deathless crown
> For sowing in thy soil the blessed Gospel seeds.[49]

In 'The Old Names' Cornish language place names are 'music everywhere'.[50] and in 'Can Gwlasol, Agan Mam-Vro/Anglice, a Patriotic Song for our Motherland' a list of Arthurian hosts is followed by an account of the saints. In 'On the Coast (Cornish Fisher-Girl's Lament)' and 'The Boats of Sennen (Cornish Fisher-Girl's Song)' the implied narrator is a woman. The former has painterly qualities of language, vivid colour and opens with the lines 'Gold the corn within the shock/Blue the water o'er the rock',[51] that are repeated at the beginning of 'The Boats of Sennen': 'The corn is in the shock,/And the fish are on the rock'.[52] The scene depicted in 'On the Coast' is shown from a more detached perspective than 'The Boats of Sennen', in which the speaker's identification, though taking a historical outlook, aims to be closer to the point of view of the working woman who in turn, in a stock image, watches and waits for her seaman. These poems attempted to move closer to a demotic, but were still expressed in a literary language aware of its distance from the world being observed. Given her husband's leading role in the language revival and the fact that he composed poetry in Cornish, Katharine Jenner's poetic language might be described as having occupied a grey area, neither exclusively Cornish nor English, but a form of condensed metaphorical expression drawing on Catholic symbolism, an emerging Celtic mysticism, and Medieval/Victorian Arthurianism, together with elements of the antiquarian, language and folklore interests Amy Hale described as emerging in the eighteenth and nineteenth centuries.[53] Alan Kent understood Jenner's poetry as having a populist and nationalist appeal, designed to find a way to consider 'how the working classes might be mobilised'.[54] If that was the case, then arguably, the poetry has retained its appeal, even now, when middle and working class ideologies often merge with a mystic appreciation of landscape that is part of the joining of on-going postmodern Romanticism to a re-imagined Celticism. The tension between and within pastoral traditions, Romanticism as cultural history and a modernity that celebrated or at least explored and appreciated the legacy of scientific and industrial inheritance, were and are vital elements in the Anglo-Cornish poetry heritage.

The two poems by Annie E. Argall 'The Charm of Beauty' (in blank verse) and 'The Fal' are celebratory nature poems, cleverly constructed (six line stanzas, second and fourth line rhyming, fifth and sixth a rhyming couplet) and creating interest with inventive phrasing. The scenery is personified as male in the first poem—'Old restless Ocean with his myriad waves'[55]—and in the second the speaker at once creates an impression of human vulnerability and strength by imagining a journey on the body of the river.

> As I, in frail and simple craft,
> Down on thy heaving breast did glide;[56]

Her 1894 collection *Poems* claims a connection to the subsequent 'interest in Cornish and other verse' but these are mainly abstractions, apart from a Fal poem, which is titled comparatively 'Our Sweet English Rhine . . . the Fal' and another on 'Our Rocky Cornish Coast'. The general striving for expression, comparisons and absence of particularity and assumption of community can be understood in terms of a moment of language transition—again the greyness of the in-between, the pleasant regularity of rhyming and conventionality that covers an uneasy relationship to the signification of place and individual as well as group identities being a mark of these poems; the images of nature, children, social concerns all recurrent themes of women's writing. It was at the end of the nineteenth century that a distinctive and localized tradition of Anglo-Cornish poetry began to emerge, a process in which these poems participated. In the leading poem 'The Inspiration of Song', poetry is a form of prayer and comforts Eve, alone after the fall. Annie Argall's poems might be compared with two published in 1899 in *The Cornish Magazine* by Nora Hopper. 'A Sea-Wife's Song' merges folklore, ballad and love poem into four line, six syllable stanzas that dramatize a struggle between a seaman's wife and the sea over his soul and body. 'Joan O' the Wad' too, subtitled 'A Pisky-song', taps into the folkloric revival, personifying nature, especially in its spring seasonal manifestations as an energetic force that disturbs men. The poem mourns the passing of such traditions from the towns while remaining cheerful about their persistence in country places. Ithell Colquhoun wrote of 'Joan the Wad' in *The Living Stones* that 'She may have been all too human, a witch who could cast spells for good or ill.' 'Joan', as Professor Margaret Murray has shown, was a favourite name among the witch covens; there is a wishing well at Lewannick called Joan's Pitcher.'[57]

Tim Saunders' periodization in *The Wheel* described 1850–1920 as a time of 'remarking the boundaries of a territory that had been abandoned and allowed to run wild'. 'In the Early Modern period (1520–1850) the use of Cornish declined rapidly. . . . The Cornish language became associated with poverty and disenfranchisement.'[58] But poverty is only one of many tropes associated with the Cornish language poetry and in *The Wheel* an 'anthology of modern poetry in Cornish 1850–1980' Tim Saunders presents a number of Cornish language poems by women, accompanied by a prose shaped English or Cornu-English translation. While a language and form-based reading of the Cornish language poems is outside the scope of this article, the translations in *The Wheel* offer many interpretive positions in the context of a study of women's writing. It includes poems by Margaret Pollard's 'Gwersyow/Verses' and 'Arlodhes Ywerdhon/The Lady of Ireland' (extract) which take up the theme of alienation within Cornwall: the role of the insider/outsider that is a feature of the poetry of many women writing in and about Cornwall. And not only women, as Alan Kent explained in *The Literature of Cornwall*:

This disruption from outside is a theme of most Celtic literatures; the disruption coming from the dominant neighbouring culture. Thus, the artist is at once a symbol of the proto-tourists or the travellers who were beginning to paint their vision of a Cornwall and Scilly, and those 'others' from outside who upset the seemingly age-old balance and cycle of life, demonstrating via this intrusion the complexity and difficulty of living in the modern world.[59]

In 'Gwersyow/Verses' the implied speaker is a Cinderella figure, claiming 'You did not rear me, you do not love me, you are a step-mother to me, I do not speak your language'.[60] The fact that the poem is presented first in Cornish seems to belie any direct connection between the implied speaker of the poem and the poet, but since her Bardic name was Arlodhes Ywerdhon, which translates as Lady of Ireland, some association can be assumed. One possible reading is that even where the poems are written in Cornish language, a disjunction might still be experienced writing or speaking in it. As Brenda Wootton's wry commentary poem 'Written in the flyleaf of a Concise Oxford Dictionary, bought with a fee from Helston Comprehensive School 6 May 1977' expressed it, to write in any language, even a first language, is to experience a sense of lack and absence as well as the satisfaction that comes with achieved expression.

For Richard Gendall's sake
The Cornish language I must learn
To freely speak, 'tis true.
But English I must comprehend,
To help me so to do.[61]

Significantly, in 'Gwersyow/Verses', the implied speaker was positioned in terms of domestic labour, as a female character, whose creativity is expressed through skill in crafts and home-making:

Lyn gay dhys y-whyaf, hag owrlyn y-whraf,
Y-tekhaf dha drygva, y-tyghtyaf dha vara,

Beautiful linen I shall weave for you, and make
silk, decorate your home, and prepare your bread.[62]

In the translated extracts from 'Arlodhes Ywerdhon/The Lady of Ireland' the stranger metaphor for Cornwall is extended into a more explicit comparative description of the 'Lady' of Ireland to:

> . . . Cornwall, the
> wonderfully rich land of the
> west, rich like a great Queen
> with copper, fish and tin; you
> never welcomed strangers, cold-
> hearted Cornwall, before you
> killed them.[63]

The combination of folkloric, courtly, romantic and saint's journey narratives with Iseult traditions, in which she comes to Cornwall from Ireland to marry Mark and falls in love with Tristran, are all represented, although it becomes a poem about nature and modernity. It concludes with a reference to the red star Aldebaran rising in Taurus in winter, a sign that spring with its prolific vegetation, will come again.

With Hilda Ivall's 'Peder Can Ver II/Four Short Songs II', 'Nebes Gwersyow: I and II/Some Poems I and II' the reader encounters poems that negotiate the urban spaces of modernity, disconnected from specific references to Cornish language locations and references. That they are written in Cornish makes this distancing a specifically Cornish one, despite the absence of particular signifiers; in their absence the distance from Cornwall marks out an indeterminacy of time and place. Gwersyow II mourns the losses of 'the war' and in a series of short poems ending with stanzas of varying lengths, it explores the painter's colours of a relationship. Helena Charles' 'A Varrak Ker/Dear Knight' is a six-line poem which pithily tells a courtly knight to mind his own business; while the implied speaker could be of either gender, the fact that the poet is a woman (Maghteth Boudycca/ Handmaiden of Boudicca) makes it possible to interpret the poem as having a feminist edge. The Cornish name is also an indication of the persistence of Celtic traditions. Its succinctness in deflating the romanticism of Arthurian legend is a reminder of the compactness of folk sayings and some of the well known short poems such as 'Crankan' by John Davey. Phoebe Procter's 'Pyu a Wor An Den A-Graf?/Who Knows the Man I Love' and 'An Gwaynten/The Spring' foregrounded natural images, as did Margaret Norris' 'Poldice', picking up the ubiquitous imagery of the 'grey' Cornish world: here both valley and abandoned mine works.

TWENTIETH-CENTURY WRITING

A further anthology of Anglo-Cornish poetry *The Dreamt Sea* (1928–2004), compiled by Alan Kent, seems to bear out the editor's own convictions that Cornish literature has a distinctive identity, as does Cornish nationalism and that the rise of regionalism and devolution has contributed to its continuity. He also suggests that the rise of multi-nationalism in the UK may have contributed to a renewed interest in questions of literary authenticity and belonging.[64] The collection makes accessible again many fine poems by women. Representing those poets born in the nineteenth century there is writing by Maud Cherrill, Ruth Manning-Saunders, Anne Treneer and Frances Bellerby. 'Trevalga Rectory' depicts the building of the title lashed by rain and winds, personifying nature and hinting at the hand of God behind mother nature's storms. It is possible to read the emphasis on the natural world as a metaphor for the challenges faced by the Christian faith, signified by the Rectory. Other poems included, such as 'Cant Hill', also emphasized the relationship between the human and the natural, personifying the hill as 'dressed in such finery/As would befit some Queen of Eastern lands' and the rivalry of 'forests of faded foxgloves' 'Who to their younger rivals hate to yield'.[65] This poem represented various elements of the landscape as female, orientalized and extended the stereotyped metaphor of female rivalry into the seasonal changes of the flora. In 'Padstow Lights' the illuminations from Padstow across the river are touchingly described as 'friendly', giving a companionable feel to the natural world around and to the implied speaker's contemplation of the journey towards life's end.

Anne Treneer's poems are closely focused on local geographies, conveying the impression of neighbourhood intimacy and knowledge shared. 'Little River at Hemmick', for example, consists of a set of directions.

Leave Mevagissey for Menagwins,
Pass Gorran School to Four Turnings,
Bear left; Carvinick and Penare
Will lead through winding ways to where
By a ferny lane you reach
Shingle and sand of Hemmick beach.[66]

Treneer's review of Jack Clemo's selection of poems *The Clay Verge* in *The Cornish Review* of Winter 1951 provided an interesting insight into her own view on poetry, life and religion through its contrast with Clemo's views. 'I cannot myself sympathise with the doctrine of "election" or with the dogmas of Calvinism',[67] she wrote, and that the intensity of his Calvinist fervour and belief in the ascendancy of the elect 'frightens me'. She admired the poet's 'immediacy' and 'courage' and recognized the appositeness of his approach to life in the 'china clay district' while lamenting the absence of the more romantic poetic elements of 'the wide horizon and the singing of the larks.'[68] In comparison, Treneer's poems do appear feminized in the sense that the masculine values of endurance in that working-class life of the clay pits is nowhere to be found in them; her celebration of cliffs, swirling water and blooming flowers is more pastoral. Ruth Manning-Sanders' 'Three Cornish Rhymes' drew on folk traditions, as did Gladys Hunkin's 'Penwith Places' with a playful list of place names in Cornish language. By drawing attention to the place names, the poet reminded readers of the importance of Cornish language, its embeddedness in the landscape and the sound of its letters and syllables.

Published in 1949 in *The Cornish Review* 'Little River at Hemmick 'is one of a number of poems by women in that journal that celebrate Cornish landscapes and identity. Gladys Hunkin's 'Cornwall', printed next to Treneer's, observes the long stretch of Cornish history in the context of landscape. The four-line stanzas rhyme the first and third lines, and the fourth line rhymes throughout—the impression created is of patterns of change and repetition; the rhythm is jaunty and the language, though clichéd at times, may well deliberately be so in order to remind the reader quickly of a series of established truths:

> On stone and leaf and scallop,
> Came saints of hoary legend;
> Or guiding a light shallop
> At dawn of history.[69]

Hunkin's collection *Cornish Crystal* reviewed the general themes of its time in short rhyming poems and often had a terse restrained approach to strong emotions. Several were specifically focused on women; 'Ancient Tomb', for example, mourns for Clarice de Boleigh 'buried in St Buryan Church in the 13th Century'.[70] In contrast to Larkin's poem 'An Arundel Tomb', which celebrates the enduring commitment of married love, this lady was buried alone:

> 'Clarice the wife of Geoffrey lieth here'—
> What grief he knew to ride away and leave
> Your beauty yielded up to death's austere
> Demand . . . No use in asking, 'Why?' No use

'The Sampler' is an appealing 16-line poem imagining the life of Mary 'who wrote her name when only ten,/Upon this sampler— "seventeen-ninety-three"', commenting on the religious ideology taught to a child who still had so much to learn about life. The sampler as it is described in the poem has a resemblance to a Hunkin poem— neat, concise, clear, reaching after big themes, its iconography a mix of

Christian—'Eve, Adam and the apple tree', an unspoiled view of natural and domestic relations 'a dog and squirrel poised beside their feet' and a 'celtic border of a quaint design'.[71] 'Triumph' was dedicated 'In Homage for Poland's distinguished daughter, Marie Curie'.[72] Hunkin's Cornish genealogy traced back at least to Elizabethan times and she was made a Bard of the Gorseth.

In *The Dreamt Sea*, 'Preparing to swim in Godrevy Pool', a poem by Anne Treneer, takes up the metaphor of swimming and a close identification with the elements and nature. While 'Little River at Hemmick' successfully works irregular line lengths and rhyming couplets to convey the twists, turns and surprises of a road equally pleasurable to those familiar with it as to new travellers, the latter consists of three line stanzas, the last one shorter than the previous two. The images associated with the implied speaker are feminine—the pool is 'snake-like', and a 'gown of green water'.[73] 'North Cliffs' again begins with a set of directions for a walk, out of town and into the summery countryside: 'I am one with the earth whose child I am' the poem claims, until drinking from the 'great grail of God', at which point 'by this draught I can/Give thanks I am not earth but man.'[74] Given that the poet was a woman, it can be seen to repeat rather than resolve the problems of patriarchal Christianity, while finding comfort in its established values. Frances Bellerby's subject matter is Cornish landscape, yet strangely emptied of specific references—even the building named in 'Plash Mill, Under the Moor' is unoccupied, 'forsaken':

> Through all the roaring maniac din
> Outside, the shadowless stillness there within
> Held. No face, all the frantic day,
> Pressed the glass, watching the green apple hailstorm,
> No child's heart at thought of where acorns lay,
> And beechnuts, treasure for harvesting safe from harm.[75]

'The Artist in Cornwall' must 'mirror this place' then 'speak as he ordered'; although the 'he' is undesignated, it could be read as God. *The West Country Magazine,* which was published from 1946 until late 1951 made available many poems by women, including Bellerby, Treneer, Hunkin and Margaret Willy. Recurrent themes included writing about the land and sea of Cornwall, seasons, childhood/children and religious belief. Perhaps influenced by the Second World War and other recent events, questions of faith loomed large in the writing. Anne Treneer's 'To Cornwall', subtitled 'After reading English Sea Literature' searched for something especially Cornish and noted that

after travel, it was the land of Cornwall that brought the speaker home
to port:

> For Cornwall knows all secrets dear,
>   The wild lore of all Time is hers;
> By solemn cromlechs, those who hear
>   Her solemn ritual worship there,
> But strangers cross themselves for fear.
>
> The runes are set by carn and lea;
>   Great rocky scroll, graved by the wind,
> Cut by the bright blades of the sea,
>   What though I walk strange poets' ways,
> In you is all my poesie.[76]

The idea that being at sea (in reading English Sea Literature) is
grounded through metaphors of Cornishness, while the speaker's
closeness to the land is indicated by the idea that the land is a
manuscript; the speaker walking the land writes and is written by it.
Arthur Gibson's farewell to Anne Treneer in *The Cornish Review*
commented: 'Most of her poems were about the impact of nature and
the elements on the spirit.'[77]

Sara Jackson's 'Looe' links a sense of timelessness to femininity
—'A horse in the field,/All horses she'.[78] The realist journalism of the
black and white photos can be read as having contributed to *The West
Country Magazine's* general post-war spirit of reaffirmation in cultural
continuity grounded in nature. Phoebe Hesketh's 'The Last Time on
Malvern Beacon' connected a memory of hearing bells in full summer
with the loss of a child and questions about life after death. Like so
many of the poems, it found a form of consolation in the endurance
of the natural world, expressed through seasonal imagery. Katherine
Garvin's 'Cornwall' took a romanticized child's-eye view of the
Cornish foreshore, its rockpools seen from the distance of adulthood as
magical:

> Sisters, stand there upon the Celtic shore,
> Your natural, wild home; and look across the years[79]

In Joan Murray Simpson's 'Besieging Spring'[80] the speaker
imagined spring as a source of seduction and magic—'and he away'
—that may have led the speaker to surrender to temptations later
regretted. Seasonal metaphors are often an obvious metaphor for
women's sexuality in the poems, and the conflicting demands of sexual

attraction, domesticity and gendered ideology of the period are a subtext of this poem.

These themes of the 1940s and 1950s continued into the 1960s and 1970s, combined with a return to an awareness of Cornwall's appeal to migrants and visitors. Frances Bellerby's poem 'There Are Five Trees of Paradise' in *The Cornish Review* No. 3, 1966 explicitly equated the destruction of nature with the suffering of Christ and flourishing nature with the blessings of God:

> Who kills the primroses in spring
> His heart the winter gales will wring.
> Who desecrates a single foxglove
> Earns summer's hate and forfeits God's love.[81]

The balanced couplets implied the possibility of stability and the maintenance of Christian values rooted in the natural world. Gladys Hunkin's 'Rat in the Atomic Age' reflected on various representations of the rat through the ages—as traveller on ships, subject of scientific experiments and voyager in space:

> Put a steel-jawed trap to catch the evil thing:
> 'A rat does not feel!'
> Oh no? Lady have you heard me squeal
> Under hob-nails on my skull,
> A shovel thrashed to my back,
> Stiletto-pike through my side?[82]

Zofia Ilinska's poetry, also published in *The Cornish Review* displayed more overt uncertainties—the long free verse poems tightly controlled despite giving the impression of casual and internally conversational construction:

> Secretly maddened by the mystery of love,
> The silent occupier of Room Number Seven
> And his skinny unsmiling mini-skirted girl
> Are leaving us this morning, having ordered early breakfast,
> After seven highspiced peakpriced
> Soda and ice days of revolving, revolving
> On the spit of one another's unrelenting scrutiny.
> Never again. Pack pack your passionate underwear;
> How do I get unhurt? How shall I ever
> Succeed to shake you off somehow, somewhere
> Amidst the seven hills of London?[83]

Her notebook style observations in 'From a Cornish Hotelier's Diary'[84] are pithy and original, demonstrating her skills as a word collector, people watcher, food lover and maker of lists mingled with allusions to literary history and alertness to signifiers of the contemporary. The Contributor's note reads 'Lives in St Mawes, which she loves. Two children. Hobbies: dogs, sailing, wines, ghosts.'[85] In 'The Tanker and Her Tugs' the journey to port becomes a metaphor for the effort that goes into easing a death. Ruth Dunstan's poem, published with Ilinska's, connected spirituality to the Landscape:

> Then to the churchyard,
> Open, windswept, ringed with old minestacks,
> Studded with daisies, gorse-kindled,
> Humming to the airs of heaven; a place that's close
> To the Almighty hand.[86]

Poetry by Betty Lane—'Love Life'[87]—was openly sensual, recording the pulsations and rhythms of life in bodily metaphors and sublime imagery. The varied line lengths created an ebb and flow of rhythm, pulses linked to world-wide events:

> Adrift on a rafted shell on a moon pulled sea
> I live, I love, I love life:
> Sudden alarm bell shatters the light-house dome
> Orgasm, slaked in sweet salt, sea-weed, diatoms
> I am drowned, but
> A secret cell survives the sea-change
> Divides, and links me to my immortality.

Ilinska's collection *Idle Rocks*, published in 1972, displayed a surrealist linguistic humour and, like the hotel-keepers whose point of view it explored, described the interaction between location, holiday makers and workers. 'Why Not Join the Women's Institute Joanna?' advises 'Women need friends./They're lonely/with needles and knitting.'[88] 'Do You Remember, Arabella', knowingly subtitled '(after H. Belloc)' reminds a familiar reader of:

> The schimozzle and the shocks
> and the ship on the rocks,
> the chambermaids down with 'flu[89]

It is a lively, witty collection, formally accomplished, referential and also, with its room by room, job by job account of the hotel's inhabitants, sensitive to the lonesomeness that can exist in public places or between people, even those who know each other well. In terms of the relationship to Cornwall, Ilinska was ideally positioned as a refugee who had settled, to make ironic observations about both locals and visitors and to comment on developments in the tourist trade. 'The Advertisement' has an Eliotesque detachment:

> You must have read it,
> our Advertisement in the Sunday Times,
> for here you are already to keep your appointment
> with the unsurpassed view, the honeymoon perfection,
> the Private Bathroom and the Lobster Thermidor
> prepared by the Chef of last season's most starred Hotel.[90]

In a different way, Ithell Colquhoun's writing, like her surrealist art, anticipated and participated in many of the aesthetic shifts of her time. 'Grimoire of the Entangled Thicket', a remarkable poem, consists of riddling poems: 'in some the Tree-Mouth speaks as an oracle, in others it is involved.'[91] Colquhoun connects the revived Gaelic Tree alphabet to the New Moon calendar, and the poems are offerings in eco awareness to the White Goddess at 'a time when wasteful technology is threatening the plant life (and with it all organic life) of earth and the waters'. This sense of an attempt to ward off impending threat was linked to the specific lunar alignments of 1972, and so tied linear time to that of the cyclical and monumental.

The implied oracular speakers in and of the poems foreground aspects of bardic/prophetic lore to women's lives and traditions. In 'Imbolic'[92] the celandines welcome and praise St Brigid 'with covens of sharp cries'; trees reveal the 'Bride-shepherdess', called 'Bride' in Gaelic, Celtic patroness of wisdom, agricultural fertility, poets, smiths and healers. According to Caitlin Matthews, St Brigid (or Brigit) has been incorporated into a Christian tradition as a mother goddess, Mary's helper, sometimes merged with her: 'Just as the Goddess was concerned with the fertility of the land, so too is St Brigit associated with the new milk of sheep at lambing time. The late winter chill of February is softened by the bounty of sheep's milk.'[93] Speakers in the poem address the goddess through elements, flora and fauna in the natural world, and the emphasis in the poems is on a polytheism evoked by seasonal changes.

Colquhoun describes herself as 'an animist'[94] in *The Living Stones*, an autobiographical /spiritual account of writing and working in Cornwall, which provides an interesting accompaniment to readings of the poetry. Born in India of 'Irish, Scottish and Welsh' descent,[95]

Colquhoun responded in the text as an artist to Cornwall, as both visitor and informant, maintaining that 'folklore in Cornwall is not a thing of the past only but a living activity'.[96] With her Celtic connections, the representations of Cornwall shifted between homely and uncanny, enhanced perhaps by her understanding of the defamiliarization inherent in surrealism. It is possible to read a queering of the text in *The Living Stones*, a deliberate moving away from established gendering to an interest in the disruption of normative directions. She commented on the exaggeration of rumours about Aleister Crowley and deconstructed the idea of 'black' and 'white' magic. In particular, the discussion of smoking kaif opened out onto a meditation on the processes of artistic creation, on differences between Occidental and Oriental practises with regard to gender (Occidental cultures exclude women from creative café style public gatherings '(to its loss)' she maintained, although such generalizations do not investigate how her own status shifted as a woman in different locations/cultural conditions). Her views on the inequalities of the social treatment of intellectual and artistic women were clearly stated:

> The tragedy of many a marriage is that the woman is seduced into becoming more of an extrovert than she would wish; and the price of a woman's self-development is all too often a boycott by the opposite sex. *Kaif* or its surrogates tend to be taboo, since any sign of introversion is, in a woman, particularly suspect; an introverted male may always be a 'genius' and as such allowed to occupy a tolerated if unacclaimed niche. But an introverted female? Society is slow to grant her a place at all, even though the means and the end of her musing are as innocent as tree and cloud.[97]

Anne-Marie Fortier has described as queer the decentring of 'the heterosexual, familial "home" as the emblematic model of comfort, care and belonging'.[98] Colquhoun's description of Vow Cave, of homing in in Lamorna can be read beside the poems. Her search for a place to nurture her talents, recover from a war-shaped mentality and take 'refuge from the claustrophobic fright of cities'[99] became a description of the discovery and purchase of Vow Cave. At first it is glimpsed through an enclosure of trees. The disused studio is likened variously to a garage, a tent and an aquarium. On the map, her plot of land leased from an elderly landowner, one of 'feudalism's last relics' is marked in Gothic letters, a 'tautological' name' 'as the first word means "cave" as much as the second being none other than the Cornish *vugha*, "a cave", which has many varieties of spelling. I called the hut

Vow Cave Studio.'[100] The doubling of the name suggested also the emergence of the uncanny—a grave/fugou—which was and/or has become a cave—a place that becomes homely, but also a strange place, old and newly discovered, both womb and grave.

Colquhuon's description of the effects of kaif, a 'creative trance' she claimed to be able to achieve without the drugs, can be read in connection with the attempt in the poetry to reach back into a spiritual past, an activity she associated with a willingness to reject obstructive Occidental ways of thinking and of measuring time.

> *Kaif* is sometimes used as a term for a certain stage of intoxication produced by hashish—after the hilarity and heightening of sensation have subsided, there supervenes a timeless musing, a direct experiencing of the moment; a wordless, thoughtless vacuum in which one can dwell on the flickering of a fire, the slant of a tree's shadow, the shape of a cloud.[101]

Expanding the readership's consciousness of multi-cultural influences on Anglo-Cornish writing, Penelope Shuttle's collections also push at cultural and gender boundaries. Colquhuon's description of the negotiation of inner space as difficult for women is borne out by Shuttle's poetry which, although exemplifying a successful negotiation of marriage and motherhood, also charts difficulties. *The Wise Wound*, co-authored with her partner Peter Redgrove, produced interpretations of representations of women and menstruation in many cultures, influenced by psychology, psychoanalysis (especially Jung) and his ideas about anima/animus, Tantric beliefs, Greek, Roman, Papuan and many more cultural references. In 'Overnight' from *Adventures with My Horse* Shuttle shifted fixed binarisms by associating the moon with a man, man and woman together, in reflected gaze:

> I look up at the moon.
> He will do his share of the work, I know,
> even though he's only at half-strength.[102]

Gender and sexual politics is a recurrent theme, overt in *Cornish Writers '75* (Published by the W.E.A. S-W District) in poems like Sylvia Richards' 'The Other Woman',[103] and 'Lament of an Un-liberated Woman' by Edith Pascoe:

But we converse politely
And I the woman
Lower my eyes, for fear
You'll see the brazen message written there.[104]

Zofia Ilinska's poetry, written in Polish and English, developed the sense of Cornwall as a contemporaneous, multi-lingual location. In 'Ruan Lanihorne', chosen with other poems on explicitly Cornish themes for *The Dreamt Sea* the title's condensed reference to a church site elaborated on folk and religious themes of the woman attached to an unworldly purity, signified through her preference for church, mistletoe and unicorn. The five-line stanzas emphasize melody and rhythm; the rhymes confirming an established chain of metaphors and so satisfy a reader's expectations (snow/go/mistletoe and thorn/ Lanihorne) for example, in the first stanza, repeated with slight variation in the final stanza (yes and no/go/mistletoe combined with horn/Lanihorne) to suggest a contained, even repressed circuit of desire. Set in December, the repeated question 'Lady, lady will you go/With a twig of mistletoe/To meet your love at Lanihorne?' positions the imagined addressee between the potential of the spring world of sexuality and a chastity both Celtic (mistletoe) and Christian (unicorn), without resolving the outcome, so that the poem evokes the circuit of seasons and poem with an effect comparable to the rondeau form. The themes of church as location /site recurr in 'Saint Just in Roseland', where again place names situate meaning in a Cornish setting, while leaving interpretation of religious faith and the natural world wide open.

Ilinska's awareness of multi-layered national identities brought to her poetry a vision of Cornwall that interwove signifiers of cultural difference without collapsing them into each other. There is a Plath-like language in lines such as:

Patterns of lines assail me: the vertical
as the line of life: masts, trees, I
still vertical, perpendicular. Boats lie[105]

Local knowledge 'Flight of the heron to Turnaware' was combined with a hint at Christianity's in- and exclusiveness. 'The dead sleep feet pointing East'. The migrant theme emerged more specifically in 'My Two Countries', in which the poet described her move from Poland during the Second World War:

Generous flatness—proud and trusting flatness
Reckless snowdrifty death-defying flatness
Unfenced and gullible—perishing for ever.

The move was to Cornwall 'my adopted land—on the granite rock/Top
of a Celtic hill. A tidal sea'[106]

Ilinska's collections explored a large number of themes, many of
them consciously linked to traditionally female imagery. In the 1992
collection *Horoscope of the Moon* the title poem predicted a fate worse
than that of earth for the moon:

> The world is sick
> And you have reached the Phase of Discontent
> To wax and wane upon concrete and brick,
> Inscrutable on mortar and cement,
> With terror-cables for your lack of trees,
> Neon-lights poking craters in your sockets,
> Pneumatic drills to drain your arid seas:
>
> A whitewashed platform waiting for the rockets.[107]

Apocalyptic imagery appears often in this collection. Like most of
Ilinska's themes the references are distinctive and personal, but also
evidently connected to recurrent and prevailing themes of twentieth
century European literature, experienced in her own life and influenced by her study for an English Literature degree. She came to the
UK at the age of seventeen as a refugee from Poland. Her pen name
was that of the Polish Spitfire pilot she was married to for three weeks
before he was killed in 1943, and the poems tell of a life in which
tragedy was never far away; the death of a youthful son, loss of parents,
husband, defamiliarization and recovery of her first language and
culture in revisiting Poland. In *Address of Paradise*, a posthumous
collection of 1996, she wrote frequently in the poems of 'The Word', a
phrase described in the Introduction by Philip Marsden as 'multifaceted':

> It represents the unifying of her dual identities. But it is
> also used in its Biblical sense, as something that precedes
> language, that Ilinska was aware of from the cradle, that was
> jostled and harried by her move from one end of Europe
> to the other, and appears sometimes in its Polish guise
> and sometimes in its English. It is also the speech of her
> conscience chastising her for abandoning her given tongue;

and in the end she recognises it as that mysterious fount of internal chatter and song which drives the poet to the page.[108]

For all this Biblical and biological emphasis, there was also an element of poststructural awareness to Ilinska's use of the term since it was on the role of poet, as her skills in it developed, that some unity between word and flesh was achieved.

Brenda Wootton's writing is represented in the collection by two poems that demonstrate her skills in Anglo-Cornish. The transcendent sweep of 'Seagulls' explores the exhilaration of Cornish landscape through references to a classical (music) sublime:

> You must shelter behind a slab of granite
> And sit . . . and stare . . . and listen . . .
> You are utterly alone
> In an immense Opera House of the Elements.
> You are the sole witness to an awesome display
> Of oceanic choreography,
> Swirling round gigantic scenery
> Against an infinite backcloth—
> The orchestration of nature's music is of such bewildering
>   complexity that it
> Is as though Wagner and Berlioz and Strauss were in battle,
> Proclaiming their respective melodic interpretation of man's
>   destiny.[109]

The conclusion brings the reader to a gentler movement, 'when the storm dies down,/It seems to modulate into C major' and the sound of the seagull, in C sharp minor' again becomes the dominant theme. Brenda Wootton's Bardic name was 'Gwylan Gwavas'—'seagull of Newlyn', a title in which condensation merges the homeliness, garrulousness and ubiquity of the seagull with its spectacular flying abilities. 'Lamorna' is a different kind of poem altogether, evoking the earthy though ceremonial experience of a blackberriers picnic with phrases in Cornu-English:

> Last September we lined the willow basket
> With rusty, curled bracken—
> Filled it to the brim with the best berries
> No scroff—cooty, coooty, eyehole
>
> Today's a damask serviette
> Silver blue-white, starch ironed[110]

Previously unpublished poems by three women show an emerging
diversity and suggest a widening framework. Martha Street's 'Well',
'Granite Landscape' and 'Cornish Haiku' develop the on-going landscape theme. In 'Granite Landscape' the land is personified as an aging
and regenerating body:

> Land worn to the bone,
> Humps of hip and pelvis
> break thin crust of soil.[111]

The historical association of Cornish land as a home to buried
dragons/dinosaurs, an ancient/mythical prehistoric fairy tale country is
evoked in images of pelt, paw and claw in a poem which merges precise
natural elements with non-specific signifiers of imaginary appeal:

> Outstretched talons dabble diamonds,
> break the brilliance—
> beyond is open sea.[112]

Read as subtle reference to a monstrous feminine, the land/dragon
metaphors ('blue elvan stones' are 'eggs you laid lifetimes ago') make
the connection between a mythological time and the present.

Emerging contemporary poems engage the eccentric forms of free
verse. Condensed, onomatopoeiac images of Street's 'Well' suggest the
emergence and flow of water, tears, since the 'Well is a dark eye in
the earth.'[113] and 'the rush of our own blood.' Like Penelope Shuttle's
poem about 'St Nectan's Fall' which describes the river and pool where
a hermit lived,

> Slippery gentleman, St Nectan,
> breathing his own weather,
>
> raising his own lather,
> custodian of spate,
>
> of the long precipice drop
> into his black begging bowl,
>
> white water-rope, spurting cascade,
> smolt and sluice of reverse fountain
>
> scouring round
> the basalt belly of the kieve,

gimping, looping and zinging;
a water cauldron for a saint

or a luck bath for a travelling sagesse?[114]

Street associates the well with religious commitment: 'In old days a saint slept here, curled on a mound/in the corner of the chapel', an earthy resignation and eternity:

Sound of water and its flow pouring endlessly
from the earth back to the earth
springing live from the earth pouring back to the earth
endlessly.

Fiona Colligan-Yano's 'The Burial Mound' also equates femaleness with earth and the passageway from life to death, even its reversal; the mound is a 'glowing hump' reminiscent of pregnancy and 'the gestalt sings awhile/Despite times menstruum'.[115] 'Mother Lode' references the metals forming Cornish land and plays on the etymology of lode as a rich source of something, a way or watercourse. Throughout, the language mines the earth/mother/mineral/flow metaphors—her wedding dress gleamed in 'a shaft of Autumn sun', she had a 'graceful alchemy', a 'golden core', and days are 'amber tinged'.[116] A third poem, 'Bodmin Moor', continues the correlation of earth, stone and rock, while working the multiple meanings of 'moor' as African Muslims of Arabic and Berber descent, a tract of high, open, uncultivated land and the making fast of a boat; Dozmary Pool, reminiscent of Street's well, is:

An inverse pupil
Sunken in the Moor's dark eye.[117]

Two poems by Natasha Cardew continue the description of earth and stone, garden and gulls; despite the fact that 'Sculpture Garden' is an evocation of Barbara Hepworth's garden it is only vaguely feminized, referring distantly to Gertrude Stein and language poetry—'An eye is an eye is an eye looking'—and to a possible maternal relation as 'a childish maul,/steps up to a hug to a height to the Atlantic in sight'.[118] 'Gorse Hatted Hills', in a faintly comic image, though it personifies the landscape in that one image, is not gender specific.

MAKING METAPHORS

The anthology omitted to include the writing of Penelope Shuttle, who has been one of the most widely published and read of women poets in the UK. Her texts pose interesting questions; she writes in metaphors that suggest an ambivalent response to the feminizing of Cornish locations. Shuttle's poetry, in its embrace of maleness, has found a range of emotions and positions through fulsomeness to delicacy, from femininity to femaleness. It is possible to read the poems as moving towards a synthesis of what Alan Kent has described as ongoing aspects of the literary construction of Cornwall: 'the debate between the visiting writer's view of Cornwall and that of the indigenous writer'.[119] Kennedy and Kingcombe maintain that 'Despite efforts to portray or market "the real Cornwall" there is no authentic version that can be unearthed as "the real thing", much like contemporary discussion of heritage Britain.'[120] Nevertheless, Shuttle has managed to steer a course midway between poems and language that are invested in historicized versions of Cornishness, with the imagined speaker's relationship often ambiguously outlined in relation to that history.

In 'Three Lunulae, Truro Museum' the antique jewellery items are described as objects closely linked to ancient and archetypal images of women: three muses, three ages of women, phases of the moon. They are 'Crescent moons of gold/from the sunken district/of the dark/out of the archaeologist's earth' and in the custodian's opinion 'Cornish, they are,/he says/dug up at St Juliot,/regalia of this soil,/and not for the British Museum'.[121] Quoting the custodian, the imagined speaker of the poem (whose gender is not stated) imagines the lives of women who might have worn the jewellery and connects Celtic to Christian Cornwall through the linking of the lunulae with St Juliot, a church name also associated with Thomas Hardy and hence also, his poetry. This strategy has enabled the poem to balance between a very general-ized, universalizing view of women and their place in a specifically Celto-Cornish-Christianized history.

As Toril Moi pointed out in her reading of Julia Kristeva's essay 'Women's Time', 'According to Kristeva, female subjectivity would seem to be linked both to *cyclical* time (repetition) and to *monumental* time (eternity), at least in so far as both are ways of conceptualizing time from the perspective of motherhood and reproduction.'[122] Representations of the stones of Cornwall, as geology, as landscape and human marks of time, even the stone buildings, touch onto this concept of time as timeless, eternity. Shuttle's poem about the Men-an-tol in which she describes the continuity of generational links between herself and her daughter draws on monumental and cyclical notions of time (the stones themselves being circular, like the womb opening) and linear time, since it refers to herself and her daughter as representatives of different generations passing through the stone.

The lunulae poem also draws on the symbolism of circular time, women's connection to the moon and menses, marking a point of intertextuality with Hugh MacDiarmid's poem 'Cornish Heroic Song For Valda Trevlyn' in which the poet described his Cornish wife wearing:

> The golden lunula I had copied for you
> From the finest of the four found in Cornwall yet,
> Linking the early Bronze Age and the Twentieth Century,
> This crescentic collar or gorget of thin gold,
> Linking Scotland and Cornwall too,[123]

In MacDiarmid's poem, written around 1930, the necklace signified a form of yoking of a wife to her husband, and of Celtic links across placed and time. Shuttle's poetry often conveys an awareness of wifely status and in her lunulae poem the woman can be the imagined narrator of the poem as subject rather than object, although women may be among its addressees.

So time—signified in 'The slight quick tap/of a clock/goes on/like the rhythm/of an insect's leg/in the grass'—links women's time to the nature time of grass and insect, as well as circular and linear time. Many of Shuttle's images of landscape, geology and monuments refer to this monumental concept of time, while specifically locking them into images and symbols traditionally associated with women: the moon, gold, jewellery, circles, apples, signifiers of fertility. 'Water-colour of Eden'[124] describes the emotions of an Eve-like figure after Adam points out to her 'the winding path':

> as a breath of terror
> hisses in her throat
> and she half-turns
> to look back at the creature
> asleep near her feet,
> the childlike unawakened Adam.

'Eve' celebrates sexuality and fertility; 'As soon as I bite it/and taste it/an ungraceful strength fills me.'[125] while 'Intimate Sketch' describes 'my daughter's grandmother' as a soul yearning to leave the ageing body:

far away, high up in golden burning air,
where her bones long to burn
and be free at last, everyone's dream;
for her it has nearly come true.[126]

Change is marked too in 'At the Old House', an autobiographical
piece, where the speaker visits the house where her grandfather died
and reflects on her daughter's experience:

For her this old house is spooky,
the link is broken,
my daughter feels only the emptiness
of a place which life has left.[127]

Poems of the 1980 collection *The Orchard Upstairs* are concerned
with recollections, memories and images of pregnancy and birth. The
dating of poems concerned with the gestation and birth of her daughter
suggests linear time; a coincidence of linear time with the circular and
monumental significant in personal as well as public and symbolic
ways. The collection's title draws attention to condensed and merged
images of domestic interior/exteriors, surreal and postmodernized consciousness. The poems negotiate the feminization of landscape and
culture with some care; as Kennedy and Kingcombe point out, the
valorization of femininity can also be turned to produce primitivizing
and othering representations that must be resisted. The class shifts of
more recent times and across location are also registered in the poetry;
images of industrialized and disadvantaged Cornwall have rarely
appeared in Shuttle's poems; they are more Falmouth than Redruth.
Children are born into the conscious absence of the industrialized past
rather than leaving it behind. 'Behind us, the empty and echoless/shafts
of worked-out tin mines,/tunnels inching out mortally/under the
seabed' 'At Perranporth, March 1976'[128] The tone of 'A Future For
Cornwall' from *A Leaf Out of His Book* is pitched between a serious
desire for 'a quiet life' and a gently comic recognition that this
tranquillity takes place in a setting of modernity and activity. 'Let
the untaught waterfalls solve/the traffic problems of Wadebridge'.[129]
Similarly, Diane Simkin's poem in *Bardhonyeth Kernow/Poetry
Cornwall* No. 7. describes a visit to, as the title suggests 'Boscawen-un',
in which the fantasy of timelessness is intersected by the awareness of
contemporary traffic:

A hundred years? A thousand? All times meet
and merge. We follow close in ancient footsteps
to Babylon. Combustion engines roar
down to Land's End, where tourist fleshpots beckon,
and the Holy Grail lies washed up on the shore.[130]

Ann Alexander's ironic observations in 'Proper Cornish' point out
that the desire for change, exchange and profit are internal to Cornwall
and not only externally imposed. When 'The Antiques Roadshow
came to town' the 'pure and perfect Cornish man' has his pedigree
recognized only to:

Know what this great thing was worth,
So he could sell it, dreckly, to
Some poor tuss living near St Erth.[131]

Her poem on 'Madron' is more ambivalent—beyond the chapel in the
woods is where 'fresh' offerings 'to an older God' are made. Most of
the poems are not precisely located in place, describing a world of
aging, commenting on the hard edged elements of gender relations, a
struggle often lost not to exist in poverty and ironic expressions on the
(often repressed) psychic/social violence of middle-class life.

Kennedy and Kingcombe have explored the way the transition to
the society of simulacra can involve a tension between visitors and
locals, for whom holding onto significant strands of history in an
increasingly heritage oriented culture can be difficult.

There are times when individuals wish to enquire and be
informed and it is then, when accuracy matters, that they find
difficulty in distinguishing fact from play. The visitor wishes to
delve into the exploration of 'otherness' whilst the native
wishes to reclaim a past which some see as suppressed history.
Both find difficulty in the over-lap between unashamed
theme-park and museum/heritage centre.[132]

It is this tendency to simulacra that Penelope Shuttle's writing
has negotiated and modified. Emphasis on the junctures between
cyclical and linear time, where distinctive historical lives intersect with
long standing female models and types, occurs across poems and collections. 'Taxing the Rain', the title poem of a 1992 collection, mocked
the Thatcherite obsession with individualism and self-sufficiency
manifested in the imposition of the Poll Tax on a widely reluctant
Cornwall, drawing on socially conscious, Biblical associations of mercy

and charity to undo the uptightness and parsimony of the voice that
would 'Make rain pay its way.'

> Make it pay for lying full length
> in the long straight sedate green waters
>
> of our city canals,
> and for working its way through processes
>
> of dreamy complexity
> until this too-long untaxed rain comes indoors
>
> and touches our lips,
> bringing assuagement—for rain comes[133]

The utopian desire to feed the world is recognized as a dream evoked
by the exigencies of reality in 'Breasts' where the speaker is 'Sleepily
watching the ten o'clock news' then fantasizes that she has 'giantess
breasts' able to 'feed all those hungry children' only to find them
'deflated back to their normal size.' Sadness and despair accompany
the concluding images as:

> Wasted children still gaze through burning air.
> Remote and hunched, their dry mothers stare.
> Drought wind toys with their brightly-beaded hair.[134]

The poems cross and re-cross boundaries between identification as
insider and outsider to Cornishness, with an awareness comparable to
that of Carol Ann Duffy's poetry about the life of the internal migrant.
Similarly, Sylvia Kantaris' poems have reflected on a move to Helston
in 1974 and on the process of becoming more local, while retaining
some sympathy with an outsider's view of Cornwall. In 'The Light at St
Ives' she explored the 'myth, he said, set up by the tourist board/to
bring in summer visitors' in contrast to the winter atmosphere:

> when grey waves beat over Men an Mor
> and all the summer restaurants are shut
> and the light is the colour of seagulls
> flying inland and the town turns its back.[135]

A poem about 'The Mermaid in Zennor Church' from the 1985 collection viewed the carving with admiration as an ancient, pagan and
queenly figure 'old and half out of her element,/biding time through

centuries of Psalms'[136] while in 'Old Haunt' from the collection *Lad's Love* published in 1993 'I didn't even get out of the car, didn't dare/ enter the church'[137] the carving of the mermaid had come to signify lost love and estrangement from a previous self.

MIGRANT METAPHORS

In Shuttle's poems, even within national boundaries, or perhaps especially because it may not be expected, the reader is made aware of a consciousness of the foreignness of the self to itself, a strangeness located both within Cornish territory and in the relationship of the self as outsider to Cornwall. While the idea of woman as homemaker and dweller is a recurrent theme for Shuttle, the domestic space often becomes an uncanny one; abode of ghosts, shadows, unborn children and locus of dreams, fantasies, menstrual pangs. Conversely, travel, and the internationalism of culture are, at times, rendered homely—in 'Appletree in America' from *The Orchard Upstairs* the implied speaker describes feelings of homesickness and alienation 'in a continent/where I flit like a ghost' but is comforted by an awareness of the qualities of an apple tree.

> I hold a branch
> and smell the apples,
> watersweet, a beginning,
> opening of energies
> to rouse me from homesickness
> as, beyond the roadside tree,
> these foreign fields and hills
> merge into the familiar loam of evening.[138]

Another sequence set in America—'Four American Sketches'— juxtaposes images of displacement and in-dwelling to suggest an ambivalent settling in that, at the same time, concedes an irresolvable alienation:

> Our personal effects are wedged into bright rooms,
> the windows are wide open,
> breathing the almost extinct summer.
> You and I are reading the bibliotheca of autumn.[139]

Ann Tevenen Jenkins' poem links America/Armorica through poems on Brittany and a piece on 'Cornish Apples' which asks:

Which American Mother travelled far
Carrying seeds of a new apple
Mated with Cornish stock in a new land?[140]

Brittany frequently stands in as a close double for Cornwall, in
historical and contemporary terms. Seasonal colours lock the reader
into a painterly scene in 'Brittany in Summer' (The poem is accompanied by a boat and beach scene painting).[141] In contrast to the apple
poem, 'Brittany—A Winter Visit' describes a trip to the supermarket
by a vegetarian in which the speaker regrets 'the bloodlust for meat'
and 'this Saturnalian riot'.[142] A third poem in this sequence 'Brittany
and Cornwall' makes the contrast/similarities explicit—family
connections—'the shape of a Breton face/Takes me back to fisherman
of Newlyn or St Ives'[143] while difference is located in churches and the
café in comparison. Poems by Ann Trevenen Jenkin selected for *The
Dreamt Sea* expand on the tropes of migration, doubling and Celtic
connections. 'Cornish Village, Western Ireland' takes pleasure in the
drive along a coast road and 'twentieth-century technology' which is
subsequently viewed as a development out of the expertise and labour
of Cornish miners 'Metal stanchions, handholds for miners/From St
Day or Camborne perhaps';[144] 'Dear, familiar, lonely,/Cousin Jack
had conquered the landscape.'[145] The fuchsia (a plant that thrives in
Cornwall, and as a poem by Penelope Shuttle points out in 'Taking
Cuttings'[146] from her collection *The Child-Stealer*, grows easily from
cuttings) becomes a metaphor for the lives lost and won from labouring
in the earth—

The drooping fuchsia petals fall
Bleeding to the Irish ground
For Cornish miners
Who stamped their presence here.

Despite the conquest metaphor, Cornish migrants are imagined to have
suffered in the process of transferring to Ireland; a reversing of the
images in the poems of Arlodhes Ywerdhon. Other poems—'The
Distant Star' and 'Calumet, Michigan' record the lives of Cornish
migrants to Canada and the US respectively, and the exchange of
culture, history and memory with the living. Philip Payton has written
in *The Cornish Overseas* that the Trevenen family 'earned a reputation
as sailors, adventurers, travellers' and settled in Russia, Argentina,
Hawaii and Canada: 'The Trevenen family experience was at once both
extraordinary in its diversity and yet typical of Cornish mobility.'[147]

Discussing the globalization of Irish histories, Breda Gray has described 'diasporization as the site where memories circulate and reimaginings of the national takes place.'[148] and a deterritorialization of belonging that simultaneously anchors it 'again in a place and practices that are seen as preserving 'traditional' and recognizable aspects of Irish identity.'[149] Similar 'memory work' can be observed in Jenkin's poems, in which diverse, diffuse and mobile relationships to constructions of Cornishness are observed—the photograph of a shared ancestry.

> The scene was posed
> Like all old photographs—
> Mother on a ricketty chair
> In the gaping doorway;
> Daughter with ragged clothes,
> Unkempt, hair awry,
> Gazing into the distance;
> Father, short, stocky,
> Like most Cornishmen,
> Wearing a dark hat
> A drab, worn jacket,
> Standing firm
> In a dull landscape.
> He holds a gleaming proud horse
> The one sign of wealth
> In this staged scene.[150]

This section from 'The Distant Star' serves to promote awareness of a Cornishness comparable with the construction of Irishness as Gray describes it in terms that are 'trans-temporal, trans-spatial and reliant on diverse narratives of cultural belonging.'[151] Maggie Mealy's poem 'Dark Journey' about her great grandfather, a stone mason who left Cornwall for New York and 'was never heard of again' demonstrates a harsher side of emigration.

> I have seen waves as big as Bodmin Gaol
> Surround this boat and heard the blasting of
> The wind explode against our trembling craft.
> If only we might haul great granite rocks
> To reach from Cornwall to America,
> Or work and bread were plentiful at home
> And meat were in our broth instead of stones.[152]

Jenkin's reading of diaspora is filtered through her own perception of the significance of a return to Cornwall; a valorization of being re-routed/rooted there. 'Cornish cousins are infinite' 'Drewsteignton Rectory'[153] while in 'Calumet, Michigan' the speaker asks:

> And what did we bring?
> Those of us lucky to live
> In our native Cornwall?
> Links with the past and present,
> Hopes for the future—
> A sense of reality
> Which might only have been
> The dry bones of history?[154]

Jenkin's style is mostly prosaic and free verse, an approach that lends itself well to open ended readings. The 'Aloha' poem explores the significance of a visit to Hawaii in terms of this 'infinite' series of connections; commenting on how Cornish people have mined in Africa and built homes in Canada and Australia;

> Chinese, Hawaiian, Cornish, American too,
> And names from every continent
> A heart-warming reflection of a peaceful world
> Where all in harmony should live content.
>
> Re-bo cres yn nor.
> May there be peace in the world.[155]

Concluding with a repetition of 'cres'—peace—the Cornish word repeated three times in the Gorseth by celebrants and bards, the poem's hope for world peace can be set beside the conclusion in 'Drewsteignton Rectory' in which:

> My world has changed
> But there is a calmness here
> A sense of space,
> Of regeneration.
> New families, children,
> A new creative centre—
> Old chairs re-covered
> New architect's designs,
> Modern sculpture in the Rectory Garden.
> Despite the Thatcher State

The quiet still lingers
And the horrors of Bosnia
Are not the only fruit.[156]

While this poem anchors the writing in linear time and place the 'Aloha' poem projects a fantasy of world peace onto Hawaii in a way that, given the difficulties of colonial history, the unresolved conflicts over the appropriation of Hawaii by the US, situates the implied speaker of the poem as a visitor/outsider to Hawaii, as much as her own awareness of the political/historical claims of her bond to Cornwall.

Penelope Shuttle's *A Leaf out of His Book* is grounded in the Cornish landscape; the domesticity of earlier collections is recast in elemental environmental settings. The poem 'Two Visits to the Men-an-Tol, West Penwith, Cornwall' links pregnancy and birth to the landscape. It opens with the suggestively masculine names of mine shafts, past disused engine houses, then the implied speaker, remembering her last visit two month's pregnant with her daughter, moves into more feminized language: 'mist looms/wove and unwove luminous chilly muslins of fog' through a 'giantess-bracelet of stone,/cervix-anchor steadying me in a sea of mist and gorse'.[157] The poem concludes by continuing the circle/spiral as 'my daughter plunge-wriggles, coquets and corkscrews/herself through the granite o,/the ever-open place's massive orbit:/now it is she who will carry the cornucopia,/roped in her turn to earth and the spring.' Jenkin poses this connection between earth, birth and women's time as a question to the future through a poem to a new born girl 'Child of Two Celtic Worlds':

What will you make of the past?
Of the cromlechs and dolmens,
Of ancient lines of stones
Of vast expanses of ocean
And the high moors,
Stretching to infinity?
Of the old villages
Little changed by time?[158]

'Riwana' is named, blessed and identified with Cornwall and Brittany through the promise of family connections, love of the land and language.

May you hear
Our old Celtic tongue
And with your cousin Trystan
Talk in Breton and Cornish
And understand each other.

CORNWALL AS CONTEMPORARY LOCATION

Discussing the complexity of regional literatures, Simon Trezise
suggests that 'the umbilical connection once noted by Baring-Gould
between local building materials and houses, local costumes and trades,
is no longer a feature of our world.'[159] Yet Shuttle's poem does not
suggest an unmediated relationship with nature; the idea that her
daughter is 'roped in her turn' is a metaphor binding and captivating at
the same time as, in climbing terminology, it might suggest a safety
device, a saving mechanism. In the Introduction to *The West Country
as a Literary Invention* Trezise reversed the general truism that people
are shaped by their environments and argued that 'Regional fiction can
enable the reader to understand that Nature may also be "nurture",
that the landscape is partly the product of centuries of human
labour'.[160] He goes on to demonstrate that region and literary creation
are intimately connected:

> The literary West Country inventories facts and events but it
> also invents a region: it is proof of humanity making itself at
> home in an environment. It is Nature connected to Nurture;
> Nature nurtured to satisfy the human need for story-telling
> rooted in past and place.[161]

Many women poets have responded to the stones—Ann Trevenen
Jenkins, for example, in 'Stone Circle' wondered about the purpose of
her own visit but called the journey to visit Grey Wethers Stone Circle
by 'New Age Travellers' a 'pilgrimmage'.[162] Jenkin also associated
the stones with a form of psychic birth into the changed world of
modernity; in 'The Old Stones' a farmer's bulldozing of stones is
described as a form of violation:

> The boulders stared naked, new,
> Starting from the earth
> In cataclysmic birth pangs
> Rupturing the soil,
> Tearing holes in the landscape.
> Their birth was untimely
> And chaotic.[163]

The images projected in 'Re-birth' are of an uncompromisingly female earth body and birth:

Moulding of granite
Sinews of heather
Blood from the bracken
Dry bones from the earth;
Pulsing vaginal life
Spirting, vibrating,
Tearing and thrusting
A ravished new birth.[164]

Newness is seen as having to negotiate biological and geographical terms in which birth from a female body and birth experience are essential elements of the living world. The short lines with long words and minimal punctuation, with line endings breaking up the flow of the sentences conveys the impression of twisting and turning; birth, like language an alternating process of contraction and thrusting expansion. The difficulty of the birth, the mass of the stones is an important feature of that experience—a world where the birth of a poem takes place into the weighty significance of culture, history and human understanding.

The coherence and continuity of countryside themes at a time when the permanence of rural lifestyle seems more unstable than in previous eras indicates the on-going significance of land and seascape as metaphor for women writers. Set beside Annie E. Argall's (1894) poem on the Fal, Ann Trevenen Jenkin's 'The River Fal—Evening' (1997) is notable for its emphasis on the boat journey and expressions of loneliness that then lift with the brightness of sunset. The opening of the poem consists of two four line stanzas that emphasize the preparations for taking the boat out on the water. The rhyming consonants and 'Noise of chatter/Bustle, clatter'[165] convey the impression of the combined sound of human preparations, the boat noises and the river's resonance. As language vehicle, the poem mimics the noise of hurried preparations, followed by longer gliding lines that suggest the boat afloat on the moving river. The rhyme sequence moves from rhyming couplets to second and fourth line rhyming, which has the effect of making the language appear less hurried, the journey of the language stream mysterious, then revelatory.

Brenda Wootton's collection *Pantomime Stew*, while it is more comfortable with sketches of town life, also evidences an attempt to span a wide range of Cornish concerns—from an exploration of family ties and Celtic connections, through nostalgic evocations of historic

Cornwall and celebrations of its contemporary cultural mix. 'Over From Scilly', for example, tells of a visitor's shocked response to a train, and 'Acupuncture' describes the poet's response to treatment at the Natural Health Centre in Penzance in 1992. Wootton's sense of Cornishness was signified especially through the specificity of language—accent, popular expressions, place names, a valuing of folk narratives, working class concerns, demotic usage. Her open view of the constitution of Cornishness is evident in the way the tone shifts through matter of fact, pathos and comedy, often in the same poem; in general the poetry fuses her characterization as Cornish Granny and internationally treasured performer. Some poems emphasize her roles of good wife and mother, while the comic treatment of sexual problems and gender points out and provokes thoughts about general inequalities. Wootton's poem 'The Mini and the Rolls' reverses the faithless husband/faithful wife stereotype and 'The Trouble with Love' is a comic tale about mutual sexual incompetence that respects the physicality of love-making without collapsing human into animal.

In a similar vein, Ann Trevenen Jenkin also takes a humorous approach to the male dominance of the Gorsedd, suggesting that the Gorsedd has been male dominated and a bit fusty 'Rak Benenes Avorow!'—'For the women (is) tomorrow'.[166] The grammatical structure of the translation locates women ('Benenes') between singular and plural, present, past and future in a way that encapsulates the spirit of the convergence of historical periods in the way women's time is measured:

> Women of Cornwall unite
> Let us burn our bras tonight
> Wave our banners on high
> Show our legs to the thigh
> Shout our views to the sky
> Women of Cornwall unite!

The use of the seventies term 'Women's Lib' in a collection published in 1997 demonstrates a dry humour at the fact that the poet herself, as a mature writer, can still appreciate the impatience and drive for change of youth. In a model of a different kind to the one proposed in 'Women's Lib For the Gorsedd!', Jenkin's poem 'Great Cornish-woman' honours the life of Kathleen Beskeen, a bard who died in 1977, observing both her dedication to Cornish ways, her speaking of 'the ancient tongue' of Cornwall and her international friendships.

Cornish produce is seen in a number of poems by women writers of Cornwall as varied, fertile, some analogy often being made with female productiveness. Both Victoria Field and Ann Trevenen Jenkin, for example, have poems celebrating the diverse array of names of apple types. Jenkin's 'Cornish Apples', accompanied by a vivid colour photo makes the connection between Eve and apples, as does Field's 'The Heart's Orchard' in her collection *Olga's Dreams*, adorned by a picture of a curvaceous Eve-like nude. The cover of Penelope Shuttle's *The Orchard Upstairs*, like a cross between a photograph and an early modernist/surrealist painting, depicts a bright green apple at the foot of a wooden stairway and banister. The eye is led in the direction of the stairs as they lead off into an indeterminate distance/space, while the round apple in the foreground hints at poems that will explore the contours of femininity and femaleness.

Jenkin likens the apple history to that of poetry—extending back into the past, fresh grown in the present. Field's poem makes a comic list of apple types as metaphor for lovers and plays on the idea of fidelity to Cornish apples as a symbol of nationalism:

> To Wadebridge with *Tregonna King* until his branches began
>   to sag.
> I put him aside for Christmas and popped a Pig Nose in my
>   bag.
>
> But now those days are over, my lovers all long gone.
>   Smoother types
> with blemish-free skins from New Zealand, South Africa and
>   France
> try to woo me in their plastic coats and turn up in tasteless
>   tarts.
> 'Get lost,' I say, 'Please go away. My heart is not for
>   scrumping.[167]

Ilinska's 'Cantata For Apple Voices'[168] dramatises and charts a mind in conflict. Deploying the classic composure of the cantata form to shape and control the voices of a woman/women—'Sister-apple, sister-apple,/That vast commotion in the trees'[169] elements of tradition recur and echo—Blake's worm, 'The Song of Songs', classical goddesses, Biblical structures such as 'The Tree, the Human and the Snake'. The conclusion is dry, ironic and not especially hopeful as the apple-woman-sisters-women:

> In our agnostic aquiescent gowns . . .
> Laugh we shall, glorified in the fruit shops
> For fifty, sixty-nine, seventy pence . . .[170]

'The Apple' a prophetic poem dreamt in Polish and published in a sequence entitled 'Three Dreams' from *Address of Paradise* was, however, more optimistic, utopian. 'I marvel at the way the rind is able to hold so much liquid and/Yet appear so hard and so firm.'[171] The flood of memories, anticipations and impressions haunting her Cornish life overflowed in *Address of Paradise* after revisiting Poland. Ilinksa's images drew on fairy and folk tale, mythologies, Biblical texts. Conflicting attitudes to science, the processes of modernity and fears for the future are explored. In 'The Moan of Cassandra' Ilinska's text became that of:

> . . . the NUCLEAR POET,
> evolving Homo Sapiens post coitum triste,
> balanced at conscious point
> of skyscraper Race?[172]

CONCLUSION

If poetry published in contemporary journals can give some indication of the future of Anglo-Cornish women's writing, then it suggests continuity and connection through the extension of established themes, with increasing emphasis on Cornwall's cultural and linguistic diversity. *Bardhonyeth Kernow/Poetry Cornwall*, edited by Les Merton, regularly publishes numerous poems by women, translations in and from a variety of languages, dialect writing and international submissions. Each edition shows the Crowdy Crawn diversity. The first issue included poems in the journal's competition—Jenny Galton-Fenzi's 'Driving Mr Watts to the Day Centre', a tender poem about the achievements of aging with love and Diane Simkin's 'The Wait' which evokes emotions unspoken between a couple in the metaphor of a stripped bed. Eleanor Maxted, a judge of the poetry competition, praised Diane Simkin's Chaucerian roundel: 'The Horse' as a poem in which 'with great economy of words the poet conjures up, in three short stanzas, the fear inherent in pagan ritual, the sinister "other side" of the music and drumming, the prancing rhythm'.[173] A supplement of four poems by Penelope Shuttle and a long dialect poem by Joy Stevenson, a Cornish Bard 'Can She Dance the Flora?' is included in this volume.

> Be tha time we reached tha Guildhall
> I wuz steamun like a crock,
> Jaw wuz sweatun like a poultice yew
> Well, twuz aff pass one a clock.[174]

Caroline Gill's 'Shaft of Light: circle of stone' links Barbara Hepworth's sculpture to this eternal concept of earth/time but also balances masculine/feminine , heaviness and lightness; a balance seen in the sculpture, radiating outwards.

> The sculptor's place was crammed
> with heavy tools, reflecting
> open palms that cast in bronze.
> Her seeds of thought were sown among
> the carefree cats, who spread their silhouettes
> in shadowed shafts like nets.
> Strong sunlit circles link her town
> with timeless tracts of standing stone.[175]

In *Bardhonyeth Kernow/Poetry Cornwall:* No.5, Jane Tozer's 'Dialect poem', which ridicules Thatcherite out-of-town visitors who make fun of local pronunciation, sits beside Caroline Carver's clever and amusing 'Assignation', which deploys Jamaican dialect to show how 'the Queen of Sheba' and 'Christopher Columbus' solve a dispute. Pamela Trudie Hodge's poem 'A dish o' tay' promises 'braid 'n' budder an' saffron caake an' craim'[176] while Penelope Shuttle's 'Roundwood Quay, August Evening' describes an evening walk in which 'we came down the rabbit lane/into the green lingua madre/of the woods'[177] and then on to the quay in the light of a 'beautymoon' 'now here, now gone in cloud,/part of autumn/August keeps up her sleeve.' Issue Eleven includes a linguistically accomplished and witty extract from Jane Tozer's translation of 'Chevrefoil: The Lai of Withywind'. Zeeba Ansari's 'Brangwain' explores the Tristran and Isolde myth from the angle of Brangwain, Isolde's maid, who has slept with Mark in Isolde's place on the wedding night. Feeling betrayed by his failure to recognize her, Brangwain as implied speaker realizes that despite his knowledge of 'hawk, hound, horse' he cannot tell the difference between the women he sleeps with—a bitter sweet ambivalence in which status is levelled by sexual desire, but too easily reinstated in daylight hours. Martha Street's meditation 'My Shirt' imagines a woman in Bangladesh wearing 'a bright sari of thin poor cloth' sewing the 'bleached denim' shirt of the speaker, and in turn imagining 'what other/woman's arms will slide//into this blue':

> My shirt is nothing
> to her mere stuff of work work
> trance of work as quick quick[178]

The colour blue in the poem signifies both distance and connection between women across nationality, class, caste, religion and race in the quick time of the present, contrasted with the long-term negotiations of woman's/women's time. If such a varied output by so many different writers can be read as an indication of a likely future expansion of poetry published in Cornwall, then there is certainly much to look forward to.

Acknowledgements
My heartfelt thanks to all who helped in various ways with this article. Thanks to Melissa Hardie and all the people at Hypatia Trust at Trevelyan House, 16 Chapel Street, Penzance TR18AW (www.hypatia-trust.org.uk) for providing access to much of the material in this essay and convivial company. Thanks to Ted Stourton for hospitality and artistic enthusiasm for Cornwall at Camelot Castle, Tintagel. Thanks to Les Merton for sharing some of his knowledge of poetry in Cornwall and to the staff at The Cornish Studies Centre, Redruth. Thanks to my father Neil Wood, whose family history research sent me to Cornwall.

NOTES AND REFERENCES

1. Brenda Wootton, ed. Sue Luscombe, *Pantomime Stew*, Hayle, 1994, p. 116.
2. Ann Trevenen Jenkin, *Gwel Kernow: A Cornish View*, Hayle, 1997, p. 163.
3. Wootton, 1994, p. 13.
4. Wootton, 1994, p. 19.
5. Wootton, 1994, p. 116.
6. Wootton, 1994, p. 43.
7. Wootton, 1994, p. 53
8 Jenkin, 1997, p. 167.
9. See Alan Kent, *The Literature of Cornwall*, Bristol, 2000. pp. 17–18. Kent describes a literary model of language usage in Cornwall as a 'continuum', a 'process within a paradigm of language shift and change over time, which has brought about a multitude of linguistic and literary features and events throughout the past thousand years.' His usage of the term Cornish Literature for texts written in Cornish, Anglo-Cornish for texts written 'about Cornwall in English' and 'Cornu-English to show those texts which form the canon of Celtic-English writing in Cornwall; that is those texts written in what some observers might label the Cornish dialect of English' is deployed here.
10. Alan Kent, '"Song of Our Motherland": Making Meaning of the Life and Work of Katharine Lee Jenner 1853–1936', ed. Derek Williams, *Henry and Katharine Jenner*, London, 2004, p. 145.
11. Kent, 'Song of Our Motherland', p. 144.

12. ed. Judy Pearsall *The New Oxford Dictionary of English*, Oxford, 1998, p. 777.
13. 'The Mabinogi of Taliesin', Idrison, *The Bardic Source Book*, ed. John Matthews, London, 1998, p. 18.
14. Ithell Colquhoun, *The Living Stones: Cornwall*, London, 1957, p. 18.
15. Penelope Shuttle, *The Orchard Upstairs*, Oxford, 1980, p. 28.
16. Shuttle, 1980, p. 42.
17. Judith Hubback, 'Women, Symbolism and the Coast of Cornwall', *Cornwall: The Cultural Construction of Place*, Penzance, 1997, p. 99.
18. Hubback, 1997, p. 99.
19. Hubback, 1997, p. 100.
20. Penelope Shuttle, *The Child-Stealer*, Oxford, 1983, p. 43.
21. Cheryl Hayden, 'Cornwall: A Very Difficult Woman? A Feminist Approach to Issues of Cornish Identity', in Philip Payton (ed.), *Cornish Studies: Nine*, Exeter, 2001, p. 205.
22. James Vernon, 'Border crossings: Cornwall and the English (imagi)nation', *Imagining Nations*, ed. Geoffey Cubitt, Manchester, p. 117.
23. Bernard Deacon, 'From 'Cornish Studies' To 'Critical Cornish Studies': Reflections on Methodology', in Philip Payton (ed.), *Cornish Studies: Twelve*, Exeter, 2004, p. 25.
24. Deacon, 2004, p. 18.
25. Deacon, 2004, p. 25.
26. Kayleigh Milden, 'Are You Church or Chapel?' Perceptions of Spatial and Spiritual Identity Within Cornish Methodism', in Payton (ed.), 2004, Exeter, 2004, p. 148.
27. Helen Dunmore, *Out of the Blue Poems 1975–2001*, Bloodaxe, Northumberland, 2001, p. 145
28. Dunmore, 2001, p. 146.
29. Phillip Payton, *Cornwall: A History*, Fowey, 2004b, p. 212.
30. W.H. Kearley Wright, *West-Country Poets: Their Lives and Works*, London, 1896, p. 10.
31. Kearley Wright, 1896, p. 146.
32. Kearley Wright, 1896, p. 265.
33. Kearley Wright, 1896, p. 146.
34. Kearley Wright, 1896, p. 220.
35. Alan Kent, *'Wives, Mothers and Sisters': Feminism, Literature and Women Writers in Cornwall*, The Patten Press in association with The Hypatia Trust, Penzance, 1998, p. 9.
36. *Bardhonyeth Kernow/Poetry Cornwall No. 11, 2005*, p. 3. N.B. Cornwall continues to be the site of contradictory representations in which 'brownness' may be interpreted as signifying a different cultural and ethnic heritage to Anglo-Saxon England and/or a primitivization, or even a reference to the effects of the warm climate. Katherine Garvin's 'Cornwall' for example begins 'Look back at the dark child swimming in the sea'. *The West Country Magazine* Winter 1948–49, Eleven, No. 4, Vol. 3, p. 267.

37. Neil Kennedy and Nigel Kingcome, 'Disneyfication of Cornwall —Developing a Poldark Heritage Complex', *International Journal of Heritage Studies*, Vol. 4. No. 1, 1998, p. 53.
38. Kent, 2000, p. 196.
39. Kent, 2000, p. 197.
40. Wootton, p. 35.
41. Alan Kent, ed., *Voices From West Barbary: An anthology of Anglo-Cornish poetry 1549–1928*, London, 2000, p. 145.
42. Kent, ed., *Voices From West Barbary*, 2000, p. 111.
43. Kent, ed., *The Dreamt Sea: An Anthology of Anglo-Cornish Poetry 1928–2004*, London, 2004, p. 112.
44. Kent, ed., 'Song of Our Motherland', p. 146.
45. Katharine Lee Jenner, *Songs of the Stars and the Sea*, London, 1926, p. 9.
46. Marina Warner, *Alone of All Her Sex*, Vintage, London, 2000, p. 265.
47. Jenner, 1926, p. 20.
48. Jenner, 1926, p. 25.
49. Jenner, 1926, p. 16.
50. Jenner, 1926, p. 18.
51. Jenner, 1926, p. 22.
52. Jenner, 1926, p. 24.
53. Amy Hale, 'A History of the Cornish Revival', ed. Tim Saunders, *The Wheel: An anthology of modern poetry in Cornish 1850–1980*, London, 1999, pp. 19–27.
54. Kent, *Wives, Mothers and Sisters*, 1998, p. 26.
55. Kent, ed., *Voices From West Barbary*, 2000, p. 204.
56. Kent, ed., *Voices From West Barbary*, 2000, p. 204.
57. Colquhoun, 1957, p. 117.
58. Saunders, ed., *The Wheel*, London, 1999, p. 17.
59. Kent, ed., *The Literature of Cornwall*, 2000, p. 139.
60. Saunders, ed., *The Wheel*, p. 115.
61. Wootton, p. 44.
62. Saunders, ed., *The Wheel*, pp. 114/115.
63. Saunders, ed., *The Wheel*, pp. 115.
64. Kent, *The Literature of Cornwall*, 2000, p. 13.
65. Kent, ed., *The Dreamt Sea*, 2004, p. 28.
66. Kent, ed., *The Dreamt Sea*, 2004, p. 35.
67. Anne Treneer, *The Cornish Review*, Winter, 1951, p. 60.
68. Anne Treneer, *The Cornish Review*, Winter, 1951, p. 61.
69. Gladys Hunkin, *The Cornish Review*, Spring, 1949, p. 73.
70. Gladys Hunkin, *Cornish Crystal*, London, n.d., p. 35.
71. Hunkin, n.d., p. 36.
72. Hunkin, n.d., p. 48.
73. See Brian Murdoch, *Cornish Literature*, Cambridge, 1993, pp. 80–81 for a discussion of the *Ordinalia* and historical precedents for representations of the serpent as feminine.
74. Kent, *The Dreamt Sea*, 2004, p. 35.
75. Kent, *The Dreamt Sea*, 2004, p. 44.

76. *The West Country Magazine* 14, Vol. 4, No. 3., Autumn 1949, p. 218.
77. *The Cornish Review*, No. 7. Autumn, 1967, p. 22.
78. *The West Country Magazine* 12, Vol. 4, No.1, Spring, 1949, p. 28.
79. *The West Country Magazine* 11, Vol. 3, No. 4, Winter, 1948, p. 267.
80. *The West Country Magazine* 8, Vol. 3, No.1, Spring, 1948, p. 45.
81. *The Cornish Review*, No. 3, Autumn, 1966, pp. 14–15.
82. *The Cornish Review*, No. 11, Spring, 1969, pp. 12–13.
83. *The Cornish Review*, No. 10, Winter, 1968, p. 9.
84. Ilinska, 'From a Cornish Hotelier's Diary', *The Cornish Review* No. 11, Spring, 1969, pp. 66–73.
85. Ilinska, 1969, p. 96.
86. *The Cornish Review*, No.12, Summer, p. 9.
87. *The Cornish Review*, No.15, Summer, 1970, p. 13.
88. Zofia Ilinska, *Idle Rocks*, London, 1972, p. 48.
89. Ilinska, 1972, p. 69.
90. Ilinska, 1972, p. 11.
91. Ithell Colquhoun, *Grimoire of the Entangled Thicket*, Stevenage, 1973, p. 12.
92. Colquhoun, 1973, p. 4.
93. Caitlin Matthews, *The Elements of the Celtic Tradition*, Dorset, 1996, p. 100.
94. Colquhoun, 1957, p. 12.
95. Colquhoun, 1973, p. 20.
96. Colquhoun, 1957, p. 169.
97. Colquhoun, 1957, p. 29.
98. Anne-Marie Fortier, 'Making Home: Queer Migrations and Motions of Attachment', *Uprootings/Regroundings*, eds Sara Ahmed, Claudia Castaneda, Anne-Marie Fortier, Mimi Sheller, Oxford, 2003, p. 115.
99. Colquhoun, 1957, p. 13.
100. Colquhoun, 1957, p. 19.
101. Colquhoun, 1957, p. 27.
102. Penelope Shuttle, *Adventures With My Horse*, Oxford, 1988.
103. *Cornish Writers '75*, Published by the W.E.A. S-W District, p. 11.
104. *Cornish Writers '75*, Published by the W.E.A. S-W District, p. 13.
105. Kent, ed., *The Dreamt Sea*, 2004, p. 113.
106. Kent, ed., *The Dreamt Sea*, 2004, p. 114.
107. Zofia Ilinska, *Horoscope of the Moon*, Padstow, 1992, p. 9.
108. Zofia Ilinska, *Address of Paradise*, Padstow, 1996, p. viii.
109. Kent, ed., *The Dreamt Sea*, 2004, p. 129.
110. Kent, ed., *The Dreamt Sea*, 2004, p. 130.
111. Kent, ed., *The Dreamt Sea*, 2004, p. 166.
112. Kent, ed., *The Dreamt Sea*, 2004, p. 167.
113. Kent, ed., *The Dreamt Sea*, 2004, p. 166.
114. Penelope Shuttle, *A Leaf Out of His Book*, Oxford, 1999, p. 137.
115. Kent, ed., *The Dreamt Sea*, 2004, p. 192.
116. Kent, ed., *The Dreamt Sea*, 2004, pp. 192–3.
117. Kent, ed., *The Dreamt Sea*, 2004, p. 194.

118. Kent, ed., *The Dreamt Sea*, 2004, p. 200.
119. Kent, *The Literature of Cornwall*, 2000, p. 147.
120. Kennedy and Kingcome, p. 46.
121. Shuttle, *The Orchard Upstairs*, Oxford, 1980, pp. 4–5.
122. Julia Kristeva, *The Kristeva Reader*, ed. Toril Moi, Blackwells, 1986, p. 187.
123. Hugh MacDiarmid, *Cornish Heroic Song for Valda Trevlyn and Once in a Cornish Garden*, Padstow, 1977, p. 6.
124. Shuttle, 1983, p. 17.
125. Shuttle, 1983, p. 18.
126. Shuttle, 1983, p. 35.
127. Shuttle, 1983, p. 45.
128. Shuttle, 1980, p. 42.
129. Shuttle, 1999, p. 57.
130. *Bardhonyeth Kernow/Poetry Cornwall*, No. 7, 2004, p. 8.
131. Ann Alexander, *Facing Demons*, Peterloo, 2002, p. 15.
132. Kennedy and Kingcome, p. 54.
133. Penelope Shuttle, *Taxing the Rain*, Oxford, 1992, pp. 15–16.
134. Shuttle, 1992, p. 21.
135. Sylvia Kantaris, *Dirty Washing*, Newcastle upon Tyne, 1989, p. 57.
136. Kantaris, 1989, p. 61.
137. Kantaris, 1989, p. 38.
138. Shuttle, 1980, p. 9.
139. Shuttle, 1980, p. 26.
140. Jenkin, 1997, p. 40.
141. Jenkin, 1997, p. 131.
142. Jenkin, 1997, p. 132.
143. Jenkin, 1997, p. 133.
144. Kent, ed., *The Dreamt Sea*, 2004, p. 134.
145. Kent, ed., *The Dreamt Sea*, 2004, p. 135.
146. Shuttle, 1983, p. 8.
147. Philip Payton, *The Cornish Overseas*, Fowey, 2005, p. 39.
148. Breda Gray, 'Global Modernities and the Gendered Epic of "the Irish Empire"', *Uprootings/Regroundings*, eds Sara Ahmed, Claudia Castaneda, Anne-Marie Fortier, Mimi Sheller, Oxford, 2003, p. 159.
149. Gray, 2003, pp. 162–3.
150. Jenkin, 1997, p. 149.
151. Gray, p. 163.
152. *Bardhonyeth Kernow/Poetry Cornwall No. 3*, p. 12.
153. Jenkin, 1997, p. 116.
154. Jenkin, 1997, p. 158.
155. Jenkin, 1997, p. 153.
156. Jenkin, 1997, p. 117.
157. Shuttle, 1999, p. 75.
158. Jenkin, 1997, pp. 71–3.
159. Simon Trezise, *The West Country as a Literary Invention: Putting Fiction in its Place*, Exeter, 2000, p. 231.

160. Trezise, 2000, p. xv.
161. Trezise, 2000, p. 233.
162. Jenkin, 1997, p. 113.
163. Jenkin, 1997, p. 20.
164. Jenkin, 1997, p. 54
165. Jenkin, 1997, p. 43.
166. Jenkin, 1997, pp. 167–8.
167. Victoria Field, *Olga's Dreams*, Truro, 2004, p. 78.
168. Ilinska, 1992, pp. 32–36.
169. Ilinska, 1992, p. 33.
170. Ilinska, 1992, p. 36.
171. Ilinska, 1996, p. 2.
172. Ilinska, 1992, p. 2.
173. *Bardhonyeth Kernow/Poetry Cornwall: No. 2*, 2002, p. 3.
174. *Bardhonyeth Kernow/Poetry Cornwall: No. 2*, 2002, p. 17.
175. *Bardhonyeth Kernow/Poetry Cornwall: No. 3*, 2002, p. 37.
176. *Bardhonyeth Kernow/Poetry Cornwall: No. 5*, 2003, p. 27.
177. *Bardhonyeth Kernow/Poetry Cornwall: No. 5*, 2003, p. 41.
178. *Bardhonyeth Kernow/Poetry Cornwall: No. 12*, 2005, p. 42.

NARRATIVES IN THE NET: FICTION AND CORNISH TOURISM

Graham Busby and Patrick Laviolette

'Cornish earth!' she said. 'Smell it!
It's quite different!
We're home!'

Winston Graham—*Bella Poldark*.[1]

INTRODUCTION

These closing lines to Graham's last *Poldark* novel illustrate a view that is frequently taken for granted by prospective tourists to Cornwall —that this place is 'different' and thus worthy of a visit. Literary tourism, or the hermeneutic and semiotic realization of place as a travel destination, is hardly a new concept.[2] It is, however, only in recent times that local authorities have deliberately set out to promote their tourism product through literary media and, in some cases, to extend the length of the holiday season. For example, Bradford Council has promoted the area around Haworth as *Brontë Country*. The South Tyneside Borough Council has likewise developed *Catherine Cookson Country*, based on novels by the local author. Given that the identity of a place may change as a result of tourism activity, it is pertinent to ask whether literary tourism alters any given identity in ways significantly superior, inferior or different to other types of visitation.[3]

Literature has, undoubtedly, informed the general public's affiliations with Cornwall to significant degrees. Literary inspirations have come from John Betjeman, Jack Clemo, Geoffrey Grigson, Thomas Hardy, Arthur Quiller-Couch, E.V. Thompson, James Turner,

Alfred Tennyson and Virginia Woolf to name but a few. Based on a collection of material via the internet with regard to Winston Graham's novels, this article tentatively explores the relationship between literature and tourism in Cornwall. It considers some of the impacts on local visitation that Graham's writings have had and contextualises these observations by comparison with Daphne du Maurier's fictional works.

In contemplating the concept of literary tourism with reference to Cornwall, the article examines the 'draw' factor that these iconic authors have had upon their reading publics. It also pays particular attention to the transformation of their novels into television and cinema adaptations as well as the increasing availability for commentary and purchase via the world-wide-web. The article is, therefore, set additionally within a framework concerned with virtuality, cyberspace and the idea of the hypertext. Hence, we equally conceptualize the advantages and criticisms that certain types of online research techniques raise for studying perceptions of Cornwall, while considering the interdisciplinary study of tourism more broadly.

METHODOLOGY

The primary data collection pertains specifically to Graham's *Poldark* series. Given the difficulty of measuring literary tourism over Cornwall's broad geographic extent, the decision was made to undertake an internet based study that used a web-site message bulletin-board as a method of soliciting responses. The *Poldark* web-site provides a link to the Internet Book Database of Fiction message board.[4] A message with the following question was posted there on 10 November 2003: 'Has anybody visited Cornwall specifically because of the *Poldark* books and television series?' Eight lengthy replies were obtained in ten days, from respondents in a number of countries. Because of the richness of the data, only a selection of the verbatim transcripts appear in full below. Basic content analysis, also used for other Cornish tourism research, served to identify key themes amongst the responses.[5]

The internet is one of the biggest and fastest growing activities in human history. Over the past decade, many social scientists have turned their interest to online support networks, the formation of Information Technology identities, the creation of hypertext based communities and even the study of virtual tourism.[6] A recent trend in this vast research realm has been to focus on the construction of narrative as an alternative base for examining online social phenomena, with virtual communities and identities simply acting as subsets to the many types of discourses taking place in the ethereal world of internet communication.[7] The present study falls into this newly developing category. It is concerned with narrative constructions of place through invoking mnemonic recollections of Cornwall that have been inspired from fictional literature. The data retrieved was, of course, itself a type of hypertext literature—prose compositions sent via the medium of the information superhighway.

This article is, therefore, about the linkages amid various narrative styles, and is not a study of internet use as understood by the anthropologists Daniel Miller and Don Slater[8] in their discussion of the ethnographic construction of online social identities. Nor are we proposing a study of how people navigate through media construed realities.[9] Rather we are talking about the use of the internet and conceptualizations of virtuality as newly developing research tools.[10] Online research in the social sciences introduces a number of methodological problems. Some of these are unique to this medium of exploration. For instance, while certain people argue that entering cyberspace is the equivalent of going 'into the field', there are others who feel that cyberspace is not 'real'—and thus not worthy of study. Additionally, the important question arises as to whether cyberspace conversations are public or private.[11] That is, whether we have the right to observe and analyse online discussions without the permission and explicit consent of participants. In this respect, we should state that permission was sought after collection of the data. We should also add that between the two of us, we share an intense sociological and ethnographic knowledge of issues relating to Cornish identity into which the brief analysis below fits. Hence, the study does not exist in isolation, outside a wider contextual and intellectual basis.

LITERARY PORTRAYALS OF CORNWALL

Cornwall has been portrayed in a variety of ways. Early travellers included John Leland, who visited in 1536 and 1542,[12] and Celia Fiennes in 1698.[13] The Reverend William Gilpin, instigator of the 'picturesque' debate in Britain, came in 1775: 'From Launceston we travelled as far into Cornwall as Bodmin, through a coarse naked country, and in all respects as uninteresting as can well be conceived'.[14] Uninteresting to Gilpin and yet a topographical asset to Daphne du Maurier for the setting of *Jamaica Inn*, the area referred to is Bodmin Moor. In Victorian times, Cornwall—or rather Cornishness —was portrayed by folklore compilers as 'a "primitive", dark and wild "Celtic" culture' where the very ancient superstitions had survived the impact of Roman, Saxon, Danish and Norman invasion.[15] The 1893 *Ethnographic Survey of the British Isles* studied the inhabitants and folklore of Cornwall at 35 locations, since it was presumed that

Cornwall's geographic location would provide a 'remarkably un-corrupted race of "primitive" people'.[16]

Bishop Benson in 1877 thought the Cornish 'a most peculiar people'. As Bernard Deacon observes, anthropologists today would consider this a typical expression of the concept of 'Otherness'—a category established by outsiders.[17] Indeed, since Benson's time, the deliberate deployment of a Celtic 'Otherness' has been used to attract visitors to Cornwall, many in search of a spiritual and romantic 'Otherworld'.[18] Some Cornish church visitor book comments intimate this.[19] Additionally, in the past many folkloric and ethnographic studies of Cornwall and the Cornish have—implicitly and sometimes explicitly —assessed the population as 'inferior' to their English neighbours, the 'racially superior' Anglo-Saxons. In other words, as well as creating an attractive image for visitor consumption, the con-structed 'Otherness' also ensured that power relations were never far below the surface.

Cornwall is, therefore, a contested territory, a contest with myriad linguistic, economic, political and religious dimensions. Andrew, Harvey, Meethan and Laviolette[20] are not the first observers to remark on the region's distinctive cultural identity, although they accept that there may be other 'distinct' regions in Britain that are likewise contested. The local authority—Cornwall County Council—insists, however, that Cornwall is the only 'county' with such a strong and recognizable cultural identity, so that Cornwall becomes 'unique' as well as 'distinctive'.[21] In this construction, parallels are often drawn with Brittany rather than other parts of Britain, amplifying the 'unique' as well as the sense of 'Otherness', a perspective that has also been echoed by the Celto-Cornish Revivalist movement.[22] Not surprisingly, this potent mix has provided fertile grounding for writers of fiction over the last century.

Cornish landscape features, both natural and industrial, also provide rich material for authors.[23] The extensive scenic coastline, abounding in stories of smuggling and wrecking, the sunken river valleys of the South coast and the wild prehistoric moorlands have frequently featured in fiction. Many of Cornwall's antiquities have come to symbolize its 'Celtic'/early Cornish culture: quoits, stone circles, menhirs, and ancient round houses.[24] As Philip Payton argues: 'ancient stones loom large in the imagery of Cornwall and Cornish-ness'.[25] Indeed, the highest concentration of such sites in Britain is to be found in Cornwall—1,267 scheduled monuments in 1998, a figure English Heritage considers is likely to increase to three thousand by 2007. Such sites have been portrayed by numerous authors seeking to evoke an elemental, primeval Cornwall: including D.M. Thomas in his *Birthstone*.[26] Furthermore, the characteristic medieval churches, comprising elements of so-called 'Celtic Christianity', feature dominantly in the landscape and attract significant numbers of visitors.[27] 'Heritage' is omnipresent in the landscape in Cornwall, and suggests a strong sense of historical continuity with the past.[28] The Cornish poet Charles Causley is credited with the comment 'nobody but a plastic rhinoceros could fail to be conscious of the past in Cornwall'.[29] And the representation of an area's heritage and cultural traditions are critical in the commodification for the process of tourist consumption, as the experience of Cornwall shows.[30]

If the concept of Celticity—in Cornwall and elsewhere—seems somewhat elusive, it should be emphasized that it has been the subject of a number of major critiques over the last two decades.[31] For Chapman, a key element in any definition is the location of the Celts 'on the edge of a more dominant world'.[32] For Bowman, Celticity is a state of mind, or what Hale terms elective affinity.[33] Such Celticity has been commodified in the Republic of Ireland for tourism promotion purposes.[34] And to some extent the same can be said for Cornwall, although here it is fused with a spiritual or 'alternative' dimension, a romantic construction suggestive of a simpler life close to nature. The historic landscape itself, according to Harvey *et al.*, also informs a visitor's conception of Celticity, and again this is apparent in Cornwall's experience, where such 'Celticity' permeates a number of works of fiction.[35]

Critically, Cornish culture is dynamic; some of the meanings implicit in previous centuries may not be extant today. To that extent, Cornish culture is 'subject to constant change and re-negotiation . . . [leading to] its re-definition and re-assertion' over time.[36] This culture, however re-defined, continues to permeate the landscape, reminding us that 'place' is a socio-cultural construction rather than simply a physical location.[37] No doubt this helps to explain why Cornwall is perceived by many visitors as being 'more natural and more real than the [metropolitan] centre'.[38] Such a view may result from the commodification of place but that does not necessarily make it inauthentic or destructive.[39] Although it almost certainly reinforces popularly-held stereotypical images of Cornwall, which comprise a 'guide book culture . . . of pirates, piskies and sweeping landscapes filled with exotic Celts',[40] a note of caution is made for, as Uzzell and Nuryanti point out, all destinations have some unique characteristics which, after all, create place identity.[41] Hence, as it is the case in Cornwall, literature and Information Technology can dialectically merge with these characteristics to both help create tourism identities and to be inspired or created out of them.[42]

THE CONCEPT OF LITERARY TOURISM

Butler proposes four forms of literary tourism, illustrated in Table 1. The first comprises homage to an actual location—for example, Daphne du Maurier's eponymous novel *Jamaica Inn* on Bodmin Moor. Butler notes that such pseudo-pilgrimage has as its rationale: 'on a somewhat higher intellectual level, to see the backcloth against which a work was produced to gain new insights into the work of the author'.[43] Citing T.E. Lawrence, 'Lawrence of Arabia', Butler sweepingly believes that the element of homage visitation 'appeals more to the masses' and 'the "backcloth" to those few who have actually read one of his works'. Pocock's research on *Catherine Cookson Country* indicates how 40 of 57 coach-borne 'literary pilgrims' to the area had previously read the work of the novelist (with a median figure of twenty books).[44] Herbert has conducted research into this higher intellectual level at Jane Austen's home of Chawton, in Hampshire.[45] From these findings it is clear that it is the popularity of the novelist which is the key criterion in inspiring the visit.

The second form of literary tourism concerns the places of significance in the work of fiction. 'The land of the two rivers', in North Devon, described in *Tarka* by Henry Williamson, exemplifies this form. Indeed, the 180-mile long-distance walking route, The Tarka Trail, has been constructed on the back of this piece. A difficulty for visitors is that it may not be at all easy to identify fictional locations, those from the romantic fiction of Mary Wesley's *Camomile Lawn* and Rosamunde Pilcher's *The Shell Seekers* may be easier to find in Cornwall than those of the *Poldark* series. As Moody[46] observes, *Poldark Country* is a composite creation and a certain level of geographical knowledge is required to identify many of the locations, even though two publications assist in this task.[47]

Butler's third form considers 'the appeal of areas because they were appealing to literary (and other) figures'.[48] This is a somewhat more specialist form yet there are several guides for literary tourists. Publications such as Finlayson's *Writers in Romney Marsh* and Bird & Modlock's[49] *Writers on the South-West Coast* actively promote areas of southern England to the serious literary pilgrim. At a national level, there is Green's[50] *Authors and Places: a Literary Pilgrimage*, Morley's[51] *Literary Britain*, Drabble's[52] *A Writer's Britain: Landscape and Literature*, Varlow's[53] *A Reader's Guide to Writers' Britain: an Enchanting Tour of Literary Landscapes and Shrines*, Hill's[54] *The Spirit of Britain: An Illustrated Guide to Literary Britain* and Bradbury's[55] *The Atlas of Literature*.

The fourth form of literary tourism is where the work of the writer is so popular that the entire area becomes a tourist destination *per se*.

A classic British example is Charles Kingsley's *Westward Ho!*, published in 1854 which gave rise to the development of the upmarket sea-side resort of this name in North Devon.[56] Interestingly, the college established there educated Rudyard Kipling between 1878–1882 prompting his 1899 publication of *Stalky and Co*.[57] As Pocock observes, 'treating writings as a literary quarry [. . .] to construct a more general literary topography' frequently leads to the all-out mining of the associations with an individual's or society's favourite author.[58] Arguably, this form is manifest when an area becomes a 'Literary Country' and a review of Pocock's[59] work illustrates that some are much more widely recognized than others. For instance, consider the level of recognition afforded to *Hardy Country, Catherine Cookson Country* and *Agatha Christie Country*. Consciousness of the latter may present difficulties; the English Riviera Tourist Board has promoted Torquay, multi-lingually, on the basis of Christie's connections although Busby *et al.* emphasize the area around Burgh Island and Bigbury.[60] The point here is that recognition is dependent on either the level of marketing invested in any given area or translation to the mass media, the small screen frequently being as effective as the large. This leads to another possible kind of literary tourism.

This fifth form is concerned with how travel writing influences tourism decision-making. As suggested by Busby and Klug, it is a broad category that ranges from guide-books to semi-fictionalized descriptive accounts—literature nonetheless.[61] A good example of the latter, relating to Cornwall, is Jeremy Seal's *The Wreck at Sharpnose Point*.[62] A key point here, as Herbert suggests, is that visitors to literary locations possess a range of motives. He highlights the need for a reappraisal of the representation of the literary pilgrim as being the image of a dedicated scholar; 'literary places are no longer accidents of history, sites of a writer's birth or death; they are also social constructions, created, amplified, and promoted to attract visitors'.[63] It is because of this, that most visitors certainly have multiple motivations.

A sixth form of literary tourism exists, predicated by film-induced tourism, whereby the visitor has read the author's works after viewing what may well have been changed by the screenplay. McAleer in his study of popular reading between 1914 and 1950 comments on how a 'selection of fiction was influenced by the cinema'.[64] The book here is a souvenir, providing a permanent reminder of having seen the film. Interestingly, the Mass-Observation research of 1944 suggested that the most frequently purchased works of fiction 'are definitely those which have been filmed';[65] with reference to Cornwall, du Maurier's *Rebecca* is one of those cited in the M.O. research. Clearly, measurement of this type of literary tourism is dependent on substantial on-site empirical research, such as that conducted on Cephallonia in the wake of production of the film *Captain Corelli's Mandolin*.[66]

Table 1. Forms of Literary Tourism

Form	Description
1) Aspects of homage to an actual location.	To see the background against which a work was produced to gain new insights into the work and the author. This form involves the emergence of the literary pilgrim.[67]
2) Places of significance in the work of fiction.	The novel 'Tarka the Otter' by Henry Williamson brought tourists to the rural part of North Devon, where it was set.[68]
3) Appeal of areas because they were appealing to literary and other figures.	The form of tourism which is connected with literary figures. Widely used by the private and public sector to promote areas and to gain economic benefit.
4) The literature gains popularity in a sense that the area becomes a tourist destination in its own right.	This form is illustrated by Charles Kingsley's *Westward Ho!* which resulted in the creation of the eponymously-named seaside resort in North Devon.[69]
5) Travel writing.	A vehicle through which places and people have been re-interpreted and communicated to wider audiences illustrated by the work of Bill Bryson.
6) Film-induced literary tourism.	Tourism resulting from enhanced interest in a destination, secured through reading the literature after viewing the screenplay.

Source: Adapted from Butler (1986) and Busby & Klug (2001).

TWENTIETH-CENTURY AUTHORS IN CORNWALL

Authors of fiction have long been associated with Cornwall, some still well-known and others forgotten. A small sample from the last century is provided here. Perhaps drawn by his perceptions of Celtic imagery,

D.H. Lawrence arrived in Cornwall in December 1915 and stayed for nearly two years. However, his two works featuring Cornish material, *The Fox* and *Kangaroo*, were written after he had left. Amongst those largely forgotten are Howard Spring, Hugh Walpole, and Leo Walmsley. A literary visitor centre in Fowey provides interpretation panels for Walmsley and the locally famous Sir Arthur Quiller-Couch. Westland and Moody, amongst others, have discussed the importance of modern literature in Cornwall;[70] as they note, the evocative place-name prefixes Tre, Pol and Pen are employed by many of these novelists, including Susan Howatch, Winston Graham, Victoria Holt, Mary Williams and Mary Lide. Indeed, *Penmarric* is said to have 'provided Susan Howatch with an income for life'.[71] With their adaptation to television, Alan Kent maintains that *Poldark* and *Penmarric* had a 'cultural impact . . . [that was] massive'.[72]

Two twentieth-century authors predominate when the relationship between literature and tourism in Cornwall is considered: Daphne du Maurier and Winston Graham. Both possessed the 'evocative power of literary description' when dealing with the Cornish landscape and culture.[73] Both authors are considered here, whilst the influence of Graham's *Poldark* oeuvre on tourism is reviewed through an online data collection exercise. The fact that neither was Cornish emphasizes Alan Kent's observation that non-indigenous writers have had a major impact on the cultural construction of Cornwall.[74]

Daphne du Maurier 1907–89
It has been suggested that du Maurier's first novel, *The Loving Spirit* romanticized the Fowey area. It certainly created what was to become a life-long association with Cornwall in her fiction. Her last novel, *Rule Britannia*, set in the countryside around her homes at Menabilly and Kilmarth, near Fowey, was published in 1972. Uncannily, her last home was very nearly acquired by Winston Graham before she moved in.[75] The intervening four decades saw multiple translations and conversion of her work to the large screen, culminating in the creation of the annual Daphne du Maurier Festival, established in 1997. It has also seen the creation of a world-wide web-site, established in 1996, which receives approximately thirty thousand visits, or 'hits', per month.[76] (du Maurier's novels are listed in Appendix 1).

Jamaica Inn, Rebecca, Frenchman's Creek and *My Cousin Rachel* were published in Omnibus format by Gollancz, in 1978, under the title of 'Four Great Cornish Novels'. However, in all, nine of her novels feature Cornwall, providing a range of evocative landscape descriptions and characters. These range from the inhospitable Bodmin Moor to the gentle Helford River, the latter encapsulated in *Frenchman's Creek*. A critic in the *Observer* in August 1996 stated he would take the novels on his Cornish holiday because of 'their evocation of Cornwall's mysterious, history-sodden landscape'.[77] The portrayal of Cornwall and the past 'as dark countries'[78] is evident in *My Cousin Rachel* as well as *Jamaica Inn*, emphasized by the opening line of the former: 'They used to hang men at Four Turnings in the old days.'

For Horner and Zlosnik, du Maurier is a regional novelist. They comment that, with her work, more than providing a suitable setting '*for* the plot . . . it is inflected *by* the plot'.[79] Without doubt, as Busby and Hambly, observe 'freedom, delight, temptation and danger are to be found in du Maurier's Cornwall'.[80] Although certain authors suggest that her Cornish novels are primarily romantic fiction, appealing mostly to women,[81] a darker Gothic *genre* is readily apparent in *Jamaica Inn*. Hughes refers to the image of Cornwall, portrayed in this novel, as possessing an attractiveness because of the harshness of the landscape.[82] Does this help to attract a male readership? More recently in *The Power*, bestseller Colin Forbes utilizes the harshness of the Bodmin Moor landscape.[83] In her biography, Margaret Forster suggests that du Maurier 'felt all No.2' when writing, that is with her repressed, masculine aspect. Foster hints that, to some extent at least, this is why du Maurier's work actually appeals to both genders.[84]

Whilst numerous other authors have included Cornish locations in their plots, du Maurier was the first to attract significant popularity. Perhaps, more importantly, she was producing the novels during the period when conversion to the big screen first became a serious possibility. As Payton has recognized, although he thinks du Maurier's work more subtle than the stereotype suggests, 'it is easy to characterise Daphne du Maurier as the first of the big-house-with-windswept-woman-on-a-cliff-top genre of romantic novel writers, her works the forerunner of the multiplicity of "Cornish fiction" books that were to appear after the Second World War'.[85] *Daphne du Maurier Country*, announced on the boundary signs of Fowey and surrounding villages, shows how Restormel Borough Council has chosen an author who, whilst not indigenous, is associated with this part of South Cornwall. When this fabrication of identity is added to the recently created annual Daphne du Maurier Literary Festival, we can see clearly an instance of the cultural construction of place. Undeniably, most of the locations in her novels exist—either under their real or fictional names—and several of the characters were genuine. But the question remains: does her work portray Cornish culture as it really was, in any century? Jamaica Inn has indeed suffered many of the dead hand characteristics of Disneyfication, as Horner & Zlosnik put it.[86] Were she alive today, it is likely that Dame du Maurier would be horrified at the level of commodification of her work for tourism purposes—ironic when she wrote *Vanishing Cornwall* to depict a culture very much under threat from a range of sources including tourism.

Winston Graham 1910–2003

The books in Winston Graham's *Poldark* saga, written between 1945 and 2002, have now sold millions of copies (Appendix 2 identifies the year of publication for each title). Amazingly, the first of the titles sold seven hundred copies in the Truro branch of W.H.Smith in the month of December 1945. However, as Sinfield observes, it is only with adaptation of literature for film and television that the 'full audience' is reached.[87] Cornish tourism was certainly stimulated following conversion to the television screen, attracting fifteen millions viewers. This was further reinforced by the BBC's best-selling video-tape of the series achieving sales in 1983 and 1984 of 'about 50,000 copies'.[88] This imagery continues today through the www.poldark.com web-site. (Table 2 highlights the possibilities of the forms of literary tourism associated with Graham and du Maurier in Cornwall).

Like du Maurier, Betjeman and others, Winston Graham was not Cornish. He did, however, believe that he understood Cornwall, disparaging authors who merely used the setting. Whilst acknowledging the rich material of smuggling and wrecking available to the author, he found the social and political history of 'rotten boroughs' and mining just as useful for fictional purposes. Indeed the *Poldark* series chronicles in its own semi-researched, semi-fictional style, many of the ways in which Wesleyan Methodism brought a rejuvenated hope to the people of Cornwall. It is the relationship between Graham's *Poldark* saga and Cornish tourism which is now considered via internet message board statements.

Table 2. Forms of literary tourism associated with the works of du Maurier and Graham

Author	First Form	Second Form	Third Form	Fourth Form	Fifth Form	Six Form
Daphne du Maurier	√	√	√	√	√	√ ?
Winston Graham	√	√	√	√ ?	√	√ ?

WORDS CAUGHT IN THE WEB

As stated above, the following question was posted on an internet message board on 10 November 2003: 'Has anybody visited Cornwall specifically because of the *Poldark* books and television series?' Within ten days, eight very lengthy responses were obtained and, because of the richness of the data, some of the verbatim transcripts are displayed in full. Demonstrating the potential speed-enhanced nature of internet-assisted research, a British respondent (A) provided the following statement within a few hours of the question being posted:

> Sort of. I used to go with my aunts as a child but went back last year for the first time in nearly 20 years. I went because of Poldark but immediately recognised places that I had been to as a child and fell in love with the place.
>
> So, I went back this year and will go again next etc. It's lovely to see all the locations and put views to places mentioned in the books but that alone wouldn't sustain repeated visits if it wasn't such a beautiful county in the first place. It's strange. I know my way round Cornwall better than I do my own area. I felt instantly at home.

Respondent B, from the USA, also on 10 November stated:

> In February 2003 we travelled from Commerce, Michigan specifically to see 'Poldark country'. We were not disappointed. We took our lives in our hands and rented a car in Truro so we could see it on our terms. We loved every minute of our time there. The spectacular vistas rival our own American West for pure grandure (*sic*). I highly reccommend (*sic*) a trip to Cornwall for any Poldark fan.

Australian respondent (C) on 11 November:

> Partly we went to Cornwall firstly in 1979 because of Poldark. I had first fallen in love with Cornwall from the Derek Tangye and Howard Spring Books. It was great to visit the Poldark sites and imagine how they were back then and also knowing where it was filmed. We visited again in 2000 and some things had changed drastically. We couldn't believe what had happened at Tintagel—it was just a sleepy little village when we were there in 1979 and there were lots of tacky (sorry, but they were tacky) touristy things there when we revisited in 2000—but nothing could detract from the scenery.

> In 2000 we stayed longer and saw Bottalack (*sic*) manor . . .
> [the BBC used Botallack as Ross Poldark's home, *Nampara*,
> in the television series]

Evidently, some message board users met up physically to pursue their
common touristic interest as a result of their online interactions. The
following statement from a British respondent (D) on 12 November
reveals this:

> X (name removed)—Y (name removed) and I—who
> originally met through the Board [internet message board]—
> all visited Botallack Manor and the nearby mine ruins and
> stayed the night. We also visited—and stayed in—Truro. We
> were very impressed with the city—it seems to have retained
> many of its Georgian features. We also went to St Agnes
> (Stippy Stappy Lane), Perranporth and to Bodmin Jail [*sic*].
> My only bugbear is that a lot of places were closed such as
> Bodmin Jail—have these people not heard of year around
> tourism? But I can certainly recommend doing a Poldark trail.
> We hope to do some of the places we missed in a couple of
> years time.

Here, all the locations that she names feature in the Poldark novels,
some under their real name, others because the BBC chose to use them
in filming. The first site mentioned, Botallack Manor, now provides
Bed and Breakfast accommodation. An American respondent (E)
reveals, on 12 November, 'we have been staying at the Manor Farm
since 1990'.

On 14 November another British respondent (F) comments:

> Yes. . . . that is eventually!
> Unfortunately I never knew of or saw any of the original
> books or TV series as I was living abroad throughout most of
> the '70's, so the first I knew of Poldark at all was in 1979 when
> I bought 'The Angry Tide' in a Swedish railway station!
>   So in reply to your question 'Has anybody visited Cornwall
> specifically because of the Poldark books and television
> series?' the answer, I'm slightly embarrassed to say is yes—
> about a couple of months ago, though I've lost count of the
> number of times I've been down to Cornwall since 1985!

Links to previous respondents in answering questions is another
interesting phenomenon made possible by online message board

interactions. An American respondent (G) on 18 November 2003 demonstrates this:

> Having visited some of those Poldark places in Cornwall with Z (name removed) and Q (name removed) brought the Poldark saga that much more to life for me! I just loved Truro to bits, and I wouldn't mind living there. As Maggie said, it has maintained a lot of its Georgianess (*sic*). Cornwall would be an absolutely lovely place to live!

Finally on 20 November, another American respondent (H), made the following comment which moves away from direct reference to the question concerning Poldark and addresses wider issues to do with Cornwall's sense of difference:

> I loved Cornwall so much, I have told my sister we should retire in Truro. It's a nice size town, but does not have the overwhelming crowds that central London does. Oxford street is like that. You get swept into the crowds of walking people, and get swept along, even if you don't want to go. Give me Cornwall any day!

With no previous experience of this form of data collection, it was pleasing to achieve these lengthy responses quickly. It appears, however, that interest in message board postings wears off quickly —although there were 227 visits to the message in total. The following discussion is thus tentative, given the small, and self-selecting, sample. Nonetheless, the material is significant enough to identify certain interesting research issues.

From just these few responses, a number of themes emerge. Firstly, there is the issue of Cornwall as a literary destination *per se*. Respondent C, whilst citing Howard Spring, confirms the view that non-fiction has a place in literary tourism as well—an example of the fifth form. Derek Tangye produced The Minack Chronicles, over twenty autobiographical books, about life with his wife on a flower farm, on the West Cornwall coast, emphasizing the various animals in their life and the trials of earning a living from a small plot. The books were bestsellers in the 1960s and 1970s.

A second theme emanating from these responses is that of *loyalty*. Respondents A and F emphasize the repeat visit aspect; this has been remarked on by Busby in his study of 725 visitors to Cornwall and through content analysis of visitors' books.[89] The 'childhood and nostalgia' theme is emphasized only by respondent A and, yet, one cannot help feeling that, given an empirical study, this would be more to the fore.

Respondents A, B, C, D and G, to varying degrees, illustrate the theme of location-seeking which, as Moody[90] observes, requires a certain level of geographical knowledge because it is a composite creation. Winston Graham in his memoirs identifies some of the locations, acknowledging that some are actual and others composite. Undoubtedly, there are multiple motivations for the vast majority of visitors to Cornwall. Almost certainly, for most of the respondents cited here; the likes of respondent B, travelling from Michigan specifically to see *Poldark Country,* must be the exception rather than the rule. Table 3 summarizes the literary tourism types from the collected data.

Table 3. Forms of literary tourism associated with the *Poldark* **novels emanating from message board respondents**

Author	First Form	Second Form	Third Form	Fourth Form	Fifth Form	Sixth Form
Winston Graham	√	√	√ ?	√	√	√ ?

CONCLUSION

Novels have, undoubtedly, influenced tourist decision-making. In Cornwall particularly, Winston Graham and Daphne du Maurier are the noteworthy exemplars. Other authors have, arguably, had a subliminal effect to a greater or lesser extent; the negative imagery of Bodmin Moor in Colin Forbes' *The Power* being an unexpected example. Additionally, conversion of a novelist's work to the small or large screen brings significantly greater awareness. For instance, the *Wycliffe* books of W.J. Burley reached a much smaller audience than that achieved by adaptation for television. Indeed, Lowerson suggests that the constructed appeal of modern Cornwall depends on:

> media exploitation of Daphne du Maurier's works and the Poldark sagas, and the production of such local guides as 'Poldark Country', with its building on 'the romantic imagination of so many viewers' (Clarke, 1977: 5) to provide a text for the glove-compartment of the tourist's car.[91]

This view is perhaps too extreme. It does, however, emphasize the importance of literature and, especially, the potential viewing numbers when converted to small and large screen. Contrarily, Alan Kent makes the observation that the 'often false yet, to the outside world at least, convincing romanticisation of place' is what promotes Cornwall.[92] Local authorities and DACOM (Devon and Cornwall Overseas Marketing) deliberately use the romanticization of place in their marketing strategies. The latter organization has published a thirty page booklet, entitled *Cornwall and Devon Literary Inspiration*, detailing literary places and trails. DACOM is a consortium, established in 1995 and comprising 'all district authorities, the County Councils and Prosper, as well as the support of West Country Tourist Board'.[93]

This article has located Cornwall, as a case study, within the framework of literary tourism. A number of forms, many of which can be illustrated in the region, emanate from this research. These are: places as literary destinations *per se*; visitor loyalty; location-seeking; and the mnemonic recollections of childhood and nostalgia. Given the increasing popularity of the internet and its inherent connection with both literature and tourism promotion, the article further widens this framework to consider a contemporary expression of literary tourism as relating to the hypertext. An important caveat concerning methodology must be noted at this point: whilst internet message boards harbour a rich potential for data collection, no assumptions can be made about the representativeness of the population selected.[94] Furthermore, message board respondents are, by definition, a self-selecting group. A significant lack of ethnographic and participatory interviewing is also present in soliciting answers in this way. The intimacy of face to face contact is replaced by an electronically mediated form of communication.

On the other hand, volunteer respondents do provide evidence for a specific market. Additionally, online billboards are an incredibly quick and low cost method which can identify important themes for further research. The qualitative data collection here has demonstrated value, albeit limited in terms of external validity, for reaching specific populations. Indeed, in this case, the richness of the responses and the scope that they open for further research has been vast. Nevertheless, we would ultimately suggest that the use of open-ended internet questioning as a data gathering technique only becomes interesting or powerful when combined with other techniques.

What it has provided in this case, however, is an insight into how the development of a spirit of hyperreality has come to manifest itself in relation to Cornishness and to tourism in the area.[95] Examples of an expanding global-local nexus in the region abound. To an extent, Cornwall already exists as a sort of testing ground for the promise of social benefits from Virtual Reality technologies. The installation of a pan-regional channel of underground fibre optic cables that connects Cornwall to the outside world has been hailed for years as the solution to many of Cornwall's socio-economic plights and peripheral isolation. Interestingly here, there exists equally a significant relationship be-tween the metaphors of 'surfing the Net' and the associations towards Cornwall's surf culture and water-based leisure industry.[96] The Net is also a particularly fitting metaphor in Cornwall since nets, ropes and binding are powerful social symbols in relation to Cornwall's industrial fishing heritage.[97]

In these senses, we are beginning to witness increasingly inter-connected narrative constructions of identities in Cornwall, whereby the relationship between the newer forms of hypertext travel and the more traditional types of literary tourism offers a telling case for globalized locals and localized globals. As our ability to distinguish between reality and the imaginary dissolves, new kinds of hyper-realities develop. This is particularly connected with the messenger of the hyperreal, the electronic media. As we have seen here with the assistance of the internet, Daphne du Maurier and Winston Graham have become literary examples *par excellence* of the potential tourism draw factors that continue to influence Cornwall's local/global con-struction of place and social identities.

APPENDICES

Appendix 1. The novels of Daphne du Maurier.

The Loving Spirit	1931
I'll Never Be Young Again	1932
Julius	1933
Jamaica Inn	1936
Rebecca	1938
Frenchman's Creek	1941
Hungry Hill	1943
The King's General	1946
The Parasites	1949
My Cousin Rachel	1951
The Scapegoat	1957
Castle Dor (with 'Q')	1962
The Flight of the Falcon	1965

The House on the Strand	1969
Rule Britannia	1972

Appendix 2. The Poldark novels of Winston Graham

Ross Poldark	1945
Demelza	1946
Jeremy Poldark	1950
Warleggan	1953
The Black Moon	1973
The Four Swans	1976
The Angry Tide	1977
Stranger From The Sea	1981
The Miller's Dance	1982
The Loving Cup	1984
The Twisted Sword	1990
Bella Poldark	2002

NOTES AND REFERENCES

1. W. Graham, *Bella Poldark: A Novel of Cornwall, 1818–1820*, London, 2002, p. 688.
2. See G. Hughes, 'Tourism and the semiological realization of space', in G. Ringer (ed.), *Destinations—Cultural landscapes of tourism*, London, 1998. And I. Ousby, *The Englishman's England*, Cambridge, 1990.
3. M. Kneafsey, 'Tourism, place identities and social relations in the European rural periphery', *European Urban and Regional Studies* 7 (1), 2000, pp. 35–50.
4. www.ibdof.com viewed on 10 November 2003.
5. G. Busby, '"A true Cornish treasure": Gunwalloe and the Cornish church as visitor attraction', in Philip Payton (ed.), *Cornish Studies: Eleven*, Exeter, 2003, pp. 168–91.
6. R.V. Kozinetz, 'E-tribalized marketing?: the strategic implications of virtual communities of consumption', *European Management Journal* 17 (3), 1999, pp. 252–64.
7. S. Jones (ed.), *Doing Internet Research: Critical Issues and Methods for Examining the Net*, London, 1999.
8. D. Miller and D. Slater, *The Internet: an Ethnographic Approach*, Oxford, 2000.
9. G.E. Marcus (ed.), *Connected: Engagement with Media*, Chicago, 1996.
10. M. Crang, P. Crang and J. May (eds), *Virtual Geographies: Bodies, Space and Relations*. London, 1999.
11. C. Hine, *Virtual Ethnography*, London, 2000.
12. T. Gray, *Cornwall—The Travellers' Tales*, Exeter, 2000.
13. A.K.H. Jenkin, *The Story of Cornwall*, London, 1934.
14. Gray, ibid., p. 54.

15. J. Vernon, 'Border crossings: Cornwall and the English (imagi)nation', in G. Cubitt (ed.), *Imagining Nations*, Manchester, 1998, p. 157.

16. Vernon, 1998., p.159.

17. B. Deacon, '"The hollow jarring of the distant steam engines": images of Cornwall between West Barbary and Delectable Duchy', in E. Westland (ed.), *Cornwall—The Cultural Construction of Place*, Penzance, 1997, p. 8.

18. J. Lowerson, 'Celtic tourism—some recent magnets', in Philip Payton (ed.), *Cornish Studies: Two*, Exeter, 1994, pp. 128–37; A. Hale, 'Representing the Cornish', *Tourist Studies* 1 (2), 2001, pp. 185–96.

19. See, for example, Busby, 2003, ibid.

20. B.P. Andrew, 'Tourism and the economic development of Cornwall', *Annals of Tourism Research* 24 (3), 1997, pp. 721–35; D.C. Harvey, 'Land-scape organization, identity and change: territoriality and hagiography in medieval west Cornwall', *Landscape Research* 25 (2), 2000, pp. 201–12; K. Meethan, 'Selling the difference: Tourism marketing in Devon and Cornwall, South West England, in R. Voase (ed.), *Tourism in Western Europe—A Collection of Case Histories*, Wallingford, 2002; P. Laviolette, 'Landscaping death: resting places for Cornish identity', *Journal of Material Culture* 8 (2), 2003, pp. 215–40.

21. Cornwall County Council, *Cornwall Heritage and Culture Strategy*, Truro, 2000.

22. N. Baron-Yelles, 'Literature, tourism and the politics of nature: the making of a grand site national at La Pointe du Raz, Brittany, France', in R. Voase (ed.), *Tourism in Western Europe—A Collection of Case Histories*, Wallingford, 2002.

23. C. Brace, 'Cornish identity and landscape in the work of Arthur Caddick', Philip Payton (ed.), *Cornish Studies: Seven*, Exeter, 1999, pp. 130–46; J. Hurst, 'A poetry of dark sounds—the manuscripts of Charles Causley', in Philip Payton (ed.), *Cornish Studies: Seven*, Exeter, 1999, pp. 147–64; P. Laviolette, 1999. 'An iconography of Cornish landscape images in art and prose', in Philip Payton (ed.), *Cornish Studies: Seven*, Exeter, 1999, pp. 107–29.

24. A. Hale, 'Whose Celtic Cornwall?' in D.C. Harvey, R. Jones, N. McInroy and C. Milligan (eds), *Celtic Geographies: Old Culture, New Times*, London, 2002.

25. P. Payton, *Cornwall*, Fowey, 1996, p. 26.

26. D.M. Thomas, *Birthstone*, London, 1982.

27. G. Busby, 'The Cornish church heritage as destination component', *Tourism* 50 (4), 2002, pp. 371–81. 'The contested Cornish church heritage', in Philip Payton (ed.), *Cornish Studies: Twelve*, 2004, Exeter, pp. 166–83.

28. D.C. Harvey, 'Heritage pasts and heritage presents: temporality, meaning and the scope of heritage studies', *International Journal of Heritage Studies* 7 (4), 2001, pp. 319–38.

29. J. Hurst, 'Literature in Cornwall', in P. Payton (ed.), *Cornwall Since The War*, Redruth, 1993, p. 296.

30. D. Inglis and M. Holmes, 'Highland and other haunts', *Annals of Tourism Research* 30 (1), 2003, pp. 50–63.

31. A. Hale and P. Payton (eds), *New Directions in Celtic Studies*, Exeter, 2000.
32. M. Chapman, *The Celts: the Construction of a Myth*, Basingstoke, 1992. M. Kneafsey, 'Tourism images and the construction of Celticity in Ireland and Brittany', in D.C. Harvey, R. Jones, N. McInroy and C. Milligan (eds), *Celtic Geographies: Old Culture, New Times*. London, 2002, p. 124.
33. M. Bowman, 'The commodification of the Celt: new age/neo-pagan consumerism', in T. Brewer (ed.), *The Marketing of Tradition: Perspectives on Folklore, Tourism and the Heritage Industry*, Chippenham, 1994, cited in Kneafsey, 2002, ibid. Hale 2002, ibid.
34. Kneafsey, 2002, ibid.
35. D.C. Harvey, R. Jones, N. McInroy and C. Milligan, 'Timing and Spacing Celtic Geographies', in D.C. Harvey, R. Jones, N. McInroy and C. Milligan (eds), *Celtic Geographies: Old Culture, New Times*, London, 2002.
36. B. Deacon and P. Payton, 'Re-inventing Cornwall: culture change on the European Periphery', in Philip Payton (ed.), *Cornish Studies: One*, Exeter, 1993, pp. 62–79 (p. 63).
37. A. Pritchard and N. Morgan, 'Culture, identity and tourism representation: marketing Cymru or Wales?', *Tourism Management* 22 (2), 2001, pp. 167–79.
38. N. Kennedy and N. Kingcome, 'Disneyfication of Cornwall—developing a Poldark Heritage Complex', *International Journal of Heritage Studies* 4 (1), 1998, pp. 45–59 (p. 58).
39. J. Boissevain, 'Ritual, tourism and cultural commoditization in Malta: culture by the pound', in T. Selwyn (ed.), *The Tourist Image: Myths and Myth Making in Tourism*, Chichester, 1996.
40. B. Deacon, 'Cornish culture or the culture of the Cornish?' *Cornish Scene* NS1, 1988, pp. 58–60, cited in Hale 2001.
41. D. Uzzell, 'Creating place identity through heritage interpretation', *International Journal of Heritage Studies* 1 (4), 1996, pp. 219–28; W. Nuryanti, 'Heritage and postmodern tourism', *Annals of Tourism Research* 23 (2), 1996, pp. 249–60.
42. N. Morgan and A. Pritchard, *Tourism Promotion and Power: Creating Images, Creating Identities*, Chichester, 1998.
43. R. Butler, 'Literature as an influence in shaping the image of tourist destinations', in J.S. Marsh (ed.), *Canadian Studies of Parks, Recreation and Tourism in Foreign Lands*. Canada: Department of Geography, Trent University, 1986, p. 115.
44. D.C.D. Pocock, 'Catherine Cookson Country: Tourist Expectation and Experience', *Geography* 77 (3), 1992, pp. 236–43.
45. D.T. Herbert, 'Heritage as literary place', in D.T. Herbert (ed.), *Heritage, Tourism and Society*, London, 1995.
46. N. Moody, 'Poldark Country and National Culture, in E. Westland (ed.), *Cornwall—The Cultural Construction of Place*, Penzance, 1997.
47. D. Clarke, *Poldark Country*, St. Teath, 1977, cited in Lowerson 1994; W. Graham, *Poldark's Cornwall*, Exeter, 1983.

48. Butler, 1986, ibid., p. 118.
49. I. Finlayson, *Writers in Romney Marsh*, London, 1986; E. Bird and L. Modlock, *Writers on the South-West Coast*, Bradford on Avon, 1994.
50. R.L. Green, *Authors and Places—a literary Pilgrimage*, London, 1963.
51. F. Morley, *Literary Britain*. London, 1980.
52. M. Drabble, *A Writer's Britain: Landscape in Literature*, London, 1984.
53. S. Varlow, *A Reader's Guide to Writers' Britain*, London, 1996.
54. S. Hill, *The Spirit of Britain: An Illustrated Guide to Literary Britain*, London, 1994.
55. M. Bradbury, *The Atlas of Literature*. London, 1996.
56. G. Busby and Z. Hambly, 'Literary tourism and the Daphne du Maurier Festival', in Philip Payton (ed.), *Cornish Studies: Eight*, Exeter, 2000, pp. 197–212.
57. Green, 1963.
58. D.C.D. Pocock, 'Imaginative literature and the geographer', in D.C.D. Pocock (ed.), *Humanistic Geography and Literature—Essays on the Experience of Place*, London, 1981, p. 13.
59. D.C.D. Pocock, 'Writers who knew their places', *Geographical Magazine* 54 (1), 1982, pp. 40–43.
60. G. Busby, P. Brunt and J. Lund, 'In Agatha Christie country: resident perception of special interest tourism', *Tourism* 51 (3), 2003, pp. 287–300.
61. G. Busby and J. Klug, 'Movie induced tourism: the challenge of measurement and other issues', *Journal of Vacation Marketing* 7 (4), 2001, pp. 316–32.
62. J. Seal, *The Wreck at Sharpnose Point*, London, 2002.
63. D. Herbert, 'Literary places, tourism and the heritage experience', *Annals of Tourism Research* 28 (2), 2001, pp. 312-33 (p. 313).
64. J. McAleer, *Popular Reading and Publishing in Britain, 1914-1950*, Oxford, 1992, p. 87.
65. McAleer, 1992, p. 87.
66. K. O'Neill, S. Butts and G. Busby, 'The Corellification of Cephallonian Tourism', *Anatolia*, 16 (2), 2005, pp. 207–26.
67. Butler, 1986.
68. P. Wreyford, *A literary tour of Devon*, Chudleigh, 1996.
69. Busby and Hambly, 2000.
70. E. Westland, 'The passionate periphery: Cornwall and romantic fiction', in I.A. Bell (ed.), *Peripheral Visions*, Cardiff, 1995. Moody 1997.
71. Hurst, 1993, p. 293.
72. A.M. Kent, 'Screening Kernow: authenticity, heritage and the representation of Cornwall in film and television, 1913-2003', in Philip Payton (ed.), *Cornish Studies: Eleven*, Exeter, 2003, pp. 110–41 (p. 116).
73. J.P. Sharp, 'Towards a critical analysis of fictive geographies', *Area* 32 (3), 2000, pp. 327–34 (p. 327).
74. A.M. Kent, 'The Cornish Alps: resisting romance in the clay country', in E. Westland (ed.), *Cornwall—The Cultural Construction of Place*, Penzance, 1997.

75. W. Graham, *Memoirs of a Private Man*, Basingstoke, 2003.
76. www.dumaurier.org 2003.
77. N. Spencer, 'Critics' favourite summer reading'. *The Observer Review*, 1996, 4 August, p.16, cited in Horner and Zlosnik, 1998, op. cit. p. 16.
78. A. Horner and S. Zlosnik, *Daphne du Maurier—Writing, Identity and the Gothic Imagination*, Basingstoke, 1998, p. 143.
79. Ibid.
80. Busby and Hambly, 2000, p. 200.
81. Horner and Zlosnik, 1998.
82. H. Hughes, 'A Silent, Desolate Country: images of Cornwall in Daphne du Maurier's Jamaica Inn', in E. Westland (ed.), *Cornwall—The Cultural Construction of Place*, Penzance, 1997.
83. C. Forbes, *The Power*, London, 1995.
84. M. Forster, *Daphne du Maurier*, London, 1993, p. 276.
85. Payton, 1996; Forster, p. 262.
86. A. Horner and S. Zlosnik, '"I for this and this for me": Daphne du Maurier and "regional writing"', *Working Papers in Literary and Cultural Studies No. 13*, Salford European Studies Research Institute, 1994.
87. A. Sinfield, *Literature, politics and culture in postwar Britain*, London, 1997, p. xxviii.
88. C. Davies, 'BBC pride as 50,000 buy Austen video', *Daily Telegraph*, 25 October 1995.
89. Busby, 2002; 2003; 2004, ibid.
90. Moody, 1997, ibid.
91. Lowerson, 1994, ibid., p. 130.
92. Kent, 1997, ibid., p. 56.
93. K. Meethan, 'New tourism for old? Policy developments in Cornwall and Devon', *Tourism Management* 19 (6), 1998, pp. 583–93 (p. 589).
94. Y. Poria and H. Oppewal, 'A new medium for data collection: online news discussions', *International Journal of Contemporary Hospitality Management* 15 (4), 2003, pp. 232–6.
95. U. Eco, *Travels in Hyperreality*, New York Harcourt, 1986; J. Baudrillard, 'The virtual illusion: or the automatic writing of the world', *Theory, Culture & Society* 12, 1995, pp. 97–107.
96. P. Laviolette, Forthcoming. 'Green and extreme: Free-flowing through seascape and sewer', *Worldviews: Environment, Culture, Religion* (special issue on the sociological dimensions of water), Jan. 2006.
97. P. Laviolette, 'Where difference lies: Performative metaphors of truth, deception and placelessness in the Cornish peninsula', in L. Hill and H. Paris (eds), *Place and Placelessness in Performance*, Basingstoke, 2005; Ships of relations: Navigating through local Cornish maritime art. *International Journal of Heritage Studies* 12 (1), 2006, in press.

CORNISH COPPER MINING 1795–1830: ECONOMY, STRUCTURE AND CHANGE

Jim Lewis

'There are few persons resident in Cornwall who are not, either directly or indirectly, interested in the prosperity of its mines.'

'AZ' writing on the copper trade
in the West Briton, 14 December 1821

INTRODUCTION

In his book *Cornwall* Philip Payton comments on the early industrialization of the Cornish economy, lamenting that 'the complex experience of Cornish industrialisation [has been] marginalised and dismissed in gross oversimplification' and underlining 'the increased interest in comparative regional industrialisation'.[1] He continues this theme in *Cornish Studies: Ten*, suggesting that Cornwall's failure to receive full recognition for its contribution to the Industrial Revolution is fed by 'a sketchy knowledge of Cornish mining history' amongst scholars.[2] Gill Burke and Peter Richardson have suggested that 'for too long the history of Cornish mining has been characterised by provincialism and anecdotalism'.[3] This overview is intended to look at copper mining in the round and to place it within a broad context. The article contains a brief comparison of Cornwall's copper and tin economies, supported by statistics in the appendix. The period reviewed covers war and peace and strong, sustained growth in British industrial production.[4] The letterbooks of William Jenkin (mineral agent to the Lanhydrock estate and later copper agent to the smelters Williams Grenfell) have been heavily used in researching this article and, where possible, cross checking has confirmed the information they contain.

THE MARKET

One estimate for the total British production of copper metal at the end of the eighteenth century (1798) is 7,500/8,000 tons with Cornish ore producing 70/75 per cent of the total and the balance largely made up by ore from Anglesey. An estimated 70 per cent of British copper went in exports, either as copper goods or the copper content of brass (approximately two thirds copper, one third zinc) items. A substantial part of the export trade was underwritten by the East India Company which was required under its charter to make annual purchases of 1,500 tons of British copper.[5] Birmingham[6] was the centre of the brass and copper trades and by 1800 brass was its most important industry.[7] The numerous end users there contrasted greatly with the number of firms who bought the copper ore from the mines. Virtually all Cornish copper ore was taken to South Wales for smelting, and throughout the period there were only about twelve copper companies who bid at the public ticketings for ore with a few firms in a dominant position. Other firms came and went. From time to time the copper companies did arrange price fixing rings between themselves and they also tried to make it difficult for new entrants to come into the market. These arrangements broke down and, despite short-term market manipulation, ultimately the price paid for copper ore reflected demand from the end users of the metal.[8] Some copper companies had major share-holdings in mines and presumably they obtained their ore direct from them.[9]

WAR

John Rowe identified that 'the high prices of copper during the years of the French Wars . . . do not accurately reflect the state of the Cornish Mines in that period'.[10] Mining costs rose significantly, with William Jenkin referring to a 70% rise in mining materials and wages in the four years to 1801, and in 1807 he wrote of a 'great advance in balk, deals, hemp and iron' as a consequence of the war in the Baltic.[11] The price of balk timber supplied to the Cornish mines rose from the pre-decimal equivalent 10p per foot in 1800 to 20p in 1810. Over the same period the price of a hundredweight of ropes increased from £3.30 to £4.20 whilst the price of bar iron per hundredweight fell from £1.03 in 1800 to 73p in 1810, suggesting that for iron the 1807 price rise was temporary. The price of a wey of coal at the mines rose from £4.08 in 1800 to £4.27 in 1810.[12] Wartime disruption of international commerce led to a decline in Birmingham's exports of copper and brass items. Napoleon's trade embargoes against Britain were put into effect in 1810 and the retaliatory Orders in Council caused further problems by disrupting the town's trade with the USA.[13] Cornish copper mining was squeezed between restricted demand and rising costs.

There is ample evidence to show that copper mining struggled during the war years. The parliamentary report of 1799 into 'The State of the Copper Mines and Copper Trade of this Kingdom' (the '1799 Report') listed North Downs, United Mines, the Consolidated Mines, Wheal Unity (worked in conjunction with the neighbouring Poldice) and Tincroft as the five major Cornish ore producers contributing about 50 per cent of Cornwall's output. The first three were described in evidence as 'old, deep mines' and, by inference, costly to operate.[14] North Downs and the United Mines had faded away by 1805 with Tincroft barely surviving after the exhaustion of its ore reserve.[15] The large price rise of copper ore that year (see appendix) was possibly the result of speculative buying and hoarding of copper in anticipation of a large government contract for a new copper coinage.[16] Ore prices peaked in June 1805 but confidence in the market was undermined when the East India Company refused to make its annual purchase of copper metal and it was further dented when the government contracted to import 1,000 tons of copper from Siberia for the Royal Navy rather than pay the high domestic price.[17] Ore prices fell heavily in the next three years and a leading producer in the early 1800s, Crenver and Oatfield, closed in 1806.[18] In its edition of 24 January 1807 the *Royal Cornwall Gazette* reported that the trade in Cornwall had sunk 'to a deplorable state', and deputations from the Cornish mining interests requested the government to give up the Russian contract and prevail upon the East India Company to take more copper.[19] The Company resumed its purchases (not always the full 1,500 tons) in a buyers' market. The *Royal Cornwall Gazette* of 27 July 1811 feared 'that more than one of our large mines will soon be stopped working owing to the high price of materials and the low rate of ores'. The Consolidated Mines closed shortly afterwards,[20] leaving only Wheal Unity & Poldice of the five top mines in the 1799 Report as a continuous long term producer. Even it temporarily stopped its pumping engines in November 1806 when it was said to be making losses on ore sales of £10,000 per month.[21]

The 1799 report shows no evidence of significant outside involvement in Cornish copper mining and the industry appears to have been largely financed from within Cornwall.[22] This changed in 1809 as London capital flowed in to reopen major mines that the Cornish had abandoned. Clearly, the new investors had an optimistic view of the industry's future and ore prices rose significantly in 1809.[23] The United Mines and Crenver & Oatfield restarted, the latter being consolidated with the adjoining Wheal Abraham. Chacewater Mine (Wheal Busy) was also reopened, the shareholders in all three of the new ventures being mainly Londoners. The costs of getting United Mines and Chacewater up and running were £80,000 and £30,000 respectively with Crenver, Oatfield and Wheal Abraham carrying a deficit of £60,000 by October 1812.[24] The impact of these reopened mines on Cornish production was significant, with the United Mines and Crenver Consolidated alone contributing 20 per cent of Cornwall's ticketed ore sales of 74,047 tons in 1813.[25] The discovery of large shallow ore deposits at Crinnis mine marked the birth of the St Austell area as a major copper producer and here the adventurers (shareholders) made profits of £120,000 between 1811 and 1816.[26] Following the end of the war, in 1816 Cornish ores supplied 85 per cent of the 8,200 tons of British copper metal produced and this dominance continued up to 1830 and beyond. From 1795 to 1816 the top four producing mines regularly supplied 40/50 per cent of the ticketed ores sold in Cornwall.[27]

PEACE

The immediate impact of peace on the Cornish mining industry is captured in a letter from William Jenkin to the smelter Pascoe Grenfell on 10 September 1816:

> I cannot say that I can point out even one mine of any considerable note that is likely to stop very soon – for although the standard[28] has dropped far below what it was once thought they could have borne yet by the late reduction in the prices of most mining materials, and by a species of economy that necessity has produced, I do not see that there is much loss sustained, in any of the mines, even in those that are very deep . . . the labourers gettings are greatly reduced, so that instead of 60/- or 70/- [£3/£3.50] per month, they are now generally reduced to about 40/- [£2] and some even lower, and when that will not support their families the overseers of the poor are frequently applied to for the remainder – to this must be added a great reduction in the stock of materials and halvans [coarse ores] in the mines . . . the Lords [landlords] of many mines have given up *all* their dues [and] others have made some abatement according as circumstances vary – I know but one mine which under the present depression can be said to be absolutely paying its present cost, and that is United Mines, but I believe there is no profit, for I understand from one of the agents of this mine the monthly regular cost is from £4,000 to £5,000.[29]

The price of many mining materials fell like a stone. Balk timber was down from 20p to 7p per foot in 1820 and 5p in 1830. Ropes similarly reduced from £4.20 to £2.43p and £2 per hundredweight respectively with a wey of coal which had cost £4.27 down to £2.67 in 1820 and £2.55 in 1830.[30] The big Cornish casualty during the post-war readjustment was Wheal Alfred which closed in 1816 having been Cornwall's leading copper ore producer from 1811 to 1815.[31] With the gradual return of normal international trade Birmingham's brass and copper industries faced a rosier future aided by a large pool of labour made redundant from the town's armament trades. A savage post war depression continued there until the start of the 1820s but by 1823 the town was in a state of full employment. Birmingham had 50 brass manufacturers in 1800 and 160 in 1830; the number of brassworks there increased from 50 to 280 in the same period.[32] In Cornwall London adventurers reopened the Consolidated Mines under the superintendence of the London mine manager John Taylor in 1819 and in 1822 it began its long period as the leading Cornish copper mine. By 1837 its adventurers had received dividends totalling £248,000 in addition to the return of their capital at £65,000.[33] Its success started a new influx of London money into Cornish mining, the *West Briton* of 26 September 1823 commenting that 'Mining speculations are becoming, more than ever, a favourite mode of investing money with the London capitalists . . . so sanguine are the expectations in those new adventures that the shares of all of them already sell at a premium, a circumstance very rare in the commencement of such undertakings when the actual expenditure is great, and the hope of a return distant.'

This was part of a general enthusiasm for mining speculation which saw huge sums invested by the British in South America.[34] Londoners bought out the Cornish interest in the United Mines and, amongst others, restarted Wheal Alfred and Chacewater Mine (Wheal Busy) under John Taylor's management.[35] Not only were the costs of mining supplies falling but major improvements in steam engine efficiency after 1825 were also reducing the costs of mine drainage.[36] Under Taylor, Wheal Alfred again failed during the financial crisis of 1825/26 with a loss of £50,000[37] but of the top five ore producers in 1826 only Dolcoath was not under his direction. In total he managed eleven copper mines producing 40 per cent of Cornish ore sold at the ticketings that year.[38] Despite Cornish opposition in 1827 a bill was passed in parliament allowing British copper companies to smelt foreign copper ores for re-export without the payment of import duties. The government maintained that import duties still gave British copper a virtual monopoly of the home market, but there were concerns in Cornwall that the bill would allow foreign ores to be smelted more cheaply which would enable foreign copper to compete more effectively with Britain in the international market.[39] By 1830 the top four producing copper ore in Cornwall were the Consolidated Mines and Dolcoath from the 'traditional' copper areas around St Day and Camborne/Redruth, with the newer ore fields represented by Wheal Leisure at Perranporth and Fowey Consols near St Austell. These four mines produced 40,000 tons of ore or 30 per cent of the total, continuing the trend where a small number of mines contributed a high proportion of the total output.[40] The amount of ore sold at the ticketings in the period 1816–30 was 52 per cent higher than that sold in the preceding fifteen years, the number of mines selling more than 1,000 tons of ore annually increasing from 17 in 1815 to 34 in 1830. Following its reopening in 1799 Dolcoath was rarely out of the top three throughout the period 1800–30 and it provided 10 per cent of Cornwall's copper ore sold at the ticketings during that time.

LANDOWNERS, ADVENTURERS AND MINING FINANCE
The evidence suggests a very difficult war for copper mining and a better peace with two major influxes of London capital into an industry previously dominated by the Cornish. What systems were in place to cope in an often volatile industry where large amounts of money changed hands? In 1821 the Cornish mineral agent of the Marquis of Buckingham told him that mines in Cornwall were much more plentiful than those who wished to speculate in them and there were, he supposed, five chances out of six that any adventurer would be a loser in a mine.[41] Given these unattractive odds it is not surprising that there is no evidence that Cornish landowners of this (or any other) period tried solely to operate their own mines. The rent they levied on mining companies was in the form of 'dues' and paid on a proportion of ore sales, from about one eighth for shallow mines down to one twenty-fourth or less for deep and expensive ventures with steam engines.[42] Mining leases lasted for 21 years and usually contained clauses requiring adventurers to complete specific tasks to ensure that they energetically worked the mine.[43] Landowners often reduced dues until new mines had recovered their initial costs and, as indicated in Jenkin's letter of 1816, cancelled them altogether in difficult times.[44] In world terms copper is not a rare metal, and the protection Cornish copper mining enjoyed through import duties was subject to government policy.[45]

Cornish landowners were uniquely well placed to promote the interests of the mining industry through their control over many of Cornwall's 44 seats in parliament. From his Governorship of the Cornish Metal Company in the 1780s through to the 1820s the landowner of Dolcoath and other large mines, Francis Basset, Lord De Dunstanville, was a major political player in Cornwall and a major campaigner for the mining industry.[46] In 1799 he played a leading role when the Cornish lobby put pressure on the government to prevent the passing of a bill originating in Birmingham which would have restricted both copper sales to the East India Company and the duties on imported copper.[47] In 1810 he helped save Cornish mining from being associated with the anti-government stance of a new local newspaper to be called the *West Briton, or Miners Journal*. Protests headed by De Dunstanville and Lord Falmouth ensured that *or Miners Journal* was dropped from the title.[48] Following a public meeting in October 1810 to discuss the distressed state of copper mining, De Dunstanville lobbied the Board of Trade requesting support for the industry. The meeting thanked De Dunstanville 'for the attention he has uniformly paid to the interests of the Cornish Miner'.[49] It was not for nothing that the monument to him was erected on the top of Carn Brea to loom over the surrounding mining district.

With its uncertainty, mining was mostly a flexible partnership between landowner and mining tenants, and owners often took minority shareholdings in mines sunk on their land.[50] The 1799 Parliamentary Report shows that the average number of shareholders in 17 major Cornish copper mines was 17 with the highest at 30 and the lowest at 11. Many shareholders had interests in several mines.[51] Contemporary correspondence does not show a large trade in shares amongst the Cornish: there was no central market and shares were bought and sold by word of mouth.[52] These 'cost book' shareholdings brought with them unlimited liability to outside creditors. Adventurers with property in Cornwall could have their assets seized under the Stannary laws to pay debts.[53] In losing mines presumably shareholders settled up amongst themselves in proportion to their shareholdings after paying off the mine's creditors. Merchant shareholders in Cornish mines have received a bad press through their reputation for overcharging.[54] When the lease on the highly profitable Tincroft Mine expired in 1803 and a new lease was being prepared, the Quaker Fox family of merchants and engine manufacturers were offered 12 per cent of the shares in the mine by the landowners.[55] Why, then, were the Foxes invited in? A look at mining finance seems to provide the answer.

Inward cashflow for mines was quite rapid; they received payment for their copper ore one month after sale by a 30 day bill of exchange, but this two month delay could be halved by borrowing against the bill.[56] The money passed through the hands of a purser who ran his own accounts on behalf of a mine and who passed cash payments and receipts through the cost book. Profits were paid away regularly to adventurers with little left as a reserve. If the mine needed to make calls on the shareholders for additional cash they had the choice of either paying up, renouncing or (if they could find a buyer) selling their shares.[57] Mines did not need a substantial cash reserve because they were supported by credit supplied to them by merchants and others against the perceived personal wealth of their shareholders. Pursers could either help or hinder the cashflow of a mine. At Wheal Alfred in 1809 the purser delayed the payment of a dividend having lent money to the neighbouring Wheal Ann.[58] In 1815 he allowed the payment of a dividend at Wheal Alfred despite the adventurers being in debt to him for £10,000.[59] Jenkin's letters show an ambivalent attitude to merchant shareholders. In 1802 he wrote that they 'become adventurers in [mines] for the purpose of promoting their trade . . . merchants are more likely to keep up deep mines, than others who adventure with hard cash only—consequently [they are] the best people for proprietors to have recourse to'.[60] In 1817 he told a copper smelter that merchants prolonged mines to benefit their trade but it had the beneficial side effect of employing labourers for longer.[61]

Merchants played a significant role in providing extended credit to mines leaving the shareholders to provide less capital themselves. Jenkin described the Foxes as 'by far the greatest Adventurers in Mines in the County' and 'the principal props of mining' in Cornwall.[62] When De Dunstanville's mine at Dolcoath reopened in 1799 he and the Fox family were amongst the shareholders: in 1802 the adventurers owed the Foxes £34,000. Following losses by the mine they were still owed 'enormous sums' in 1804.[63] After Herland mine closed in 1817 the Neath Abbey Co and the Perran Foundry Co (both owned by the Foxes) and the Hayle Foundry agreed to take back equipment they had supplied to the mine in part satisfaction of debts.[64] Chacewater mine had 1,000 employees in 1817 and when it faced closure local merchants and traders agreed to supply it for a further two months even though its London adventurers and local banks had withdrawn their support.[65] Capital accumulated from profits by the wealthy Cornish merchant-bourgeoisie identified by Bernard Deacon[66] was lent back to the mines in the form of credit granted. It is not difficult to see how money percolated through the system from mining into the pockets of local businessmen. Taking 1798 as an example, Cornish copper mines paid away £250,000 in wages and £150,000 for materials and equipment.[67] Merchants supplying Cornish mines can probably be seen as heroes rather than villains because they reinvested their profits in mining, unlike many shareholders and landowners who syphoned their mining profits into other less risky areas.[68] The self-regulating side of Cornish merchants' mines can be seen at Cardrew Downs mine in 1825 which was supplied jointly by the Foxes and John Williams of Scorrier. William Jenkin had been succeeded in his various roles by his son Alfred by this time and, in his opinion, the 'high character' of the Fox/Williams partnership ensured the prices paid at Cardrew Downs were in conformity with other mines and that the mine was 'conducted fairly'.[69] It was not just the commercial classes that supplied credit. To the extent that it was used at this time the 'month in hand' system meant that the workforce employed on contract were paid two months in arrears which synchronized with the mines' own cycle of payment from the copper companies.[70]

THE WORKFORCE
In common with other mining areas of Britain, work in Cornish mines was mainly carried out by contract. Cornwall was unusual in putting these contracts out to competitive tender every two months, the system procuring 'a great deal of effective labour in proportion to the money paid for it'.[71] Mines granted subsistence payments to workers to tide them over delays in the payment of wages. Many of the workforce used credit provided by shopkeepers to purchase food with hardware and clothes bought with a form of hire-purchase.[72] In 1787 the labour force in Cornwall's copper mines was thought to be 7,200 and a rough calculation suggests that about 8,000 were employed in 1800, 11,000 in 1816 and 20,000 in 1830.[73] About 40 per cent of those employed were women, boys and girls.[74] During the difficult war years there are frequent references in Jenkin's letters to hardship in the mining areas.[75] The payment of poor rates by the mines was calculated on the landowners' dues. They were considered an 'odious burden' and a matter of negotiation between landowner and adventurers on which party should pay them.[76]

Major mine closures brought major problems in their wake. Having employed over 1,000 workers in 1815 the post-war demise of Wheal Alfred in 1816 brought an end to mining in the parishes of Phillack and Gwinear. A total population of about 4,500 lost its economic mainstay, and in 1817 'many stout young men offer[ed] to bind themselves to farmers, in the same manner that parish apprentices are bound'.[77] After Wheal Alfred reopened it was found to be 'a poor mine' in 1825 and it when closed in May 1826 it threw the 500 then employed out of work once again.[78] By this time their chances of finding alternative employment were much greater. Cornish miners were following London capital and emigrating to mines in the New World, and at home their industry was expanding.[79] In June 1825 Alfred Jenkin wrote of 'so many captains who have lately been raised from the ranks of common miners that I do not know one half of them'.[80] This says as much about the close-knit mining community of former years as it does about the new opportunities arising.

THE LONDON ADVENTURERS

A lack of investment in mining by the Cornish during the difficult years of the early 1800s left the door open to London capital. Traditionally, Cornish shareholdings were expressed in (sometimes complicated) fractions but to simplify matters the prospectus circulated in London for the reopening of Herland mine in 1815 divided the venture into 1,000 shares whilst the Consolidated Mines reopened in 1819 with 100 shares.[81] The Londoners soon found that they were operating amongst webs of long-established personal, business, political and family interests bound together by trust, unwritten rules and accepted standards of behaviour maintained through respect or fear. Life outside this Cornish club could be harsh. A study of the reopening of the United Mines in 1809 taken from a newspaper report of a court case in 1818[82] provides a Londoner's view of the industry and an insight into their difficulties. In many cases they were major investors in businesses which they little understood and over which they had little control. For them dividends were all important, whilst the Cornish benefited generally from mining money circulating through Cornwall in terms of labourers' wages and social stability, increased profits for traders and lower poor rates.

The prospectus for the reopening of the United Mines was circulated in London in 1809 by Capt Joseph Sowell of Penryn, a sea captain of a coastal trader. The adventurers paid a premium to Sowell of £50 for every one-sixty-fourth share sold and Sowell received a salary of £50 per month.[83] The opening capital of £40,000 was soon exhausted and 'loss followed loss until the ruin of some adventurers was complete'. At this stage the adventurers discovered that Sowell was charging them 1/12th dues and paying the landowners 1/24th, pocketing the difference. He was taken to court, made to refund £3,000, and the management of the mine and pursership was put into the hands of the Williams family of Scorrier with the stipulation that double-entry bookkeeping should be adopted. By May 1815 the mine accounts showed that it was carrying accumulated losses of £11,000 and the adventurers paid up to settle the debts. The Williamses then sent the adventurers a letter from the Fox family stating that they were owed more than £20,000, but the duplicate cost book held in London showed that much of this money had already been paid. There was a subsequent dispute about who had paid what to whom, the adventurers contending that the duplicate cost book did not show a true state of affairs, only enough to encourage them to keep the mine going. In July 1818 mine profits had reduced outstanding debts to £18,500 'no part of which has yet been charged to the cost book or, if charged, not divided and collected, as it was the duty of the defendants as pursers to do'. The adventurers then sent down a John Swan from London to look after their interests and supply the mine with 1/5th of its materials, but 'no sooner had this gentleman procured wharves and conveniences for supplying these mines with coals than the price of that article was lowered by the Portreath Company of which the defendant, Mr John Williams, is the managing partner, from 72/6d [£3.63] to 59/- [£2.95] a wey, a price at which he knew Mr Swan could not deliver coals at the United Mines with profit'.

At the trial, the Williamses and Foxes were described by the plaintiff's solicitor as 'opulent' and that 'either directly or by their connections they are able to influence the whole trade and mining interests of the county'. The Williamses were accused of forcing out competition and attempting to 'absorb the capital of rivals by length of credit'. They were alleged to have paid a dividend although the mine was in debt in order to recover money they had lent to an adventurer in their capacity as bankers. Their counsel contended that their conduct had been 'fair and honourable' and dictated by a 'desire to benefit the adventurers and secure the continuance of the United Mines, an object of the greatest consequence to the county at large'. The case was thrown out on a technicality and the matter seems to have died down although suspicions remained, partially based on the accounting problem. The events illustrate the difficulties in transmitting the true state of a business to remote shareholders who were not prepared to rely on trust, a problem which still tests the accountancy profession today. Despite the criticism of Williams' management, between 1816 and 1822 the United Mines were in the forefront of Cornish copper producers. Following a change of shareholders in 1823, the mine passed into the managership of John Taylor.[84]

JOHN TAYLOR

Taylor was a trusted conduit through which outside capital flowed into Cornish mining. His early career started about 1800 in west Devon where he managed mines for the banking, brewing and sugar refining Martineau family of Norwich.[85] Their support continued as his business expanded in the 1820s and his reputation as a mine manager was aided by favourable publicity following his profitable reopening of the Consolidated Mines in 1819. Through articles in national and local journals and newspapers he established himself as the promoter and voice of mining modernization and progress.[86] It is no coincidence that Charles

Babbage obtained information on Cornish mining from Taylor when writing his influential *The Economy of Machinery and Manufactures* in the 1830s.[87] Taylor was independent of the local financial and trading interests which had helped sustain Cornish copper mining through its difficult years: with adequate London capital at his disposal[88] he was doubtless able to drive hard bargains with his local suppliers. His reputation was burnished after his death by Robert Hunt in his book *British Mining: A Treatise* published in 1887:

> The influence exerted by Mr Taylor on mining generally was most remarkable, and as it regards Cornish mining was of especial importance. Every branch of mining was improved, new machinery was introduced, and the condition of the steam pumping-engines was during his reign so greatly improved that the Cornish engine became a pattern to the civilised world . . . By honesty of purpose, by well directed industry, and by devotion to the business of subterranean exploration, he restored mining to a healthful and profitate state . . . an important industry was saved from ruin by the energy of one mind.[89]

Taylor patronized the engineer Arthur Woolf. This same passage, however, could equally well have been written about John Williams who employed William and James Sims as engineers.[90] Cornwall's mining industry was 'saved' by a changed economic climate. The practical side of Taylor's Cornish business was founded on the knowledge and skills of William Davey of Redruth[91] and men like him, and Taylor introduced Cornish captains and methods as his business expanded beyond Cornwall.[92] What he did bring to Cornwall was a talent for sophisticated marketing and publicity which enabled him to present himself as the new man for the new era. The London capital which brought him to prominence in Cornwall had largely ebbed away by the mid-1830s, leaving the industry mainly in local hands once again.[93]

TECHNOLOGICAL CHANGE

Cornish metal mining and its techniques developed at a time when the study of geology was in its infancy. In 1837 Taylor wrote that he did not know of any major mining improvements that had recently come about through improved geological knowledge, stating that 'hitherto geology has rather been indebted to mining, than mining to geology'.[94] In 1814 the Royal Geological Society of Cornwall was founded to promote its study, acquiring its royal patronage through De Dunstanville's friend the Prince Regent. It was the second oldest geological society in Britain.[95]

Cornwall's important role in the development of the steam engine is well known. A contemporary estimate suggests that the average engine in Cornwall was consuming 60 per cent less coal in 1835 than its equivalent elsewhere would have done in 1814.[96] There has been a struggle to explain why its development in Cornwall, apparently stalled between the expiry of Boulton & Watt's engine patent in 1800 and 1811, the latter being the year when Arthur Woolf returned to Cornwall and the publication of Lean's *Engine Reporter* commenced. It is less of a puzzle if accounts of 'wretched', 'miserable' and worn-out steam engines and leaking boilers during that time are seen as descriptions of a generally unprofitable and demoralized industry struggling to survive rather than of declining engineering standards as such.[97] London capital flowing into Cornwall in 1809 gave copper mining a major boost and probably accounts for Woolf's return.

Writing in 1827 Joseph Carne cited longer working hours, the introduction of underground tramways, better underground ventilation (comparatively) and better maintenance of adits and surface drains as recent improvements. He felt that the widespread recent introduction of overhand stoping (sinking below an ore deposit and mining it from underneath) required less timbering and was more efficient than the underhand stoping it replaced. He commented on the crushing mills that had been recently introduced, and these were later followed by the invention of mechanical separators to process poorer quality ores. He highlighted the change from the 'make do and mend' of the war years when equipment was only bought when needed, writing in 1827 that 'in most of the large mines of Cornwall there is a perfect command of capital . . . there is a sufficiency of power for all occasions—everything is in readiness before it is wanted, and in consequence an interruption of the work rarely happens'.[98] Transport in the mining areas was also being improved. 1809 saw the commencement of a tramroad built by the Fox/Williams partnership from De Dunstanville's port at Portreath to serve the area in which the United Mines and Chacewater had recently reopened.[99] It later found itself in competition with the Redruth and Chasewater (sic) railway which was built circa 1825 by John Taylor and his London partners to run from the port of Devoran to serve their Consolidated Mines and United Mines and the area around Redruth.[100]

COPPER AND TIN COMPARED[101]

It is perhaps artificial to distinguish between copper and tin mines when some mines produced the ores of both metals. During most of the period reviewed however the great 'copper' mines overwhelmingly produced copper ore. When significant amounts of tin started to appear in the copper lodes of Dolcoath and the neighbouring Cook's Kitchen mine in the mid 1820s Alfred Jenkin looked upon it as a contaminant, describing it as an 'objectionable' metal. With its numerous small mines and smelting houses scattered across western and central Cornwall, tin mining at this time contrasted with copper and its huge mines which were largely centred around St Austell, St Day, Redruth and Camborne. In the appendix the proceeds from selling unsmelted copper ore are compared with the sale proceeds of tin metal.[102] Tin was smelted in Cornwall and there was often shared ownership in tin mines and smelters. A gross income from copper ore and tin metal of over £1,000,000 is first seen in 1805. Comparing the years 1801–15 with 1816–30 the proceeds from metallic tin sales averaged 52/53 per cent of ticketed copper ore sales for both the war and peacetime periods with the production of metallic tin increasing by 62 per cent from 38,362 tons in 1801–15 to 62,033 tons in 1816–30. Much of this increased production came from Wheal Vor which produced 25 per cent of Cornish tin in the period 1824–30.

Unlike copper, Cornish tin at one time enjoyed a virtual world monopoly but lost it after Straits tin increasingly came onto the international market about 1816. At this time Welsh tinplate works became Cornwall's most important customers. Both metals were protected by import duties and supported by purchases by the East India Company. In 1813, the year it lost its monopoly in the India trade (it retained the China trade), the Company purchased its full quota of 1,500 tons of British copper which was about 20 per cent of Cornish production and 650 tons of Cornish tin which represented about 30 per cent of its sales.[103]

CONCLUSION

Anglesey had previously flooded the market with cheaply produced copper ore from the 1780s, which badly damaged Cornish copper mining and forced some large mines to close. Hopes for a brighter future as Anglesey's output and domination declined in the 1790s[104] were ended when the war with France forced up mining material and labour costs and restricted Britain's export market in copper and brass goods. Through their many shareholdings in mines, ownership of foundries, provision of credit and general trade in mining supplies the Fox family underpinned copper mining in Cornwall. They probably acted as a sort of clearing house, helping to balance out profits and losses across much of the industry. The arrival of substantial London capital in 1809 revitalized copper mining in Cornwall. Like the Cornish, the Londoners suffered from the instability of the wartime copper market, and their bruising financial losses coupled with inadequate accounting practices helped generate distrust between them and the Cornish. This was exacerbated by their differing aims, with one side driven by the expectation of profits and dividends and the other benefiting generally from money circulating through Cornwall. In the improved post-war economic climate London investors coalesced around John Taylor, and his writings brought a better understanding of Cornish mining to a national audience and publicly stimulated competition with the Fox/Williams partnership as he sought to expand his business. This competition helped accelerate the development of the steam engine. After the war many Cornish miners took the opportunity to leave their unstable home industry and follow British capital to the ore fields of the New World in search of higher wages.

The industrial organization and structure of Britain at this time operated in 'a climate of unlimited liability and ubiquitous credit' where 'confidence and trust were pivotal' and in a business environment which changed rapidly and which was 'unstable, high risk and information poor'.[105] This is reflected in the Cornish experience, but the Londoners' comparative information deficit contributed to the breakdown in confidence and trust between them and the local business community. In terms of comparative regional industrialization, Cornwall is significant because it provides this example of a clash between outside capital and local vested interests operating within a mature and highly organized industry. Those vested interests largely funded Cornish copper mining on credit and, in many cases, provided a form of risk capital which was effectively guaranteed by the personal wealth of shareholders in the mines. What drew outsiders into Cornish mining and sustained its local interests was summed up by John Taylor in 1814: 'On the whole probably mining does not yield any great profit to the adventurers, but there are numerous cases of extraordinary gain, and these are probably nearly balanced by more numerous concerns, in which loss is incurred, the latter however, if taken individually, being generally much less in amount than the former.'[106]

APPENDIX
Cornish Copper & Tin Statistics 1794-1831

Year	Copper ore (tons)	Produce*	Price per ton of ore	Copper (tons)	Sale of copper ore	Metallic tin (tons)	Sale of tin
1794	42,816		£7-49		£320,875	3,351	£320,020
1795	43,589		£7-48		£326,189	3,440	£319,920
1796	43,313		£8-23	4,920	£356,564	3,061	£295,386
1797	47,909		£7-88	5,201	£377,838	3,240	£314,280
1798	51,358		£8-23	5,600	£422,633	2,820	£265,080
1799	51,273		£9-16	4,923	£469,664	2,862	£277,614
1800	55,981	9 1/4	£9-84	5,187	£550,925	2,522	£254,722
1801	56,611	9 1/4	£8-41	5,267	£476,313	2,328	£244,440
1802	53,937	9 5/8	£8-25	5,228	£445,094	2,627	£285,029
1803	60,566	9 1/4	£8-81	5,615	£533,910	2,914	£317,626
1804	64,637	8 3/8	£8-83	5,374	£570,840	2,993	£326,237
1805	78,452	7 7/8	£10-99	6,234	£862,410	2,742	£308,475
1806	79,269	8 5/8	£9-21	6,863	£730,845	2,855	£344,027
1807	71,694	9 3/8	£8-49	6,716	£609,002	2,426	£285,055
1808	67,867	10	£7-30	6,795	£495,303	2,330	£265,620
1809	76,245	8 7/8	£10-10	6,821	£770,028	2,508	£305,979
1810	66,048	8 1/2	£8-63	5,682	£570,035	2,006	£314,942
1811	66,786	9 1/8	£8-34	6,141	£556,723	2,384	£337,336
1812	71,547	9 3/8	£7-68	6,720	£549,665	2,373	£303,744
1813	74,047	9 1/4	£8-03	6,918	£594,345	2,324	£311,416
1814	74,322	8 1/2	£8-44	6,369	£627,501	2,611	£408,621
1815	78,483	8 1/4	£7-04	6,525	£552,813	2,941	£413,210
1816	77,334	8 5/8	£5-79	6,697	£447,959	3,348	£383,346
1817	76,701	8 1/2	£6-44	6,498	£494,010	4,120	£385,220
1818**	86,174	7 7/8	£7-96	6,849	£686,005	4,066	£344,593
1819	88,736	7 5/8	£7-03	6,804	£623,595	3,315	£249,453
1820	91,473	8 1/8	£6-59	7,508	£602,441	2,990	£219,017
1821	98,426	8 5/8	£6-15	8,514	£605,968	3,373	£255,235

Year	Copper ore (tons)	Produce*	Price per ton of ore	Copper (tons)	Sale of copper ore	Metallic tin (tons)	Sale of tin
1822	100,364	8 5/8	£6-36	8,569	£638,715	3,278	£313,049
1823	97,017	8	£6-24	7,730	£605,083	4,213	£399,182
1824	103,710	7 3/4	£6-14	8,004	£636,741	5,005	£440,440
1825	110,964	7 5/8	£7-39	8,468	£820,215	4,358	£398,060
1826	122,846	8	£5-76	9,767	£708,268	4,603	£354,431
1827	131,876	7 7/8	£5-94	10,440	£783,818	5,555	£422,180
1828	124,272	7 5/8	£5-75	9,447	£714,992	4,931	£361,196
1829	130,449	7 7/8	£5-79	10,292	£754,904	4,434	£328,116
1830	141,263	8 1/8	£5-69	11,554	£802,979	4,444	£327,745
1831	137,893	8 5/8	£5-78	11,838	£798,308	4,300	£316,050

* The Produce figure shows the amount of copper metal in the ore.

** The figures for tin after 1817 include the output from Devon. All the tin statistics are taken from the *Memoirs of the Geological Survey—The Geology of Falmouth and Truro and of the Mining District of Camborne and Redruth*, 1906, p. 311. It is likely that the price paid for black (unsmelted) tin was about 55 per cent of that paid for metallic tin. In the period 1853–72 the price paid for black tin averaged 56 per cent of the price paid for metallic tin and for 1895–1905 it averaged 53 per cent. See D. B. Barton, *A History of Tin Mining and Smelting in Cornwall*, Truro, 1967, pp. 110, 231.

Copper statistics for 1794–99 are taken from R. Hunt, *British Mining*, London, 1884, p. 892. Figures from 1800 are transcribed from *A Synopsis of the Cornwall Ticketings for Copper Ores from 1800 to 1849* held at the Cornish Studies Library at Redruth.

The output figures above cover only the copper ore sold at ticketings. Figures for private contract sales are available in the *Transactions of the Royal Geological Society of Cornwall* for the following years ended 30 June:

Year	Tons of ore	Proceeds £	Tons of copper
1818	1,132	7,790	98
1819	1,900	18,000	177
1820	4,000	28,600	338
1821	4,800	29,200	393
1822	2,230	13,200	191
1823	1,720	10,900	142
1824	2,500	16,700	198
1825	2,546	16,900	191
1826	1,460	9,819	113
1827	1,750	10,200	140
1828	500	3,000	40
1829	1,400	8,500	106
1830	1,760	10,150	141
1831	2,100	11,650	174

NOTES AND REFERENCES

1. Philip Payton, *Cornwall*, Fowey, 1996, p. 198.
2. Philip Payton, 'Industrial Celts? Cornish Identity in the Age of Technological Prowess', in P. Payton (ed.), *Cornish Studies Ten*, Exeter, 2002, p. 118.
3. G. Burke and P. Richardson, 'The Adaptability of the Cornish Cost Book System: A Response', *Business History*, XXV, No. 2, 1983, p. 193.
4. N. Crafts, The Industrial Revolution', in R. Floud and D. McCloskey (eds), *The Economic History of Britain Since 1700,* London, 1994, p. 49.
5. J. R. Harris, *The Copper King: a Biography of Thomas Williams of Llanidan*, 1964, pp. 131, 132, 134, 135; 33 Geo III cap 52, LXXXIV. Copper used in brass ranges from 55 per cent to 95 per cent. 'Yellow brass' contains 70 per cent copper.
6. Liverpool, Bristol , London and Sheffield were also centres of the copper trade but no reference to them has been seen in Cornish correspondence. Birmingham's primacy and Cornish attitudes to it are summarized in a letter from W. Jenkin to C. B. Agar on 23 May 1806 held at the Royal Institution of Cornwall [RIC] HJ/1/8.

   At the time Jenkin supported a proposal to erect a new smelting works in Cornwall to smelt its own ores 'instead of seeing such enormous profits carried out of the County by Birmingham Copper Smiths and Tinkers'.
7. E. Hopkins, *Birmingham: The First Manufacturing Town in the World*, 1989, pp. 46, 47.
8. Harris, 1964, p. 12; R. R. Toomey, *Vivian & Sons 1809–1924: A Study of the Firm in the Copper and Related Industries*, 1985, pp. 58, 316–27. Annual figures for British copper production and the ore purchases of

the various copper companies for 1818–30 appear in the *Transactions of the Royal Geological Society of Cornwall*, Volumes II (1822) to IV (1832).

9. Report from the [Parliamentary] Committee Appointed to Enquire into the State of Copper Mines and Copper Trade of this Kingdom 7 May 1799 ['1799 Report'] pp. 159, 160 re the Birmingham Company.

10. John Rowe, *Cornwall in the Age of the Industrial Revolution*, Liverpool, 1953, p. 117.

11. [RIC] HJ/1/5 Letter W. Jenkin to to W. Phillips 8 May 1801, HJ/1/9 letter to C. B. Agar 11 December 1807.

12. C. Babbage, *The Economy of Machines and Manufactures*, London, 1835, p. 155. The page notes that the figures were provided by John Taylor.

13. J. Lowe, *The Present State of England in Regard to Agriculture, Trade and Finance*, London, 1823, p. 81; Hopkins, 1989, pp. 36, 72, 73.

14. Fifty per cent based on adventurers' ore sales. The 1799 Report pp. 102, 158.

15. Neither mine appears in the ticketing lists published in the *Royal Cornwall Gazette* by that date; [RIC] HJ/1/6 Letters W. Jenkin to A. M. Hunt 17 June and 11 November 1803.

16. R. Doty, *The Soho Mint and the Industrialisation of Money*, London, 1998, p. 297.

17. [RIC] HJ/1/8 Letters W. Jenkin to G. Wilbraham 13 March 1806 and HJ/1/9 Letter to C. B. Agar 11 December 1807.

18. [RIC] HJ/1/8 Letter W. Jenkin to R. Hunt 25 October 1806. Copper ore production figures for mines are available in the volumes of *The Transactions of the Royal Geological Society of Cornwall* from 1815. They have been extracted from the ticketing lists appearing in the *Royal Cornwall Gazette* before that.

19. [RIC] HJ/1/8 Letters W. Jenkin to C. B. Agar 13 March 1806 and 17 January 1807, Dr Colwell 2 February 1807; HJ/1/9 C. B. Agar 11 December 1807. RCG 17 January 1807 and 12 December 1807.

20. [RIC] Letter W. Jenkin to W. Phillips 3 September 1811.

21. [RIC] HJ/1/8 Letter W. Jenkin to W. Phillips 14 November 1806.

22. 1799 Report, pp. 159–62.

23. *Royal Cornwall Gazette*, 29 April 1809.

24. [RIC] HJ/1/10 Letters W. Jenkin to W. Phillips 22 July 1809 and C. B. Agar 24 August 1809; HJ/1/11 Letter W. Jenkin to G. Wilbraham 22 October 1812.

25. See footnote 18.

26. S. Drew, *The History of Cornwall* , 1824, Vol II p. 70.

27. *Royal Cornwall Gazette,* 28 September 1816; *Transactions of the Royal Geological Society of Cornwall* , Vol. I, 1818, p. 252.

28. A measurement of price: the price of a quantity of copper ore sufficient to produce one ton of copper metal after the deduction of returning charges' which notionally covered the smelters' costs in turning the ore into metal.

29. [RIC] HJ/2/2.
30. Babbage, 1835, p. 155.
31. [RIC] HJ/1/13(1) Letter W. Jenkin to A. M. Agar 4 May 1816. Wheal Alfred sold 50,000 tons of ore through the ticketings from 1811–1815.
32. Hopkins, 1989, pp. 46, 74–8.
33. J. Lewis, 'Captain William Davey of Redruth and the Reopening of the Consolidated Mines in 1819, in *Journal of the Trevithick Society*, 2004, p. 53.
34. Sharron Schwartz, 'The Making of a Myth: Cornish Miners in the New World in the Early Nineteenth Century', in P. Payton (ed.), *Cornish Studies: Nine*, Exeter, 2001, pp. 106–11.
35. *West Briton*, 26 September 1823.
36. D. B. Barton, *The Cornish Beam Engine*, Truro, 1965, p. 46.
37. A. K. Hamilton Jenkin, 'The Rise and all of Wheal Alfred', *Journal of the Royal Institution of Cornwall*, 1959, p. 137.
38. [RIC] HJ/2/6 Letter A. Jenkin to P. Grenfell 9 June 1826: the copper mines under Taylor's control were East Crinnis*, Pembroke*, East Wheal Basset, Consolidated Mines*, Wheal Buller*, Wheal Hope, Wheal Fortune, United Mines, Wheal Busy, Condurrow, and South Roskear. Mines in the top five ore producers are marked with an asterisk. Pednandrea, Wheal Sparnon and Polgooth were tin and cobalt mines under his management.
39. *West Briton*, 22 June 1827.
40. *Transactions of the Royal Geological Society of Cornwall,* Vol. III, 1832, p. 494; R. Burt, P. Waite and R. Burnley, *Cornish Mines*, Exeter, 1987, p. xii.
41. [RIC] HJ/1/13(2) Letter A. Jenkin to T. Craufurd 9 June 1821.
42. [RIC] HJ/1/8 Letter W. Jenkin to C. B. Agar 22 May 1806, HJ/1/13(2) Letter A. Jenkin to Sir S. B. Morland 25 January 1820.
43. [RIC] HJ/1/9 Letter W. Jenkin to C. B. Agar 28 February 1809, Letter A. Jenkin to T. Craufurd 24 September 1821.
44. [RIC] HJ/1/9 Letter W. Jenkin to C. B. Agar 28 February 1809.
45. Harris, 2003, p. 130; Rowe, 1953, p. 122; *Mining Journal*, 9 September 1848.
46. Sir Lewis Namier and J. Brooke, *The History of Parliament—The House of Commons 1754–1790*, London, 1964,Vol. II, pp. 62-64; R. G. Thorne, *The History of Parliament—The House of Commons 1790–1820*, London, 1986, Vol III. pp. 149–51.
47. Harris, 1964, p. 130; [RIC] HJ/1/5 Letter W. Jenkin to S. Bernard 26 April 1799.
48. Brian Elvins, 'Cornwall's Newspaper War: The Political Rivalry Between the *Royal Cornwall Gazette* and *West Briton* 1810–1831', in Payton, (ed.), 2001, p. 151; *Royal Cornwall Gazette*, 30 June 1810.
49. *Royal Cornwall Gazette,* 3 November 1810.
50. For instance see [RIC] HJ/1/13(2) Letter W. Jenkin to A. M. Agar 30 April 1819.
51. 1799 Report, pp. 159–163.

52. [RIC] HJ/1/2 Letters W. Jenkin to R. Wilbraham 20 February and G. Hunt 15 March 1794.
53. [RIC] HJ/1/13(3) Letter A. Jenkin to G. Wilbraham 15 October 1824.
54. John Taylor, 'On the Economy of the Mines of Cornwall and Devon', 1814, in R. Burt (ed.), *Cornish Mining*, Newton Abbot, 1969, p. 26.
55. [RIC] HJ/1/6 Letter W. Jenkin to R. Hunt 18 June 1804.
56. Toomey, 1985, p. 58.
57. G. Burke and P. Richardson, 'The Decline and Fall of the Cost Book System in the Cornish Tin Mining Industry 1895–1914', *Business History*, XXIII, No. 1, 1981, p. 4.
58. [RIC] HJ/1/10 Letter W. Jenkin to W. Phillips 3 November 1809.
59. [RIC] HJ/1/13(1) Letter W. Jenkin to W. Phillips 6 June 1815.
60. [RIC] HJ/1/5 Letter W. Jenkin to A. M. Hunt 19 June 1802.
61. [RIC] HJ/2/3 Letter W. Jenkin to P. Grenfell 6 September 1817.
62. [RIC] HJ/1/6 Letters W. Jenkin to R. Wilbraham 14 September 1802 and R. Hunt 18 June 1804.
63. [RIC] HJ/1/5 Letters W. Jenkin to A. M. Hunt 19 June 1802 and HJ/1/6 5 May 1804.
64. [RIC] HJ/1/13(1) Letter W. Jenkin to G. Fox 25 August 1817.
65. [RIC] HJ/2/2 Letter W. Jenkin to P. Grenfell 9 and 17 January 1817.
66. Bernard Deacon, 'The Re-formation of Territorial Identity: Cornwall in the Late Eighteenth and Nineteenth Centuries', unpub. Ph.D thesis, Open University, 2001 p. 179.
67. 1799 Report p. 158. The three biggest mines alone in the parish of Gwennap (the St Day area: Consolidated Mines, United Mines and Wheal Unity & Poldice) paid £57,000 in wages and £50,300 for materials in 1798.
68. [RIC] HJ/4/50 In the 5 years to 1802 the absentee Agar family of Lanhydrock received £26,000 in mine dues (mainly from Tincroft) and this money was remitted regularly to the family's London bankers and not spent locally.
69. [RIC] HJ/1/13(3) Letter A. Jenkin to G. Wilbraham 5 April 1825.
70. 1864 Parliamentary Commission to Enquire into the Conditions of All Non-Coal Mines in Great Britain, Evidence of J. Bankart.
71. John Taylor, 1814, pp. 20–1.
72. 1842 Parliamentary Commission on the Employment of Children in the Mines of Devon and Cornwall, Evidence of J. Phillips p. 815.
73. John Rule, 'Some Social Aspects of the Cornish Industrial Revolution', in R. Burt (ed.), *Industry and Society in the South West*, Exeter, 1970, p. 82. Calculation for 1800, 1816 and 1830 based on the ticketed ore sales divided by a factor of 7 to represent an estimated average tonnage per person. The lowest output per person identified was 4 tons at Chacewater in 1816, the 7,200 employed in 1787 suggests 5 tons, at Wheal Alfred in 1815 1,000 employees produced 8 tons each and workers at the Consolidated Mines and Fowey Consols in 1836 also produced an average of 8 tons per person.
74. Estimate extracted from Sir Charles Lemon, 'Statistics of the Copper

Mines of Cornwall, 1838', in Burt (ed.), 1969, p. 72. See also [RIC] HJ/2/2 Letter W. Jenkin to P. Grenfell 17 January 1817.

75. For example [RIC] HJ/1/5 Letters W. Jenkin to A. M. Agar 22 November 1800, HJ/1/8 to R. Hunt 25 October 1806, HJ/1/9 to C. B. Agar 5 January 1808, HJ/1/11 to A. M. Agar 17 April 1812, HJ/1/13(1) to A. M. Agar 9 November 1816.

76. [RIC] HJ/1/8 Letter W. Jenkin to C. B. Agar 11 January 1806; *Royal Cornwall Gazette*, 27 November 1819.

77. [RIC] HJ/1/13 (1) Letters W. Jenkin to A. M. Agar 12 August 1815 and 7 June 1817.

78. [RIC] HJ/1/13(3) Letters A. Jenkin to A. M. Agar 31 January 1825 and 15 May 1826.

79. Schwartz, 2001, pp. 106–10.

80. [RIC]HJ/1/13 (4) Letter A. Jenkin to T. Craufurd 10 June 1825.

81. [RIC] HJ/1/13(1) Letter W. Jenkin to ? 9 January 1815, *West Briton* 26 September 1823.

82. *West Briton*, 13 March 1818, Report on Stannaries of Cornwall Vice Warden's Court, 3 March 1818.

83. [RIC] HJ/1/11 Letter W. Jenkin to W. Phillips 3 September 1811.

84. *West Briton*, 26 September 1823 re change of shareholders.

85. R. Burt, *John Taylor, Mining Entrepreneur and Engineer 1779–1863*, 1977, pp. 9, 15, 18, 21; [RIC] HJ/2/8 Letter A. Jenkin to P. Grenfell 15 August 1823.

86. Burt, 1977, pp. 11, 77, 78.

87. Babbage, 1835, p. 155.

88. [RIC] HJ/2/8 Letter A. Jenkin to P. Grenfell 7 August 1823, '[John Taylor] has extensive connections with monied means, principally Bankers, so that he appears able to command capital to almost any amount.'

89. R. Hunt, *British Mining: A Treatise*, London, 1887, p. 872.

90. Burt, 1977, p. 76; Barton, 1965, p. 39; *West Briton*, 16 November 1821.

91. Lewis, 2004, pp. 49–55.

92. Burt, 1977, p. 23, 25.

93. Roger Burt, 'Segmented Capital Markets and Patterns of Investment in late Victorian Britain: Evidence from the Non-ferrous Mining Industry', *Economic History Review*, LI, 4, 1998, p. 715.

94. John Taylor, 1837, in Burt, (ed), 1969, p. 45.

95. C. M. Bristow, *Cornwall's Geology and Scenery*, Exeter, 1996, p. 3. The world's oldest geological society was the Geological Society of London founded in 1807.

96. T. Lean and Brother, *Historical Statement of the Improvements Made in the Duty Performed by the Steam Engines in Cornwall*, 1839, p. 146. Lean's Engine Reporter was published monthly and recently doubts have been expressed over the integrity of some of the engine statistics they contain: see Bridget Howard, *Mr Lean and the Engine Reporters*, 2002, pp. 18–43.

97. Barton, 1965, pp. 28, 29; J. Carne, 'On the Period of the Commencement

of Copper Mining in Cornwall, and on the Improvements which have been Made in Mining', in *Transactions of the Royal Geological Society of Cornwall*, Vol. III, 1827, pp. 58, 59: Carne writes of engines 'less than thirty years ago'. Shortly before it closed in 1814 the engines at Wheal Towan were described as 'quite worn out, as [were] generally the whims, ropes and other materials'. [RIC]HJ/1/13(1) Letter W. Jenkin to W. Phillips 18 June 1814.

98. Carne, 1827, pp. 63–73; B. Earl , *Cornish Mining*, Truro, 1968, p. 81; J. Lewis, *A Richly Yielding Piece of Ground: A History of Fowey Consols Mine 1813–1867*, St Austell, 1997, pp. 38–41.

99. D. B. Barton, 'Portreath and its Tramroad', in *Essays in Cornish Mining History*, Vol 2, Truro, 1971, p. 133.

100. D. B. Barton, *The Redruth and Chasewater Railway 1824–1915*, Truro, 1966, p. 23.

101. Most of the information in this section is taken from D. B. Barton, *A History of Tin Mining and Smelting in Cornwall*, Truro, 1967, pp. 18, 19, 26, 28, 29, 36, 44, 45, 53, 58, 59.

102. [RIC] HJ/2/6 Letter to P. Grenfell 30 March 1827.

103. *Papers respecting the negotiation for the export of Tin from Cornwall to China during the East India Company's Exclusive Privileges*, 1813.

104. Harris, 1964, pp. 40, 54, 90, 135.

105. P. Hudson, 'Industrial Organisation and Structure', in R. Floud and P. Johnson, (eds), *The Cambridge Economic History of Modern Britain Vol 1 1700–1860*, Cambridge, 2004, pp. 48, 49.

106. Taylor, 1814, p. 29.

THE 1913 CHINA CLAY DISPUTE: 'ONE AND ALL' OR 'ONE— THAT'S ALL'?

Ronald Perry and Charles Thurlow[1]

INTRODUCTION

Paradoxically, while the 1913 strike of china clay workers, lasting eleven weeks and involving five thousand men, must be one of the most widely and continuously discussed events in Cornish labour history, its coverage is deficient. Is it a coincidence that most accounts have appeared during periods of acute industrial strife, initially by contemporary journalists and ballad-mongers, sixty years later by historians, politicians and a television film producer? Their agenda was to create political heroes and villains and they portrayed the strike as anything from the doomed saga of a small but gallant band of independent Cornish china clay men fighting against employers determined to starve them into submission, to honest but naive labourers persuaded by outside agitators to take part in a vast conspiracy to overthrow the capitalist system. And it still excites passion among descendants of those who took part in it, as Garry Tregidga and Lucy Ellis have shown.[2]

What these commentaries failed to recognize, let alone investigate, was why china claymen in West and North Cornwall and West Devon took no part in the dispute, why half the workforce seemed reluctant to join in, or how Mid Devon ball clay workers, led by a rival union, managed to bring a parallel strike to a successful conclusion whereas the Mid Cornwall china claymen failed.[3] Nor is the role of political and religious leadership in a Methodist-Liberal stronghold adequately explored. This article examines these issues of solidarity and parochialism in the light of other neglected factors, including the existence of wide pay differentials, the state of trade union finances and a spatial division in support for the strike.

THE BACKGROUND TO THE STRIKE[4]

The year 1913 opened full of promise for the china clay industry. For decades output had been rising by leaps and bounds, reaching a record level of almost a million tons in 1912. Cornish and Devon clays enjoyed a world-wide reputation for quality and three quarters of production was exported. Labour relations were generally harmonious and no significant dispute had occurred since 1876, when clay workers had suffered a humiliating defeat after trying to form their own union. This failure had discredited the organized labour movement in the workers' eyes and tales still circulated of broken promises of financial support from other unions and, even worse, of 'wagon loads of gold sovereigns' that had arrived in Cornwall for the strikers, only to disappear into the pockets of local officials.[5]

On the face of it, the clay country seemed an unlikely background for industrial strife, especially within the context of a Cornish labour market in which employment in the dominant mining sector had dwindled from over 36,000 to seven or eight thousand, and mass emigration had robbed the region of potential labour leaders. But both clayworkers and their masters were aware of a wave of unrest that was sweeping through Britain. While wages had risen fairly steadily through the nineteenth century, in the Edwardian period they stayed constant while prices rose. According to a Board of Trade survey of industrial towns, general prices increased by 14 per cent between 1906 and 1912 and food prices by a quarter. Seizing upon the discontent that this caused, some labour leaders, inspired by French *'syndicalisme révolutionnaire'* and American worker militancy, were calling for mass action by formerly non-unionised unskilled workers to overturn capitalism and local newspapers reported these events in the belligerent terms of class warfare.

Readers of the *St Austell Star*, self-proclaimed voice of Gladstonian Liberalism in the clay country, learned that 'The Great Shipbuilding Lockout' of 1910 was followed by 'The Great Industrial War' of cotton textile workers, 'The Great Railway Wars' and 'The Great Miners' Strike' of 1911 and 1912. Even hitherto conservative and deferential groups like farm workers went on strike, following the example of others in demanding higher minimum wages of £1.20 a week and recognition of the rights of a union to negotiate with the employers.[6] British Trade Union membership escalated to four million by 1913, perhaps 30 per cent of all eligible workers, while in 1911–13 disputes cost 20 million working days each year.

As the impact of these strikes in shortages and higher prices began to make themselves felt upon the Cornish population, attitudes towards them changed. The *St Austell Star* had sympathised with railwaymen when they threatened to strike in 1907, but turned against them when they struck in earnest four years later, condemning their 'propensity for causing the greatest amount of inconvenience for the public'. The 1910 lockout of 120,000 cotton textile workers affected demand for china clay which, used to impart weight and smoothness, made up a high proportion of the cheap cotton cloth sent to the colonies. Seamen's, dockers' and coalminers' strikes stopped production in industries using china clay as well as preventing maritime and overland trade in clay. When 850,000 coal miners downed tools, some Cornish coal merchants, who had not replenished stocks after the seamen's and dockers' strikes, put up their prices by as much as 60 per cent, but clay merchants such as J.W. Higman and John Lovering, who had wisely built up reserves in advance, were able to keep their steam engines and drying kilns going. They even had enough to help out the Great Western Railway with coal for trains to take clay to the ports, and also supplied clay families with coal at the old price. In this way they reinforced distrust of unionism and weakened working class solidarity.[7]

THE UNION BIG GUNS MOVE INTO CORNWALL

It was in this incendiary atmosphere that union organizers began recruiting among the clay workers of Cornwall and Devon. They were not the first in these regions. In the early 1890s Martin, the master of Lee Moor china clay works of Plymouth, had warned his landowner Lord Morley of the intrusion of 'labour agitators' and predicted that they would soon be fermenting strikes,[8] while powerful unions were signing up Cornish railwaymen, despite intense opposition from local employers. It was not until 1911, however, that two rival unions began to recruit among clay workers in Mid Cornwall, the Gasworkers' Union led by Jack Jones and Will Thorne, both powerful labour leaders, and the Workers' Union, who appointed Charles Robert Vincent as their organizer. A Truro bookseller and stationer, Vincent was an early member of the Socialist Democratic Federation, the first such organization to be established in the south west in 1894, a year after Vincent was first listed as a newsagent (Plymouth's first branch came a year later). Truro was a hotbed of radicalism in those days and Vincent was probably involved with Jack Jones when the latter stood unsuccessfully as Parliamentary Candidate in 1906.

At first Vincent found recruitment heavy going. Neither a clay worker nor a clay country man, he was asked to explain why he was urging claymen to make financial sacrifices by striking when, as an organizer, he was paid two or three times as much. He replied that he had given up a trade that paid him twice as much again, although it was said that he was only saved from eviction from his bookshop, when he could not pay his rent, by the clemency of the landowner Lord Clifden.[9] To fight his cause, however, Vincent brought in some of the big guns of the labour movement. Chief among them was Tom Mann, architect of victory in the historic 1889 London dockers' strike, and triumphal leader of the 1911 Liverpool dockers' strike.[10]

Workers' Union officials who made frequent visits to Mid Cornwall included the Secretary, Charles Duncan, MP for Barrow in Furness; Charles Beard, local government councillor and union agent for the Midlands, Matt Giles, South West Organizer and member of the National Executive Council, A.E. Ellery, Bristol Agent and Joe Harris, Cornwall organizer, experienced in Union affairs in Dublin, Belfast and the North of England. Miss Varley, union organizer for the Black Country, later came down to rally support from the claymen's wives.

By 1913 the Gasworkers' agents had withdrawn from Mid Cornwall to concentrate upon Devon, and the Workers' Union pursued the classic strategy of combining workers in related industries that controlled production and distribution by signing up dockers at Par and Fowey and co-operating with the powerful railwaymen's' unions. When the railwaymen embarked upon a six weeks' strike in 1912, and the dockers joined in, Duncan and Tom Mann addressed mass meetings of clay workers, urging them to show solidarity by blocking movement of clay to the railways and docks. The crucial importance of this kind of inter-industrial co-operation was displayed in a 1913 Lancashire farm hands' strike when a newly organized union succeeded because railwaymen refused to handle farm produce and Liverpool dockers, after Tom Mann's victory in 1911, were rich and powerful enough not only to block all farming exports and imports but also to subsidise the strike pay of the strikers.[11]

But the claymen refused to join in and Tom Mann warned them they would pay the price for this. Nonetheless, the Workers' Union continued to recruit claymen with a programme of union recognition and 'reaching the twenty five', a minimum wage of 25 shillings (£1.25) a week instead of the current minimum of 18 shillings (90p). Union leaders urged them to set their sights even higher. If female textile workers were already earning £1.25 weekly, asserted Duncan, claymen should get more, and Tom Mann suggested a target of £1.50 like the coal miners. However, Vincent and Matt Giles, who played a leading role in local matters, cautiously followed another classic trade union practice of using threats of strikes to gain a series of small increases. Time and again they announced that their agents in every pit were awaiting an immediate call to arms, but then at the last minute postponed the strike for a variety of reasons. Sometimes they claimed that the employers were willing to make marginal concessions (which they did), sometimes that they had to await a decision from the Union Executive. Meanwhile Vincent was building up good relations with some of the claymasters (he claimed that he and Tom Mann dined with one of them) and gradually increasing pay levels towards 'the twenty five', which he now announced could be reached in stages rather than by one all-out strike.

THE CARNE STENTS MEN DOWN TOOLS

There seemed no reason why union brinkmanship and employer concessions could not have continued indefinitely, so it came as a shock when, on Monday morning of 21 July, thirty men from Carne Stents, a small works with some fifty men a couple of miles west of St Austell, downed tools. Their immediate grievance was not the minimum wage, but that their employer had reneged on an agreement to pay them fortnightly instead of a so-called monthly system which only paid out twelve times a year, resulting in unpopular 'five week months'. However, led by Vincent and a fiery United Methodist Minister, the Reverend Henry Booth Coventry, the Carne Stents men marched westwards from pit to pit towards the Fal Valley, calling upon men in the smaller pits and cajoling or coercing them to join in, before turning north east to the Bugle area where they expected, and met, with stronger reluctance to strike.

At first no one, including the press, took the movement very seriously, but within two weeks the *West Briton*, generally sympathetic to the strikers, was revealing that 'all 5000 workers are out on strike', although noting 'a strong suspicion that an unusually large proportion of men have been dragged out against their will',[12] particularly in the area around Bugle to the north east. The claymasters' reaction to these events was one of masterly inactivity. They formed a China Clay Federation to monitor the strike, but their reply to all requests for reconciliation, whether from the Union, or Methodist and Anglican Ministers, or from independent neutrals, was to put the ball back into the strikers' court. There was no lock-out, they declared, and the workers were free to return to work at any time they liked, when their grievances could be settled in the usual way, by negotiation with individual employers.

The early weeks of the strike coincided with an unusually long spell of fine weather. Every day dawned dry and sunny and something of a carnival atmosphere prevailed. But as the strike went into its fifth week, and monthly pay packets were exhausted, enthusiasm began to wane and men started to drift back to work, Bugle men to the fore. For many clay families, Booth Coventry conceded, were 'not great savers'. What they earned they spent, and some relied greatly on credit from shopkeepers, especially at the end of a 'five week month'. Only 650 Union men received the full strike pay of 12/6d (63p) a week, although perhaps twice that number were entitled to the ten shillings (50p) allowance for newly joined members. Around 160 of the most needy families were given food to the value of a few shillings (25 to 30p) a week from the Strike Relief Fund.

To try to force the employers to concede, the strikers increased their pressure. Newspapers carried accounts of men being beaten on their way to work, and of engine houses sabotaged in night raids to prevent pumps from operating, thus putting the pits out of action. Marshel Arthur, a clay captain, described how a member of the Workers' Union ordered him to stop the pumps and flood the pit. When Arthur refused, the man left but later some young men tried to disconnect the machinery running away when he approached.[13] By the end of August, claymasters were taking the fight into the strikers' camp by reopening pits in the union heartland.

Up until then, law and order had been reasonably well maintained by a force of 200 policemen drafted in from all parts of Cornwall by the County Council, which was the Police Authority, although they had problems with night raiders. To protect returning workers from pickets, the Council brought in police reinforcements from outside: 30 from Devonport, 60 from Bristol and 100 from South Wales, including the 'Tonypandy men', battle-hardened veterans of violent coal-mining and railway disputes in which men had been killed. They came equipped with bicycles, truncheons, new and improved shields and powerful electric torches to spy out the night raiders. In the opening days of September a series of bloody skirmishes broke out between police and gangs of pickets armed with staves, in which the union leaders were injured: Councillor Beard at Bugle, Matt Giles at Roche, Harris at St Stephen and Vincent at St Dennis.

Meanwhile, in Devon, near Kingsteignton, another conflict involving ball clay workers was following a different course. It had begun on 7 July when men in one pit downed tools and, led by Jack Jones of the Gasworkers' Union, brought other pits out until by mid-August two thousand workers were on strike, including dockers, ships' stokers and seamen, thus stopping ball clay from being taken down river to Teignmouth. The strikers were encouraged by the news that building employers in North Devon had conceded union demands after a 15-week dispute, and a fortnight later the ball clay masters seemed willing to follow suit. The strike ended in the first week of September with employers agreeing to pay increases and, either formally or informally, accepting the right of the Gasworkers' Union to negotiate on behalf of the workers. Interestingly, ball clay workers in North Devon and Dorset did not join in the dispute.

THE ISOLATION OF THE CLAYMEN
Cornwall's strike leaders must have been aware of these successes, but they made no reference to them in their speeches, although the Devon ball clay leaders had referred to the Cornish dispute. The china clay men seemed isolated from fellow workers and the population at large. True, allegations of police brutality had brought them declarations of moral support and condemnations from Trades Union Conferences, but as the weeks wore on it became clear that this rhetoric was of no practical use. Vincent and Booth Coventry appealed to all branches of the Workers' Union for financial aid but with little result. Booth Coventry also penned an article in the London *Daily Citizen* under the headline 'Clayworkers fight for their life' but with no greater success. In a rare example of generosity, the Miners' Union, still recovering from a loss of £10 million in an unsuccessful dispute, voted £200 to help clay families in distress and a Co-operative Wholesale Society Conference at St Columb took up a collection for them, as did a railwaymen's meeting at Penzance. But these amounts were chicken feed in a strike involving thousands of workers, and the powerful National Union of Railwaymen warned its branches not to fritter away money for outside disputes that might be needed for their own purposes later.

Vincent and Giles went to meet the jettymen of Fowey and Par and asked them to block shipments of china clay but, as Tom Mann had warned, their appeal fell on deaf ears. The china clay workers were paying the price for their earlier refusal to support the dockers and railwaymen, and the claymasters were able to dispatch quantities of clay, a psychological blow to the claymen. The clay was eventually held up by Bristol dockers, who would not unload them from coastal vessels onto ships bound for North America, but by this time the strike was nearly over.

In West Cornwall, neither the Penzance-based *Cornish Telegraph* nor the St Ives Western Echo made any reference to sympathetic action from clayworkers in their areas, and paid little attention to what they called 'the Mid Cornwall dispute'. Indeed, the *Telegraph* gave more space to a strike in South Africa involving Cornish miners, while the *Echo* reported in some detail a silver band contest at Bugle without mentioning the industrial action that was raging there at that time. According to the *Falmouth Packet* newspaper, local County Councillors' main interest in the strike was to avoid contributing to the cost of the police force drafted into Mid Cornwall, and Redruth Councillors shared the same concern.

North Cornwall Councillors, however, were less unwilling to pay, because local clayworks on Bodmin Moor had picked up orders when the St Austell pits were closed. At a dinner he gave to his workers, one North Cornwall claymaster was complimented on the excellence of his industrial relations. Another, Frank Parkyn, was criticized by fellow claymasters for paying too much attention to his workers' needs at the expense of profits. Four hundred china clay workers at Lee Moor in Devon were also unwilling to strike. They were mainly employed by the Martin Brothers, who had already agreed to wage increases, but they sent small amounts for the Strike Relief Fund, for which Booth Coventry thanked them publicly.

After the intervention of outside police forces, violence escalated on both sides. A policeman from Lostwithiel was shot, but not fatally, by a youth called Howard Vincent (no relation of the organizer) during a night raid, and a revolver and ammunition were found at his home. After 30 cases of dynamite were stolen from one of Stocker's stores, one stick exploded in a milk churn outside a clay captain's house, causing alarm but not injury, and rumours spread that a dozen Mauser revolvers and one thousand rounds of ammunition had been shipped from Plymouth to St Austell. Death threats were delivered to claymasters, warning them that they would soon find 'your souls in hell and rats eating your bodies'.[14]

After a poll in which 2,258 voted to continue the strike, Vincent was carried through the streets of St Austell amid scenes of great jubilation. Looked at from another angle, however, more than half the workers had not voted to fight on and, protected by the police from pickets, they returned to work in increasing numbers. By the middle of September over a thousand were working, by the following week 1,500 and, as September came to an end, Vincent, Giles and Booth Coventry conferred and called the strike off.

CONTRASTING INTERPRETATIONS
The first continuous account of the dispute was a 62-stanza ballad composed during the strike by an anonymous author who was clearly closely involved with its organization.[15] It began with the Carne Stents men downing tools in protest against wages that 'only just kept us alive', made no reference to previous union activity, only mentioned union leaders after they were attacked by police and failed to recognize

the contribution of the charismatic Booth Coventry. In this version it began to rain, flooding the pits and stopping production, and the employers in their desperation decided to 'import some hundreds of police' who, fortified by 'John Barleycorn', acted 'like demons or men who were insane'. This only stiffened the resolve of the men but eventually they 'decided to retreat', defeated not by the police, nor by the masters, but by 'weak kneed' blacklegs, especially the 'jelly limbed' Bugle men 'who, like Judas, their brethren they did betray'. The poem ended on a confident note, however, urging readers to 'join the Workers' Union and win victory next time'.

Some sixty years later the BBC television producer Tom Clarke dramatised parts of the strike in a film 'Stocker's Copper', which is still occasionally shown in the clay district. It begins halfway through the dispute with the arrival of a contingent of Tonypandy men and focuses upon a friendship that developed between one of them and a striker on whose family he is billeted. Inevitably, their comradeship is shattered when they find themselves face to face in a baton charge which effectively ends the strike. Again, as in the epic poem, no references are made to external union activities and the only leader mentioned is Vincent, although Booth Coventry is given a prominent role. The Tonypandy men, however, are not demonized as in the ballad but treated as functionaries carrying out their duty to maintain law and order.

Shortly after the film appeared, another lengthy account of the strike was presented by J.R. Ravensdale, historian and Workers' Educational Association Tutor in Cornwall.[16] This account explored the background of earlier and later union activities, although it did not mention the absence of backing from clay workers in other districts, nor the existence of a ball clay strike by a rival union. Ravensdale suggested that the Union would have achieved its aims if Carne Stents men had not jumped the gun and forced it into premature action, although this is subject to some doubt, since Vincent accompanied the men when they confronted their clay captain.

Of other contemporary verdicts on the strike, only Vincent and Booth Coventry attributed defeat on betrayal by 'cowardly scabs'. Some newspaper editors who were broadly in sympathy with the cause lay the blame on the strike leaders who, according to the *Falmouth Packet*, 'forced the men to down tools' and in the words of the *Cornish Guardian*, misled them with 'far too much bluff'. An influential outside opinion came from Sir George (later Lord) Askwith, the Chief Industrial Commissioner of the Board of Trade, who had played a leading part in resolving the 1912 railwaymen's strike, and who was sent to Cornwall to mediate the dispute at the request of the

Honourable T.C.R Agar-Robartes, MP for St Austell. He concluded that the men had no real grievance and had been misled by 'false prophets and self-exulting agitators'. The right-wing *Royal Cornwall Gazette* and the *Western Morning News* agreed with this verdict and only the *Newquay Express* considered that the decision to bring in police reinforcements was the main cause of defeat.[17]

An interpretation as a spur-of-the-moment action that came to nothing because of a lack of worker solidarity was also favoured by the clay historian Kenneth Hudson, the local historian R.S. Best, whose father was one of the Carne Stents men and by A.L. Rowse, who actually witnessed the dispute. For him the strike 'came spontaneously and independently of the Workers' Union, which had only a small membership'.[18] A contrasting set of interpretations lay the blame upon outside agitators who fomented an entirely unnecessary strike among a basically contented group of men. The clay historian J.M. Coon contended that 'industrial relations between employed and employers were for many years undisturbed' until a strike that was 'probably attributed to outside agencies'. Another historian of the industry, R.M. Barton, concurred with this view, but David Mudd, long-serving Tory MP for Camborne-Falmouth, went much further. For him the strike was 'a carefully planned operation of sabotage and violence falling not far short of anarchy'.[19]

PAY DIFFERENTIALS, PROFITS AND UNION FINANCES

A fundamental disparity between these two contrasting sets of explanations hinges upon the relative prosperity or poverty of the claymen. In presenting their case, the unions naturally highlighted the plight of the worst off and Booth Coventry toured the area demanding a 'living wage'. He never defined what this was, however, and the China Clay Association countered with the claim that their workers were 'the highest paid earners in the south west'. A Board of Trade enquiry noted 'bicycles, gramophones and other luxuries' in workers' cottages and concluded that by the standards of the day, claymen's pay compared favourably with that of other labourers.[20]

Several local newspapers, reporting these opposing statements, made their own investigations into rates of pay, including the *Royal Cornwall Gazette*, the *St Austell Star* and the *Cornish Guardian*. While the *Gazette* was not on the strikers' side, the *Star* was broadly in favour and the *Guardian* extremely supportive: indeed Booth Coventry publicly referred to its Editor, A Browning Lyne, as 'a dear old friend', at least before the results of the pay survey were published.[21]

According to these surveys, about half of the men already earned more than the union's target of £1.25 a week, some of them considerably more. The 'burden men' who shifted the top soil, and the 'sand men' who removed waste matter from the pits were paid on piece rates and averaged between £1.27 and £1.58 a week, while the 'drymen' in the kilns earned between £1.50 to £2 a week. The other half of the workforce, including the 'breakers' and 'washers', who removed material from the sides of the pit, were on hourly rates, amounting to £1.05 for a 7-hour day to £1.15 for a 7½-hour day. Kiln men only worked about 5 hours a day, whereas the normal working day in other industries was at least 10 hours: in the farming dispute referred to earlier the workers settled for 12 hours. Clayworkers who had time to work smallholdings, keep a pig and a few fowls were not badly off by the standards of the day. The father of the historian R.S. Best, one of the Carne Stents men, helped to run the village post office and stores at nearby Trewoon, as well as working a small holding.

No doubt the employers felt justified in their claims that the men were adequately paid, especially since they were surrounded by areas suffering from the decline of the once dominant mining industry and they had no problem recruiting labour. But given the prosperity of their industry, could they have paid more? The China Clay Federation, like the Workers' Union, made the most of its worst cases. Sir William Serjeant, a landowner who claimed to be on the workers' side, explained that a clayworks on his land, although run by the experienced claymasters J.W. Coon and William Rose, had failed to pay him a rent for over a decade.[22] Such marginal pits existed, since the industry consisted of a small number of large, efficient and profitable works producing 'best' clays and a large number of marginal pits producing inferior 'common' clays. Nevertheless the leading clay families like the Martins, Loverings and Stockers could afford to pay more and Stocker was among those who offered to do so (and did after the strike was over). In their wills, John Lovering had left £36,000 in 1900, William Martin £28,000 in 1905 and Thomas Martin £36,000 in 1913. By today's values they were millionaires.

There was another possible reason, though, why some claymasters felt no need to offer more pay—the precarious state of the Workers' Union finances. Oddly enough this was barely mentioned in contemporary accounts of the strike and the impression was given that it was a powerful force in the labour movement. Yet in 1911 the St Austell Star, on the whole friendly towards the clay workers, had reported that the Union only had in total 20,000 members, and even at the height of the strike its leaders only claimed 27,000, presumably including two thousand or more clayworkers.[23] Compared with the juggernauts of the movement, such as the National Union of Railwaymen with 188,000, or the Gasworkers with 120,000, it was small fry, and to make matters worse it had only been formed in 1898 and had no time to build up a substantial strike fund. Does this explain why its officials spent so much time on the clay country dispute? For them an additional 5,000 members represented a sizeable gain, whereas for the big unions it would be insignificant. Its limited finances also suggest why the union preferred to negotiate rather than strike.

RELIGION AND POLITICS

What part did local religious and political leaders play in such a Methodist-Liberal stronghold? The two best-remembered Methodists represented opposite ends of the political spectrum. The Reverend Henry Booth Coventry, avowed socialist and member of the Independent Labour Party, Superintendent of 29 United Methodist churches, is portrayed in the film 'Stocker's Copper' as a Christ-like figure. His reported speeches, however, suggest a mastery in stirring up resentment and envy among his audiences. He spelled out the conflict in black and white terms: those who were not on the workers' side 'had no right to say their prayers' and should not be part of the Christian Church. Such men certainly included Captain 'Sammy' Dyer, a self-made claymaster, local preacher and Sunday School Super-intendent, who had earlier created a fervour when he claimed that families could live quite comfortably on less than the minimum wage, providing that they did not fritter it away on gambling and drink. He caused an even greater outrage when he used a Wesleyan ceremony to launch a bitter attack on the way that 5,000 men had been 'pulled out of work, punishing their families and themselves' to further Vincent's career.[24] Booth Coventry attacked him for mixing religion and politics, a clear case of the pot calling the kettle black. Writers to the press denounced Booth Coventry's socialist views, and the *Western Morning News* called them 'fanatical outpourings'.[25]

The opinions of the vast majority of religious leaders however, fell between these two extremes. The Reverend Henry Gilbert Low, United Methodist Minister for St Dennis and Chairman of the Rural District Council Finance Committee, always advocated restraint at strikers' meetings, reminding them that claymasters were also fellow human beings. Ministers of all denominations advised moderation and tried, unsuccessfully, to persuade the claymasters to negotiate.[26] While sympathising with the sufferings of distressed strikers' families, they were unconvinced of the need for unions. The Primitive Methodist Minister W. A. Bryant was among those who urged the men to abandon their claim for union recognition in order to reach a peaceful settlement. The Cornish Wesleyan Synod, meeting at a crucial moment in the clay strike, refrained from passing an opinion upon the merits of the strikers' case and advocated 'moderate consensus and mutual forbearance'. An example of nonconformist neutrality was the use of the Bible Christian Sunday School at St Austell, not far from Rowse's home, to house the Glamorgan police, a 'rough crew' according to Rowse.[27]

The radical Editor of the *West Briton*, however, criticized the way that some prominent Methodists had 'laid low' during the strike, accusing them of being 'too much in with the big bugs', and the *Newquay Express* criticized their 'rigid silence', with only Booth Coventry whole heartedly on the side of the underdogs. Letters to the press called for the boycott of churches, and Alf Yelland, a well-known lay preacher on the strikers' side, was among those who claimed that the Christian church was failing in its duty and leaving it to the unions to fulfil its work of looking after the poor.[28] The 'big bugs' presumably included claymasters like Stocker and Dyer, devout Methodists and Sunday School Superintendents (a stone was thrown through the window of a chapel where Stocker was preaching), and this symbolized the divided loyalties of the clay district, where Methodism embraced workers, clay captains and claymasters.

The same divisions were apparent in political matters. Isaac Foot, a leading Liberal in Cornwall and the South West, was quick to declare that his 'sympathy was absolutely and unreservedly with the clayworkers' and the popular 'Tommy' Robartes, MP for St Austell, was said by Vincent to be on their side[29] but the *St Austell Star* was a typical example of local ambivalence. Its Editor, Walter John Nicholls, an eminent Methodist, Chairman of the Rural District Council and founder of the Strike Relief Fund, supported the right of the workers to form unions, but on occasions condemned their violence and concluded that the strikers' cause was ruined by indiscipline and disorganization.

Other newspapers inclined towards the workers' side, like the *Cornish Guardian* and the *Newquay Express*, came to similar conclusions. On the other hand these papers condemned the employers for their intransigence in refusing to negotiate and the Star rebuked some prominent Liberals, including Henry Hodge, Chairman of the St Austell Liberal Association, County Councillor and County magistrate, and H. Syd Hancock, Secretary of the St Austell Liberal Association and Parliamentary Agent for the Liberal Party, for remaining silent during the strike while always being free with their opinion on other matters. Hancock, though, as manager of a clay works and agent to the claylord Sir Charles Graves-Sawle, was on the employers' side.

Other leaders with strong clay interests, like William T. Lovering and John Wheeler Higman, were pillars of the Tory Party, but others, such as Frederick Augustus Coon, were life-long Liberals. Coon, County Councillor for Bugle, was famous for his radical views, calling for the abolition of the House of Lords and the nationalization of the railways and land, but he was chased by strikers through the streets of St Austell, escaping from the back door of the White Hart Hotel, after he spoke at a meeting advising them to go to work and hold a referendum on the decision to continue the strike.[30]

A BATTLE BETWEEN INTERLOPERS

After what had become almost a struggle between non-Cornish union leaders and policemen from outside Cornwall had ended, the chief protagonists departed. Vincent seems to have disappeared without trace, Booth Coventry was posted to Scotland and two years later resigned from the ministry, Tom Mann and the union officials went on to greater glories elsewhere, only Joe Harris remained to stand as Parliamentary Candidate (Rowse attended his election meetings). As for the police, they were demonized, sanctified and sanitized in the usual manner. To trade unionists they were brutal mercenaries of capitalist oppression; to the *Royal Cornwall Gazette* and the *Western Morning News* they were merely carrying out orders in the face of severe provocation. Bristol Council and Cornwall County Council investigated their record and found it beyond reproach. One china clay captain from Bugle received an ebony walking stick from the Tonypandy men in appreciation of his support.

But what had the strike achieved? Most commentators at the time and since have concluded that the clayworkers came off worst, forfeiting between £60,000 and £70,000 (£100,000 according to Mudd) in wages foregone, but this seems an exaggeration. Undoubtedly some families suffered distress, but while the strike disrupted production for eleven weeks, total stoppages were much shorter, and output for 1913 was only 4 per cent below the record level of 1912. Men who returned early to work, or earned overtime afterwards to make up lost production, must have received nearly as much in 1913 as in 1912. As for the employers, clay shipments through Fowey for 1913 were only 2 per cent down on 1912, implying that they had made up the 4 per cent shortfall by using existing stocks.

If the claymasters and men suffered short-term losses, however, the Workers' Union was the undoubted winner. Within months Stocker's thousand-strong West of England Company, closely followed by other producers, negotiated a three-year, no-strike contract with Matt Giles and Joe Harris which meant that a labourer working a 7½-hour day would make £1.60 a week, more than the original target. The china clay worker, by the standards of the general labourer of his day, was well paid, and the Workers' Union claimed the credit for this.

The longer-term consequences of the strike are difficult to assess, since eight months after it ended the Great War broke out. Stuart Dalley has suggested that disillusion with the establishment who had used police forces to end the strike accounted for the lack of enthusiasm among clayworkers to join the army[31] and Alfred Jenkin contended that the performance of Workers' Union officials during the strike so impressed Cornishmen that its membership rose to 15,000 in Cornwall as a whole by 1918. However by 1918 the climate of British industrial relations had changed. A general shortage of labour had shifted the balance to workers and trade union membership doubled to eight million. Even without the 1913 strike, and the powerful intervention of the Workers' Union, labour strength in the clay industry would probably have grown.

Finally, was the strike part of a carefully prepared movement to over throw the capitalist system? If so, it was surprisingly badly organized, with rival unions poaching each other's members and failing to co-operate in parallel strikes. The absence of china clay strikes in West and North Cornwall and Lee Moor, and of ball clay strikes in North Devon and Dorset, suggests that both disputes were the result of union ambitions to secure a toehold in hitherto unexplored recruiting grounds. Perhaps the key reason why the Cornwall strike failed and the Devon strike succeeded was that in Cornwall employers responded to the traditional rallying cry 'One and All' whereas claymen, did not. In Devon, ironically, the opposite was the case.

NOTES AND REFERENCES

1. The authors thank Bernard Deacon and Tony Noonan for useful comments on an earlier draft. John Tonkin has also made valuable comments on previous drafts and generously made available unpublished research from his own archives.
2. Garry Tregidga and Lucy Ellis, 'Talking Identity: Oral Culture through Group Dialogue', in Philip Payton (ed.), *Cornish Studies: Twelve*, Exeter, 2004, p. 98.
3. The strike of ball clay workers was headlined 'The Mid Devon Strike' by local newspapers, although in the ball clay world the district is known as the South Devon area.
4. Apart from the references cited in the text, information on the strike comes from the Truro-based *Royal Cornwall Gazette* (*RCG*) and *West Briton* (*WB*), the Plymouth *Western Morning News* (*WMN*), the Bodmin *Cornish Guardian* (*CG*), the *Newquay Gazette* (*NG*) and the *St Austell Star* (*SAS*). All these papers reported the events of the strike at great length. Other references include the Penzance-based *Cornish Telegraph*

(*CT*), the St Ives *Western Echo* (*WE*) and the Newton Abbot *Mid Devon Advertiser* (*MDA*).

5. For a fuller discussion of these issues see Ronald Perry and Charles Thurlow, 'The china clay strikes of 1875–6', *China Clay History Society*, 9, 2005, pp. 4–7.

6. See, for example, A. Mutch, 'Lancashire's Revolt of the Field', *North West Labour History Society*, 8, 1982, pp. 56–67.

7. *SAS* 19, 26 September 1907, 17 August 1911, 14, 21, 28 March, 4 June 1912, 7, 14 August 1913.

8. Letter of 24 April 1890, from John Tonkin archives.

9. *Alfred Jenkin Collection* in Courtenay Library of RIC Truro; *Cornish Life*, July 1981.

10. Eric Taplin, 'Unionism among seamen and dockers', *North West Labour History Society*, 1987.

11. Mutch, 1982, pp. 56–67.

12. *WB* 7 August 1913.

13. Marshel Arthur, *The Autobiography of a China Clay Worker*, Federation of Old Cornwall Societies, 1995, p. 31.

14. *WB* 25, 28 August, *WMN* 21 August, *SAS* 11, 18, 25 September 1913.

15. The ballad was issued in two parts and sold for 2d a copy in aid of the Strike relief Fund: 'A Clay Worker', *The Cornish Clay Strike: the White Country Dispute*, August 1913 (30 stanzas); 'Unskilled Labour', *A Souvenir of the China Clay Strike, Year 1913*, October 1913 (32 stanzas). The author is believed to be Tom Moyse of Meledor. We are indebted to John Tonkin for this information.

16. J.R. Ravensdale, 'The 1913 China Clay Strike and the Workers' Union', *Exeter Papers in Economic History*, 6, 1972, pp. 53–73.

17. *NE* 19 September, *FP*, *CG*, *RCG*, *NE*, 10 October 1913.

18. Kenneth Hudson, *The History of English China Clays*, n.d. Newton Abbot, p. 40; R.S. Best, 'Clayworkers' Sacrifice in Vain', WMN 18 July 1983; A.L. Rowse, *St Austell: Church, Town, Parish*, St Austell, 1960, p. 82.

19. J.M. Coon, 'The China Clay Industry', *Report of the Royal Cornwall Polytechnic Society*, 1927, p. 664; R.M. Barton, *A History of the Cornish China Clay Industry*, Truro, 1966, pp. 94, 130 *et seq*; David Mudd, *Cornwall in Uproar*, Bodmin, 1983, p. 4.

20. *RCG* 7, 14, 21 August 1913.

21. *SAS* 21 September 1911, 7 August 1913; *RCG* 7 August 1913; *CG* August 1913.

22. *SAS* 25 September, 23, 30 November 1913.

23. *SAS* 23 November 1911, 27 February 1913, *CG* 12 September 1913.

24. *RCG* 2 October 1913.

25. *WMN* 25 August 1913.

26. They included the Wesleyans Armstrong Bennett and T. Walter Cook, the United Methodist T.S. Lea, the Baptist H.C. Bailey, the Quaker J.H. Fardon and the Anglicans J.E. Carey, Vicar of Treverbyn and Frederick Thomas, Rector of St Mewan.

27. A.L. Rowse, *A Cornish Childhood*, London, 1942, repr. 1993, p. 124. The school is in Trevarthian Road, near the railway station.

28. *WB* 28 August, 11, 18, 25 September, *CT* 25 September, *NE* 22, 29 August 1913.

29. *WB* 7 August, *SAS* 14, 28 August, 4 September 1913.

30. For a discussion of the claymasters' role, see Ronald Perry and Charles Thurlow, 'The Edwardian Claymasters in Community Life', *China Clay History Society*, 2006.

31. Stuart Dalley, 'The Response in Cornwall to the Outbreak of the First World War', in Philip Payton (ed.), *Cornish Studies: Eleven*, Exeter, 2003, pp. 94, 100–1.

NATIONALIZED CORNWALL

Terry Chapman

INTRODUCTION

Introducing my article on the 'National Dock Labour Scheme in Cornwall' in *Cornish Studies: Twelve* (2004), our editor perceptively attributed the Scheme's 1947 establishment to the period's 'practical necessities and ideological aspirations'. The article itself suggested that although not strictly an integral part of the strategy, the National Dock Labour Scheme (NDLS) nevertheless bore considerable affinity to the post-war nationalization programme.[1] The practical and ideological origins of nationalization were, of course, linked intimately; firstly in the Attlee era, and later in Callaghan's. But this article will try to show that, while it may have been practical necessities that brought utilities such as gas, electricity and transport into public ownership, attempts to nationalize Cornish extractive industries (during the initial period) and (later) Falmouth Docks, owed rather more to contemporaneous ideological aspirations. The main aim here is to outline the *process* of nationalization (rather than its *performance*) in Cornwall. This approach may also shed light on the broader suggestion that it was differing approaches to socialism that determined the enthusiasm with which nationalization was pursued. If socialism aimed at the 'moral and material' defeat of capitalism, then its ideologically motivated proponents were often more concerned with that moral end rather than the practical means of achieving it.[2] Using Cornish examples, this article seeks firstly to establish the link between socialism and nationalization, and then to chart their progress from the Attlee period through to the Thatcher era, including the varying degrees of public enthusiasm and political support that they could command.

ORIGINS OF NATIONALIZATION

Although considered by some an 'arch opponent of public ownership', R. Kelf-Cohen was a senior government official closely involved in the process of nationalization.[3] To introduce his arguably tendentious but nevertheless factually authoritative reflection on *Twenty Years of Nationalisation: The British Experience*, he traces the Attlee Government's post-war programme back to the pragmatic 'gas and water socialism' of the Webbs. He quotes the Labour Party's 1918 Manifesto, which called for the national ownership of all transport and communications, 'unhampered by Capitalists, private or purely local interest . . . exclusively for the common good'.[4] Such overt commitment to public ownership was, of course, only recently abandoned with the contentiously symbolic removal of 'Clause IV' from the (New) Labour Party's Constitution. But signs of movement towards the post-Second War public ownership programme can be found during the First War and intervening years. To add to the local municipal provision of utilities such as gas and water, the State was becoming increasingly involved in emerging industries: broadcasting (BBC formed 1922), electricity distribution (CEB 1926) and civil aviation (BOAC 1939). Of local note was the formation of Cable and Wireless in 1934, following a conference to standardize above and sub-surface international communications.[5] Labour's pre-war Manifestos also made clear its commitment to a whole swathe of public ownership.[6] Based on his experience when successfully running London Transport, Herbert Morrison's 1933 *Socialisation and Transport* (note the conflation) provided the prototype public board corporation subsequently adopted by most of the industries taken over by the State. Herbert Morrison (1888–1965) was Minister of Transport in MacDonald's Government, then Leader of London County Council before becoming Home Secretary in Churchill's Coalition and finally, Attlee's Deputy.

That nationalization was seen by many to have failed to deliver the anticipated social and economic benefits may in part be attributed to undue interference, particularly financial, by successive governments, beginning with the one that started the process: Attlee's. The industries selected for nationalization were also inappropriate and doomed to failure, it has been argued, while the generous compensation paid and a lack of worker participation also hampered the new State enterprises. K. Morgan has added that post-war arrangements were 'hurriedly put together' and 'ill-thought out', setting the scene for industrial relations 'crises' three decades later: to which this article will return.[7] This is not the place to discuss the merits and demerits of nationalization in general or the Attlee programme in particular, although there is broad support in this article for C. Barnett's contention that the thinking behind public ownership was often based 'too much in terms of moral ends and too little in terms of practical ways and means'.[8] The primary aim here is to try to show how the Attlee programme and its successor impacted upon local industries.

ATTITUDES TO NATIONALIZATION BEFORE THE SECOND WORLD WAR

The origins of the socialist movement in Cornwall have been well documented, as has its subsequent faltering consequent upon industrial decline (particularly tin mining), together with the 'fossilization' of Cornish politics as a Liberal versus Conservative contest.[9] Yet A.L. Rowse (1904–1997) was not disastrously unsuccessful when he stood for Labour in the Penryn and Falmouth seat before the Second World War. At the very least he is considered to have exerted an important 'energetic influence' in preparing the ground for Labour's first Cornish electoral success in 1945 and even, perhaps, for its more recent (transient?) revival.[10] The brand of socialism that Rowse advocated had an 'Overtly Cornish agenda, attempting to popularise Labour's image and engage with local issues—to create in effect a Cornish Socialism'.[11] That up-country Labour's 'interfering and centralist' policies were viewed at the time with suspicion by many 'independent and individualistic' Cornish people was suggested by E.G. Retallack Hooper, later to become Grand Bard of the Cornish Gorsedd and Chairman of Mebyon Kernow, the Cornish nationalist movement. Retallack Hooper attempted to define an alternative Cornish Socialism, one that included a 'new economic system' better suited to Cornwall's unique industries. These industries, he said, 'demand treatment that cannot be dictated by ready-made up-country methods'.[12] Cornwall's pre-war socialists, then, were not all avid supporters of 'centralist' nationalization. But that is not to say that there were not some intent on nurturing seeds here that were already growing in firmer electoral ground beyond the Tamar.

Although printed in Derbyshire, *Cornish Labour News (CLN)* was established in 1932 as the 'official monthly organ' of the local socialist movement in Cornwall. Like Retallack Hooper, A.L. Rowse—leading Labour activist and a frequent contributor to *CLN*—supported 'community' socialism rather than the 'State' variant advocated else-where.[13] Yet his disappointment in the Penryn and Falmouth con-stituency epitomized the difficulty experienced by Labour in attempting a broader socialist breakthrough in Cornwall. Nonetheless, arguments deployed in early editions of *CLN* about the future of the Cornish extractive industries reflected the weight and influence of strategies and ideas being formulated elsewhere, beyond the Tamar.

Writing in the second edition of *CLN*, Sir Stafford Cripps KC MP (1889–1952, member of Churchill's War Cabinet, then President of Board of Trade in Attlee's Government before becoming Chancellor) acknowledged that the advance of socialism would be difficult amid the 'sturdy independence' of Cornish Liberal-radicalism. Yet the period's straitened economic circumstances had convinced him that capitalism now survived only by cutting workers' wages and reducing social provision. Thus, in Cornwall as elsewhere, 'the one salvation of civilisation lies in the *planned* and *co-ordinated* control of production'.[14]

There was much circumstantial evidence in Cornwall that served to support Cripps' analysis. F.H. Hayman (1894–1966) was later to hold the re-drawn Falmouth and Camborne seat for Labour from 1950. His 1951 Election leaflet revealed that it was his experience as a local government official working among the mass-unemployment in West Cornwall before the War that had convinced him of the need for a 'socialist approach'. A local historian, J. Higgans, noted that with few ships and no alternative employment, there was 'hardship' among the Hayle dockers of the period. Even the frequently unsympathetic Exeter Survey described the Camborne-Redruth-Hayle area's pre-war unemployment as 'onerous'.[15] In the similarly depressed clay country, a youthful Jack Clemo found himself surrounded by 'extreme squalor, illiteracy and inarticulate conflict'. He told the story, for example, of a family being thrown out of their cottage for non-payment of rent. When the hovel they had built for shelter collapsed, they were removed to the work-house. Although he recognized that socialists might view his self-confessed 'mysticism' with suspicion, he also knew 'that there was something terribly wrong with a system' that forced him at the age of 18 (and disabled) to live on his mother's charity from her weekly pension of 26/8 (£1.34).[16] As Attlee's pre-war, pre-Keynsian analysis insisted: 'The cause is private property; the remedy is public ownership'.[17]

Two other articles in the second edition of *CLN* identify the deleterious local effects of capitalism in order to lend support for the argument for more State ownership, the strategy advocated by the likes of Attlee and Cripps as the panacea for Britain's economic and social ills. In that year, 1932, the English China Clay Company had merged with its two main rivals, Lovering's and Pochin, to become ECLP. Discussing the merger under the headline 'The Workers Must Keep and Act Together', H.W. Mott focussed on the human costs of capitalism. The merger in his view would save the companies money by reducing competition, a monopolistic position which he believed would be 'wasteful and wrongful' for those clay-workers who had already endured—as Clemo attested—widespread 'poverty and privation'.

Indeed, Mott thought that unemployment in the clay industry was fast becoming as bad as that in tin-mining, and nearly as bad as that in the decimated pit villages of South Wales. For Mott, the answer was to remove industrial production from the hands of a selfishness system which sought only to exploit workers for profit. Capitalist unity, as evidenced by the ECLP merger, should be met with 'workers' trades' union unity' through support for Labour: the only party which sought to give workers 'their full share of the commodities and chances of life which they produce and make possible'.[18]

Although D.B. Barton, the mining historian, subsequently dismissed the proposal as 'specious', A. K. Hamilton Jenkin's slim volume *The Nationalisation of West Country Minerals* presented a case for State intervention that was welcomed as timely, relevant and realistic. It was reviewed in that same, second edition of *CLN*.[19] Payton has described Cornwall's inter-war years as a 'puzzling paradox', seeking to unravel the conundrum of 'socio-economic paralysis' occurring at the same time as a 'romantic Revivalist reinvention' of Cornish identity. Payton numbers Jenkin, hailed then as now as an authority on Cornish mining history, among those 'reluctant Revivalists' who—perhaps against their better judgement—were persuaded to lend their support during the inter-war years to the Cornish-Celtic Revivalist project. This included, Payton argues, a post-industrial yearning for a pre-industrial Cornish culture, a romantic longing that may unwittingly have contributed to the very paralysis from which the Revivalists sought to escape. But Jenkin at least cannot be accused of failing to confront the problems then facing Cornwall, his advocacy of the nationalization of mineral rights being designed to improve the lot of those engaged in Cornish extractive industries.[20] His mineral right nationalization pamphlet—seen as a key document—was reissued in 1932 by the Fabian Research Bureau (with Attlee as its chairman) for use by the Cornish Branch of the Society for Socialist Inquiry and Propaganda. Jenkin's main criticism was of the 'scandalous mismanagement, not to use a nastier phrase' inherent in what he called 'over capitalisation', the financial dereliction that wasted resources, to the direct detriment of the working men. To illustrate his point, Jenkin claimed that in the Cornish mining industry's 'boom-year' (*sic*) of 1926, only half of the £8 million invested actually went into the working of mines, the rest seemingly evaporating in administration.[21]

Significantly, while national figures such as Attlee and Cripps—together with some locals such as Mott—had advocated public ownership principally on ideological grounds, Jenkin's proposals were more practically based. He believed that *when* the time came for the State ownership of coal, as then recently recommended by two independent commissions, it was of the 'utmost importance' that Cornish and West Country mineral (and water) rights be included. This he would extend to china-clay because that too suffered 'many of the same disabilities resultant from the private ownership of minerals'. Suitably empowered local agents would be engaged to prevent capitalist abuses such as 'sett sitting': holding but not working rights in the hope that their value might increase. If ownership of a sett was contested, this would trigger the intervention of a Mining Court equipped with powers to impose settlements 'on public grounds'. Jenkin believed that 'centralising the ownership of minerals offers at least a partial means of controlling and *planning* the development of the industry'. This was an 'obvious' first step, he said, towards both increasing employment and the freeing of resources likely to be of 'benefit to the country at large'.[22]

ATTITUDES TO NATIONALIZATION DURING THE SECOND WORLD WAR

Cornwall's two main extractive industries—china-clay and hard-rock mining—provide a particularly useful illustration of wartime thinking on nationalization. While there was an excess of china-clay during hostilities, shortages of vital wolfram, tin, lead and zinc first brought their extraction into serious consideration for public ownership. But after the War, when exporting became vital for economic recovery, the position was reversed, and it was clay that came into consideration for nationalization.

Those involved in wartime metalliferous extraction formed the Cornish Tin Mining Advisory Committee (CTMAC) in early 1942. Minutes of most of their meetings and some related correspondence have been retained in the Cornwall Record Office in Truro. This article aims merely to examine the Committee's thinking on post-war nationalization, but the collection—loose-leafed and uncatalogued as it is—would merit much closer examination for its insights into contemporaneous industry in general, and its contribution to the war-effort in particular. Barton notes the drafting into Cornish mines of Canadian sappers, Polish miners, Italian prisoners under certain restrictions, and the often troublesome 'optants': men opting for mining rather than military service. The records also show that were Irish labourers, china-clay workers, and women for surface-work. Barton believes that despite a 'crash prospecting programme', little additional output was actually achieved and that within two years of the War's end, only Geevor and South Crofty were left in even depleted production.[23]

Under its chairman, Cornwall's then Lord Lieutenant Lt Col E.H.W. Bolitho, and with many locally famous mining names in its ranks, the CTMAC appears to have acted as the local agents for the Ministry of Supply's Non-Ferrous Mineral Development Control.[24] Its exact relationship and the respective responsibilities exceed the limits of this article, but of passing interest is that the Secretary to the Advisory Committee to the Ministry's Control appears to have been one Dr W.R. Jones. His paper advocating the nationalization of mineral rights was considered by the CTMAC, and he later chaired the post-war Working Party examining the china-clay industry's future. Wartime experience seems to have changed the Cornish Committee's attitude to public ownership. At their very first meeting, while force-fully pointing out that the needs of the present were then far more pressing than those of the future, the Chairman also reminded Ministry attendees that 'Cornishmen were prejudiced against outside inter-ference'.[25] Perhaps later appreciating the parlous position that the industry would be in at the War's end, the Committee had gone as far as publishing a Memorandum proposing the establishment of a national Metalliferous Mining Commission. The proposed Commission would own mineral rights, with owners in production being suitably recompensed, while something akin to the CTMAC would administer the industry locally. This would be nationalization with a Cornish face, public ownership managed from within Cornwall.

The Committee's proposal was supported at a conference to consider Cornwall's future convened in Camborne as the War ended. Attended by two local MPs and representatives from all geographic and economic areas, J.H. 'Jack' Trounson, long-term advocate of Cornish Mining, urged every effort to secure the proposed Com-mission's investment in existing mines and other 'propositions' before it was too late. While other attendees naturally wanted their areas also considered, Commander Agnew MP (Cons. Camborne) thought the delay in establishing the Commission was largely due to a transfer in Ministerial responsibility from Supply to Fuel and Power: presumably because of its association with the mining of coal. More broadly, something of the differing approaches between the main parties to post-war reconstruction can perhaps be seen in the meeting's eventual outcome. Commander Agnew's proposal that only specified areas need be included was defeated, and the meeting decided to call for the whole of Cornwall to be scheduled a Development Area under the prospective Distribution of Industry Act. They also agreed to set up a local Development Council.[26] Thinking that the MP's proposal might have been more effective, the *Cornish Guardian's* 'Whispers and Echoes' columnist urged more local initiative. With a bit of a swipe at the Government's avowed New Jerusalem, the columnist believed that 'waiting for the Government to build a new heaven and earth' would be asking for trouble beyond the purely industrial.[27] Determining exactly what became of the proposal would exceed the limits of this study; with it perhaps only being necessary to note here that the Commission was not in the end established. However, recalling the Treasury's initial lukewarm response to the proposal as seen in the CTMAC records, it might reasonably be inferred that any help for particular Cornish industries got swept up in general assistance nominally provided under such as the Distribution of Industry Act; as F.H. Hayman MP later acknowledged. But of incidental note is one subsequent analyst's finding that under the Act, the three main Development Areas (South Wales, North East England and all of Scotland) tended to divert attention and funds away from other worthy claimants.[28] Meanwhile locally, Jack Trounson helped form the purely Cornish Mining Development Association in 1948, being made an Honorary Life Member in 1986. The Association's aim of furthering possibilities for the industry's permanent revival has yet to reach fulfilment.[29]

In tracing the story of the biggest UK operation in the industry to 1966, K. Hudson divides his upbeat *History of English China-Clay* into two periods. The industry's organization up to the Second World War is described as 'primitive': characterised as being 'fragmented and under-capitalised'. Much more dynamic were the industry's post-war years, marked by 'Large production units . . . [and the] . . . application of scientific research to all aspects of the business'. Much of the transition is attributed to the serious re-thinking done during the War, not least to 'escape' the prospect of post-war nationalization.[30] Whether the 1947 Exeter Survey team wanted full public ownership of china-clay is unclear, but—as has been seen—before the War there had been a body of opinion favouring nationalization of Cornish and West Country mineral rights. Of particular note here is the Survey's insistence that since china-clay was an exporter, and since exports would be vital to any post-war economic revival, the industry could 'count upon the solicitous interest of the State'.[31]

During the War, with men machinery and materials all diverted to War work, domestic demand for clay fell to half that of 1939, and export to only 17 per cent. Two developments, however, set the scene for the post-war debate over nationalizing the industry. Firstly, there was a wartime 'conspiracy case' following governmental moves to concentrate production in 'designated nucleus firms'. As well as revealing some of the industry's more 'Alice in Wonderland' features, the case is also thought to have confirmed its innate hostility towards concentration. The 1932 merger, discussed earlier, that had brought ECLP into being, with its diverse activities ranging from clay-works to docks, farms to warehouse and to say nothing of a complex system of dues payable by tiers of leaseholders to various freeholders, had been a 'legal nightmare'. Later, as the conspiracy case collapsed, the Judge and a defending Counsel had come close to agreeing that china-clay was the most confusing industry they had ever encountered. The case did, however, bring home to the industry's leaders how fragmentation weakened their position in dealing with the advancing State machine. On the other hand, Hudson also counts such fragmentation as a strength when it came to the industry subsequently seeking to avoid post-war nationalization. The conspiracy case prompted the second wartime development: the complete re-think of the industry to produce ECLP's Post-War Development Plan. When the Government's initial Working Committee on the industry published its findings in March 1946, the report is thought to have read very much like a 'paraphrase' of the company's own post-war plan.[32]

The wartime gestation of Labour's post-war nationalization programme has been the subject of much critical analysis by scholars of the period. Many seem to support the contention made here, that the process was often driven more by ideology than practicality. P. Hennessey, for instance, recalls the famous activist ambush at the 1944 Party Conference that supported a massive post-war programme, but which none other than 'Mr Socialisation' himself (Morrison) thought likely to have cost them the forthcoming Election. Nevertheless, A. Calder finds the ensuing manifesto *Let us Face the Future,* a 'cosy and un-provocative document' that included many old favourites for nationalization, omitted a few and postponed that of land indefinitely. C. Barnett goes on to blame Morrison's managerialism for subsequently steering the Cabinet Socialisation of Industry Committee towards establishing 'steady-state utilities rather than dynamic enterprises'. Most commentators agree, however, that—to echo a Barnett chapter heading— 'The Spotlight has always been on Coal.'[33]

Many in the Labour movement saw the coal industry as the most archaic bastion of capitalism, and it therefore undoubtedly became (and remained?) 'the most passion-laden of all nationalisations'. But, in attributing Labour's industrial strategy to the two earlier discussed principles, firstly the long-term partisan and moral objective of public ownership (particularly coal), and secondly the practical increase in efficiency, P. Addison argued that it was never exactly clear how the two were related. For him, the twin principles seemed sometimes to over-lap, sometimes to coincide, and sometimes to even conflict. However, Fielding's analysis is probably nearer the mark, offering a plausible resolution of the differing readings of the post-war period made at the time by Labour Party members. There were certainly fundamentalists who believed that socialism meant both the moral and material defeat of capitalism. But most voters were far less interested in the ethical transformation of society. More prosaically, they were on the whole content with 'a welfare state and full employment'.[34] The resultant argument over more rather than less socialism, as represented by more rather than less nationalization, became henceforth a recurrent theme—both within the Labour Party, with the continuing tension between idealists and pragmatists, and in the wider Labour-versus-Conservative contest. The argument also informs the remaining part of this article.

NATIONALIZATION AFTER THE WAR
The sequence in which the evocative if ill-defined 'commanding heights' (totalling some 20 per cent) of the economy was taken into public ownership can be stated simply.[35] First nationalized in 1946 were the Bank of England, Cable and Wireless and the coal and civil aviation industries. In 1947 the whole transport industry, which included rail, canals and road haulage was nationalized; as was the electricity industry. Next was gas in 1948, followed finally by iron and steel in 1949; the latter being immediately de-nationalized on return of the Conservatives in 1951. Nationalization of the Bank of England and civil aviation do not have a particularly Cornish dimension. Nor does iron and steel. More important for Cornwall, perhaps, was watering down of Labour's proposals in the face of determined opposition. With the growing acceptance of Keyensian demand management economics, there were some early signs of wavering commitment toward public ownership. But the nationalization of Cable and Wireless, and the power and transport industries, certainly did affect Cornwall and is discussed further below. Coal, for many the crucible in which much of Labour's programme was forged, seems only to have indirectly affected Cornwall.

Much like BOAC and the Bank of England, the nationalization of Cable and Wireless, with its cable-head at Porthcurno, was relatively painless. Cable and Wireless, specialized in overseas communication, although few knew of the company when it came 'into public ownership but not public scrutiny' in 1946. It was similarly quietly returned to private hands in 1981.[36] But, the post-war period's practical necessities brought the much more prominent gas electricity and transport industries, those that Hennessey terms the State of Emergency industries, into public ownership.[37] These essential services had been used mercilessly during the War, with production considered more important than productivity. Hugely under invested might be one description; clapped out, another. If nothing else—and it is hardly a trifling consideration—public ownership in these conditions provided much needed capital as well as 'co-ordination': the so-called 'blessed', 'key-word' of the period.[38]

With the distribution grid already publicly owned, electricity generation was in many ways also relatively painless in transition. While there seem to have been other minor companies, the main local concern appears to have been the Cornwall Electric Power Company (head office at Pool, between Camborne and Redruth, where today's power distribution company has a depot), an 'associated company' of the Edmunsons' Electricity Corporation Limited. While its chairman could rail against the 'ruthless extinction' of a great company, some argued that rural areas in particular benefited from electricity's nationalization. Before the War's end, the Central Electricity Board had reportedly 'directed' CEPC to expand their capacity at Hayle to help bring power to more out-lying areas. Even so, and while Edmunsons' could claim to have been working toward reducing distribution construction costs, following nationalization, the incoming chairman of the South West Electricity Board reported that only about 20 per cent of Cornwall's then 37,000 farms had power. Of those, only about a third used it for more than just lighting.[39] The extension to Hayle's by then publicly owned coal powered station was on line by the time of the 1952 County Council Survey, which was advised that with Hayle and smaller oil powered stations at Bude and St Austell, Cornwall's foreseeable power needs could be met.[40]

Far more fragmented was gas supply, the rationalization that came through the nationalization of gas was considered not only politically desirous (at least in some circles) but industrially necessary.[41] Before nationalization there were apparently over 1,000 private gas suppliers of varying efficiency in Britain, of which 27 were in Cornwall.[42] Nationally, the number of suppliers was halved in the ten years following nationalization, with plans 'well advanced' by the 1952 Survey to reduce those in Cornwall to just three. To serve the west of Cornwall a new production plant would be built in Truro, with those at Penzance and Newquay being improved. The east would be supplied from Plymouth, with Bude serving as a northern distribution point.[43]

The Central Electricity Authority was established in 1948 as the single power generator for the 14 (later reduced to 12 on Scottish re-organization) regional distribution Boards; the Chairmen of which sat on the CEA. Gas differed in that there was no centralized authority; rather Chairmen of the 12 Area Boards met in a more 'federal' Gas Council to agree general policy, while retaining their regional autonomy in gas production and financing.[44] Both industries at the time were almost entirely dependant on coal, but both were to move increasingly towards the inclusion of other energy sources. Locally, one result was that, having already been reduced to only supplementing the national grid when needed, Hayle's power-station closed in 1973.[45] Cornwall's gas-works closed in the 1950/60s as natural gas first supplemented then supplanted coal as primary energy source. Later nationally, the Government's advertising campaign encouraged us to 'tell Sid' about the sale of British Gas in 1986. But the public mood cooled after such early successful privatisations. Sale of the Electricity Boards was delayed to the early 1990s, showing that for some observers Mrs Thatcher's later de-nationalizations were 'out of dogma, [ideology] without having made the case on managerial or cost [practical] grounds'.[46] This was, of course, exactly what her predecessors had accused Attlee and Callaghan of doing; albeit in the opposite direction.

Transport is often seen as the Attlee government's most ambitious, if least successful, nationalization. P. Hennessey views the attempt as doomed from the outset, describing the arrangement as a 'blueprint for unmanageability'. Contemporaneous local reaction called the proposal, 'Ideology gone mad', and the industry's co-ordinating body, the British Transport Commission, 'A crazy edifice of centralisation'.[47] Under funded and under resourced, the Herculean task of the five-man Commission involved simultaneously running, integrating and re-organizing the canals, rail and road transport, both passenger and freight, while surveying all ports with a view to their re-organization. Some ports, of course including neighbouring Plymouth, were nationalized already with the railway companies that owned them. Canals and ports had little in common except water, and the problems of the railways alone were almost overwhelming. Little wonder that the Commission was rewarded with only scant success. Little wonder too that the incoming Conservatives quickly set about reducing the BTC's responsibilities.

Much has been written about Cornish railways, both before and after nationalization, and little new can be added here. One local note on the impact of the brief period of nationalized road transport will, however, be taken to illustrate the broader difficulties encountered. A short recap shows that from 1933, only road hauliers holding what were known as A and B licences could carry for reward; while the carriage of own goods needed a C license. Following the 1947 Act, A and B license holders also needed a further permit to carry over 25 miles. Long-standing Conservative opposition meant that in 1953 road freight was denationalized, with the Road Haulage Executive abolished along with the 25 mile limit. K. Hudson notes ECC's (by then ECLP's parent company) maneuvering to ensure that its Heavy Transport Division was devolved into 'declared subsidiaries'. That way, until denationalization, operations qualified as own goods carried under the unlimited C licence.[48]

Many factors contributed to Labour's ousting just six years after their unambiguous 1945 landslide: continuance of wartime controls and rationing, resurgence of the Conservatives, even the weather. But perhaps, most significant was the series of economic calamities which befell it. The first was the ending of America's Lend-Lease programme just six days after V J Day, and the last the arguably disastrous over-estimate of likely Korean War expenditure. Details, although vital in understanding the period, need not overly delay this narrative. Suffice here to say that throughout the period exports, particularly to the dollar area, were vital to the Attlee Governments' economic recovery programme: even survival. As well as reminding readers that the paper used contained up to 25 per cent china-clay, the industry's governmental Working Party's 1948 report is discussed further below. Of note though is its recording that even in normal times as an export, clay was second only to coal in both value and tonnage; currently, 'because of coal shortages it ranks first'.[49]

Even if its importance was then largely unrecognized up-country, the industry's requests for scarce resources, including manpower, at the War's end brought it to official note. An already discussed, initial governmental Working Committee looked at the industry's immediate post-war recovery and recommended the establishment of a full Working Party to look further ahead. Made up of ministry officials, academics and local leaders of both sides of the industry, the Working Party produced its report, as noted above, in 1948. It had met under the chairmanship of geologist Professor W.R. Jones of Imperial College London; described as being 'well to the left of the Labour Party' and, as seen in his wartime dealings with the CTMAC, a supporter of nationalizing mineral rights.[50] Recommendations this time ranged from better housing welfare and training for workers, across the need for more mechanization, long-term planning and research, with perhaps most significantly the formation of a tri-partite China-Clay Development Council. But, unable to agree on full nationalization, the Working Party recommended merely that how best to bring all mineral rights under 'single ownership should be examined'.[51]

With his father working in an ECLP laboratory, and sister teaching in the St Austell area, the then President of the Board of Trade, Harold Wilson, supported many of the Working Party's recommendations.[52] But, a conference he later chaired on whether the recommended China-Clay Development Council should *control* or merely *advise* the industry was over-shadowed by a dramatic fall in home and European demand. Within a year of its reporting that labour shortages had helped secure an advantageous pay award for clay workers, the *Cornish Guardian* reported the laying-off of 150 men. Continuing local concerns over possible State involvement in the industry can not only be seen in debate of the proposed Clay Development Council's powers, but even in consideration of the 1947 Town and Country Planning Act.[53] Incidentally, J. Penderill-Church concludes his unpublished 1980 survey of *The China Clay Industry and Industrial Relations* with the claim that from its formation in 1950, the eventually purely internal China Clay Council 'safeguarded' relations in the industry.[54]

NATIONALIZATION REMISSIVE 1951–74

The Conservatives' return in 1951 meant an end to any discussion of nationalizing the clay industry. It is generally agreed that, for reasons touched on above, it was the loss of middle-opinion, if not necessarily middle-class, support that turned Labour's 1945 victory into defeat at the end of the decade. This was despite their traditional support remaining solid, and despite the fact that in Cornwall local support had, thanks in part to the almost moribund Liberal challenge, actually been growing.[55] *Cornish Labour Voice (CLV)*, incorporating the previously cited *Cornish Labour News*, first appeared in October 1949. Front page headlines appeared to celebrate local electoral victories, despite reversals in the national campaigns. 'Cornish Labour in Good Heart' greeted Attlee's narrow win in 1950; and 'Magnificent Increase in Cornish Labour Vote' followed his defeat the following year.[56] To take Falmouth and Camborne in 1950, F.H. Hayman's election pamphlet praised the success of nationalization in general, and coal and railways in particular. In it he also confirmed the Government's intention to press ahead with the further nationalization of cement, sugar and 'industrial assurance'. For the same contest, his Conservative opponent's leaflet denounced further nationalization as a 'socialist remedy' that had failed; saying bluntly that Conservatives would stop all further nationalization and denationalize road transport. Blunter still, the Liberals' pamphlet declared that 'nationalization for the sake of nationalization is nonsense—and socialism'.[57]

K. Morgan finds Labour 'clearly in retreat' on nationalization in the 1950 Election, describing industries further selected for such as 'random in the extreme'.[58] Labour faltering can perhaps also be discerned in Hayman's Maiden Speech. He called merely for the Minister to consider 'whatever proposals may be brought forward' to revive tin and sustain Falmouth Docks, while also thanking the Board of Trade for directing new lighter industry to his constituency. Similarly, and in marked contrast to his previous leaflet, his 1951 Election communication says nothing about nationalization, merely praising the Government's general policies towards full employment.[59] Analysis of the campaign at the national level confirms Labour's emphasis on 'consolidation' (new watchword), and concrete proposals such as had appeared in Hayman's 1950 leaflet were replaced by another evocative but vague aspiration, merely to take over business concerns that were 'failing the nation'.[60] Implicit, but nevertheless important, was the point made in *CLV* between the two Elections: nationalization had by then become, 'an essential instrument in maintaining full employment'.[61]

There were, as noted above, differences within Labour over the pursuit of more rather than less socialism, and therefore, about the efficacy and desirability of further nationalization. In their early years in Opposition after 1951, before defence became the dominant issue, 'Bevanites' to the left of the Party, had come to see socialism as 'largely a matter of implementing Clause IV'. Others behind the new leader, Hugh Gaitskell, thought that regaining power meant 'dispensing with the commitment'. From the right, Anthony Crossland published what some see as the 'revisionists' bible', *The Future of Socialism* in 1956.[62] At Labour's head, Gaitskell has been said to have found his 'heart drawing him towards public ownership while his analytical brain recoiled from its dubious results'. But his proposal to the Labour Conference for revision of Clause IV received little support. And presciently, Kelf-Cohen concludes his 1969 analysis of the episode with the view that public ownership 'remained a fundamental tenet of the Labour Party. If that were not so, the Party would cease to be the Labour Party'.[63]

The Tories, however, were also having difficulties over nationalization. Despite electioneering rhetoric to the contrary, on coming to office, iron and steel were denationalized but the industry remained under significant governmental control; and only road haulage was removed completely from what has previously been described as Labour's overly ambitious plan to integrate all transport. Of nationalized industries in general, notwithstanding 'a political distaste for their success' the Conservatives remained 'fearful of the industrial consequences of their failure'.[64] Conservative ambivalence in contrast to Labour's overt commitment, kept nationalization a live issue in all the Elections up to, and including Labour's return in 1964.

In continuance of the highly regarded 'magisterial series', David Butler's joint analysis of the 2005 Election appeared recently.[65] He had found nationalization a particularly important feature of the 1959 campaign, devoting a whole Appendix to the subject. During the contest, perhaps in response to Labour's re-commitment, a privately funded market research project had sought to establish the electorate's attitude towards nationalization. Butler believes the effort succeeded in both showing and stimulating the unpopularity of nationalization, even to proponents.[66] Almost 2 million questionnaires were completed in 129 marginal constituencies, which by their definition included Cornwall North, and Falmouth and Camborne. Customarily anti-metropolitan, local results were even more marked than the national. Results nationally showed 18.6 per cent for more nationalization with 63.5 per cent against; while in the two Cornish seats the averaged figures were 13.1 per cent for and 71.4 per cent against (don't knows at both levels around 18 per cent).[67]

Other Cornish differences among apparent similarities with elsewhere included a local 'Liberal renaissance' that culminated in the Liberals taking Bodmin in 1964, confirming a broader picture of a 'society in the process of change'.[68] Payton argues that Cornwall in this period was moving from the 'second' to a 'third' stage of peripheralism, perpetuating and redefining Cornwall's peripheral relationship with the metropolitan 'centre'. Nationally, increasingly strident calls for economic modernization to halt perceived decline were seemingly answered by the 1964 return of Labour under Wilson, albeit with a narrow majority. Since becoming leader on Gaitskell's death, Wilson had sought to bridge the gap between the emphasis on equality from the revisionist right of his party, and the more militant left wanting more public ownership. 'Modernization' was the new watch-word, with new Ministries of Economic Affairs and Technology to show that 'planning rather than nationalization was the way forward'.[69] Their hopes, this time for planned growth, were again dashed by a series of economic catastrophes. But just as in the Attlee years, while such are central to understanding the period, they are largely beyond the scope of this study. Here it is necessary to note only the Government's climb-down in face of opposition from within its own ranks to Barbara Castle's counter-inflationary industrial relations White Paper, *In Place of Strife*. This had the effect of helping the Conservatives to return under Heath, almost unexpectedly, in 1970.

As already noted, Wilson's first Administration was not ardently in support of public ownership. Even so, they could not resist reversing the Tories' 1953 return of iron and steel to private hands. In 1967, the British Steel Corporation took over the 14 companies producing 90 per cent of the industry's output and employing 70 per cent of its workforce. But under-investment had left the industry ill-equipped to compete with Far Eastern mass production, with the Conservatives eventually re-returning its rump to private hands in 1988.[70] Labour under Wilson also proposed nationalizing the port transport industry or at least the 30 ports (of 83 in the Dock Scheme plus those operated by British Transport), each handling over 5 million tons per year and employing a staggering 95 per cent of the registered dock-labour force.[71] Of course, none of these were in Cornwall, and the whole plan sank with the Conservative's return in 1970.

On coming to power the Heath administration may have famously claimed to be unwilling to re-float lame ducks, but events, again largely beyond the scope of this study, forced a 'u-turn' in more than just industrial policy. In many ways the Heath years can be seen as a period of transition, with 1972 perhaps proving the cusp. Amid national strikes in the pits and docks, unemployment was heading for what were then politically unacceptable levels; while inflation and prices were also rising steeply. Previously unseen, 'stagflation' was afflicting an economy supposedly being readied for the competitiveness of the European Economic Community. In response, and a direct reversal of their original disavowal, Rolls Royce the aero-engine manufacturer was taken over in the national interest. More controversially, Upper Clyde Shipbuilders were rescued to ward off perceived threats of civil unrest. The Secretary of State for Trade and Industry, Peter Walker, sponsored an interventionist Industry Act in 1972 to modernize (again) Britain's industrial and regional infrastructure, speaking enthusiastically about a 'socially responsible new capitalism'. Originally hands-off, the Heath administration then lavished public money into attempts to modernize old industries such as coal, steel and textiles, and into the one notable new one, computers. British Nuclear Fuels was established, and the remainder of the electricity and gas industries re-organized, readying them—sceptics might say— for subsequent disposal to the private sector.[72] A second miners' strike then induced the 'Who Governs Britain?' Election of 1974. In answer, those to starboard concluded that it would not be another administration that adopted the ultra-interventionist course taken after 1972.

NATIONALIZATION'S LAST GASP 1974–79

Labour had been tacking to port during the troubled Heath years, with some taking their pyrrhic 1974 victory as vindicating such a position. Reminiscent in some ways of the post-war era, 'misdiagnosis' of both the 1970 defeat and 1974 victory led the then ascendant left to press for more state intervention: in the hope of radically altering the balance of industrial and social power. Having campaigned against membership of the Common Market, the left (and right) were to some extent defeated by the emphatic 'yes' vote in the 1975 European Referendum.

Nevertheless, the Party's manifesto commitment to more public ownership formed part of the ambiguous Social Contract entered into with trades' unions while in Opposition. Under this arrangement, the unions agreed to moderate wage demands in return for reforms that included more public ownership. A National Enterprise Board (NEB) would be formed, while mineral rights would yet again come under scrutiny, with other initiatives of Cornish interest including plans to nationalize ship-building and repair, along with North and Celtic Sea gas and oil. But, notwithstanding its high hopes of encouraging new industries, the NEB when established instead found itself pouring money into declining industries, notably this time car manufacture. M. Holmes suggests that, in the car industry at least and probably beyond, the strategy produced the exact opposite of that desired: rather than 'industrial regeneration—industrial fossilisation'.[73]

David Mudd MP (Cons. Falmouth and Camborne) witnessed 'pandemonium' in the House following the Division on the Bill to nationalize aircraft and ship-building.[74] Being a minority government reliant on the minor parties, the left's then champion, Tony Benn admits that Labour 'cheated' to get the Bill passed by sending a Member known to be Paired through the Aye Lobby. In response, Michael Hesseltine's brandishing of the Speaker's Mace then helped establish his 'Tarzan' reputation.[75]

Citing a Labour Minister's admission that intense competition made winning orders difficult, Mr Mudd also repudiated the Government's claim that only nationalization could save the Falmouth yard. For their part, P & O, the then owners, had been trying to sell it since before the 1974 Election, but takeover indecision had seemingly frightened off potential buyers.[76] Prospects were further complicated by Falmouth's being numbered initially among twelve ship-repair yards included in the nationalization Bill which were subsequently dropped following opposition in the Lords.[77] Just ten days after the decision, however, P & O reportedly sought the Yard's re-insertion in the Bill, saying that although they did not support nationalization commercially, neither did they any longer wish to be in the ship-repair business. The Falmouth Docks Group and P & O's other interests in Tilbury were eventually among six ship-repairers taken over by British Shipbuilders in August 1977. Locally, financial negotiations had reportedly been 'going very well' but the whole had slowed trying to get 'satisfactory undertakings from the unions on certain practices'.[78] What exactly was at issue lies again beyond the limits of this study, but the Yard's unhappy industrial relations record (among many other stoppages, there had been a disastrously protracted boilermakers' strike in the cusp year 1972) must be recalled in the national context. When, following his inquiry into Britain's then torrid industrial relations, Lord Bullock (Bevin's biographer) published his proposals for greater industrial democracy, David Penhaligon MP (Lib. Truro) thought such an initiative likely to 'achieve the virtually impossible task of actually making our industrial relations worse'.[79]

The economic and industrial context might also be usefully recalled. In 1976 Callaghan's Government elected or was forced, depending on standpoint, into seeking a huge IMF loan. The inevitable conditions imposed included selling off most of the State's holding in BP, making Dennis Healey then Chancellor, 'the first privatiser'.[80] Industrially, the national manifesto commitment to take over shipbuilding came at an internationally unpropitious time. The downturn in global economic activity that followed the 1970s oil price explosion caused a dramatic decline in demand for shipping, with a consequent ferocious rise in foreign competition. Trying to weather the storm meant that British Shipbuilders were willing, with Government blessing, to take any orders, even uneconomic ones.[81] The contentious decision to subsidize the building of twenty four ships for Poland resulted had the additional unwelcome effect of assisting the Polish shipping business in undercutting British shipping operations.[82]

The local effects of other nationalizations merit brief consideration. For example, the Energy Secretary, Tony Benn, saw the considerable interest shown in oil and gas exploration 'blocks' off the Cornish coast as vindicating the Government's newly formed British National Oil Corporation holding a 51 per cent stake in all blocks.[83] My earlier study of the local Dock Labour Board found a flurry of expeditionary work during the late 1970s, with its subsequently 'stagnating' to leave only two companies working by 1986.[84] One slightly amusing footnote came as part of MP 'Willie' Hamilton's (Lab. Central Fife) 'one man crusade to topple the British monarchy'. Although the plan was doomed from the outset, Hamilton nevertheless moved a Private Member's Bill to nationalize without compensation the Duchies of both Cornwall and Lancaster. Believing Cornwall to have been looted from local Earls in the fourteenth century, he would 'in the sacred name of the people' apparently loot it back from Prince Charles.[85] Less amusing, at least for the people of Camelford, was one incident during de-nationalization of the water industry. Pre-war interest in its nationalization did not actually reach fruition until 1973. Some 1600 differing local operations were then absorbed in ten autonomous Regional Water Authorities: Cornwall coming under that for the South West. The industry's return to private hands had been announced by the Tories early in 1986.[86] Before the transfer, however, the Lawrence Inquiry into the Lowermoor water poisoning incident of July 1988 criticised both laxity at the works and the poorly coordinated initial response. A state of management limbo can hardly have helped dispel what the report termed 'a culture in which the public are told as little as possible and expected to trust the Authority to look after their interests'.[87]

Falmouth Docks was also caught up in the Tory's reversal of public ownership. Commentators see the initial Conservative policy as merely reversing the latter-day nationalization of aircraft and ship-building, broader privatization only being pursued as the Party's more ideological wing gained ascendancy after Election victories in 1983 and 1987. Despite hopes in some quarters that nationalization would secure employment (and orders), 1979 was another bleak year for Falmouth Docks. Almost 1,000 redundancies had left the workforce at a care-taker level of under 200. Local man Dennis Pascoe then staged a 'dramatic revival' to more than double the workforce by 1985, when a consortium including the current owners finally bought Falmouth Ship Repair Ltd., following the 1978 name change, for £1.75m.[88] While negotiations may have become embroiled in those over proposals to build a container terminal at Falmouth, the hiatus of the intervening period and modest price may also have reflected the claim that 'British Shipbuilders proved impossible to sell or even give away'.[89]

In 1979 the Conservatives won a massive 339 Seats on 43.9 per cent of the vote, with Labour's share falling to a post-war low of 36.9 per cent to take 268.[90] Cornish results mirrored the national. Across the five Cornish Seats, Labour support fell by 5.4 per cent between 1974 and 1979. In the former Labour stronghold, Falmouth and Camborne, the fall was even more dramatic. There, while Liberal support remained fairly constant around 13 per cent, Conservative support rose by 10 per cent while that for Labour fell by a similar amount, with the gap between them correspondingly widening from 11.5. per cent to 30.8 per cent.[91] While there may have been no Labour MPs for the Cornish electorate to unseat, the emphatic move towards the Conservatives seen across the UK in 1979 was undoubtedly evident in Cornwall. D. Butler and D. Kavanagh found the campaign 'a good example' of a Government losing rather than their opponents winning an Election: singling out the preceding Winter of Discontent for 'blighting' any signs of Labour's retention. Alongside the many similarities in the main Party's Manifestos, there was also an obvious clear choice between the Conservative promise of a smaller industrial role for the State and Labour's 'clearly more interventionist' proposals. In the detail, Labour would extend industrial democracy while the Tories would reverse the most recent nationalizations. But in contrast to the campaign two decades earlier, when the nationalization debate warranted a whole appendix in the Labour Manifesto, the word 'nationalization' had only a single entry in the index of that for 1979.[92]

CONCLUSION

This article began by attributing post-war nationalization to the ideological aspirations and practical necessities of that period. It has ended by looking at the impact on Cornwall of the differing aspirations and necessities holding sway during the Thatcher years. As we have seen, the Conservatives had to some extent been prepared previously to veer and haul in managing a mixed economy, aiming towards full employment. While there had also been some tentative movement away from public ownership following the IMF crisis of 1976, it was the coming of Thatcherism that was the real break. As we have also seen, the pace of reform then increased as 'big government' was replaced in the interests of more market-orientated 'efficiency'. Although originally ideologically driven, privatization also enabled a politically astute practical reduction in public funding and bolstered 'popular capitalism' through participatory share-schemes. Industrial relations were also reformed. On one level there was less Government intervention, and what there was aimed largely at strengthening management resolve. On another, the unions' complete exclusion meant the 'ending of tri-partite political exchange'.[93]

For the Labour Party, nationalization was always problematic in practice. Since before the Second World War, more or less nationalization was equated by Labour with more or less socialism. The differing stances of subsequent ideologues and revisionists, of left and right, and old and new have been examined in this article. Perhaps the new right (defined as those offering an 'electable reforming alternative to the Conservatives) had decided that, other than in the truly unique early Attlee years, Labour has always done best electorally when it has restrained its left wing (defined as those seeking 'more fundamental social and economic change').[94]

Although it might be argued that their monopoly status was in many ways as significant as ownership in determining the *performance* of nationalized concerns, this article has sought only to show the *process* in Cornwall. Practical necessity suggested that Cornish mining would have benefited from an injection of public funds after the War, but the industry probably lacked the clout to secure such support. On the other hand, in an expanding market, the china-clay industry, although attractive to the State, could resist its advances. Cornish industries were then largely unaffected by the ebb and flow of the nationalization debate, until later ideological aspirations that largely disregarded practical necessities, brought ship-building and repair into public ownership. But by then Falmouth Docks could be said to have lain on several peripheries, geographic economic and industrial, and was therefore unlikely to benefit even from what have proved to be the largely chimerical advantages of the centralist model of nationalization.

Of the two mainstays of the original programme, coal and the railways, the former has at least for now all but disappeared as a major industry. Still publicly subsidized, the latter—although in some respects improved—continues to face significant challenges. Possible water shortages in the South East of England recently became the 'national problem' that higher water bills in Cornwall and the South West have never been. But, the inverted ideological aspirations and practical necessities of privatizing lighter service type industries— aviation, banking, communications—has so far proved generally beneficial. In the energy sector however, as short-term anxieties over rising prices and instability of supply compound those over longer-term environmental costs, both Cornwall and the UK as a whole face some tough choices. As this study of nationalized Cornwall has helped demonstrate, separating the ideological from the practical in such considerations can prove difficult.

NOTES AND REFERENCES

1. P. Payton (ed.), *Cornish Studies: Twelve*, Exeter, 2004, pp. 7 & 229.
2. S. Fielding *et al.*, *England Arise*, Manchester, 1995, p. 216.
3. P. Hennessey and A. Seldon (eds), *Never Again Britain 1945–1951*, London, 1992, p. 207.
4. R. Kelf-Cohen, *Twenty Years of Nationalisation: The British Experience*, London, 1969, p. 19.
5. Institute of Electrical Engineers Review. *Cable and Wireless: From Victorian to Modern Times*, 1989, p. 65.
6. A. Pendleton and J. Winterton (eds), *Public Enterprise in Transition: Industrial Relations in State and Privatised Corporations*, London, 1993, p. 2.
7. R. Saville, *Commanding Heights: The Nationalisation Programme*, in J. Fryth (ed.), *Labour's High Noon*, London, 1993, p. 58; M. Caedel, 'Labour as a Governing Party: Balancing Left and Right', in T. Gourvish and A. O'Day (eds), *Britain Since 1945*, Basingstoke, 1991, p. 266; K.O. Morgan, *The People's Peace: British History 1945–1990*, Oxford, 1992, p. 36.
8. C. Barnett, *The Lost Victory*, London, 1995, p. 212.
9. G. Tregidga, 'Socialism and the Old Left' in P. Payton (ed.), *Cornish Studies: Seven*, Exeter, 1999, p. 79.
10. P. Payton, *The Making of Modern Cornwall*, Redruth, 1992, pp. 159 & 223; and *A.L. Rowse and Cornwall: A Paradoxical Patriot*, Exeter, 2005, pp. 111–13 & 129.
11. Tregidga, 1999, p. 89.
12. *Cornish Labour News*. 11.32. Held Cornish Studies Library, Redruth.

13. Tregiga, 1999, p. 89.
14. *CLN*, 11.32.
15. F.H. Hayman, *Election Pamphlet: 1951*. Held CSL, Redruth; J. Higgans, *The History of the Cornish Port of Hayle*. Unpublished 1991, held CSL Redruth, p. 76; & J. Murray *et al., Devon and Cornwall: A preliminary Study*, Exeter, 1947, p. 247. Note: P. Payton's *Cornwall* (Fowey, 1996, p. 249) records over 30 per cent unemployment in the area.
16. J. Clemo, *Confessions of a Rebel*, London, 1998 edn., pp. 40, 55 & 116.
17. Barnett, 1995, p. 213.
18. *CLN*, 11.32.
19. D.B. Barton, *A History of Tin Mining and Smelting in Cornwall*, Exeter, 1989, p. 179.
20. Payton, 1996, p. 272 and Payton, 1992, p. 130.
21. A.K.H. Jenkin, *The Nationalisation of West Country Minerals*, London, 1932, p. 16; & *CLN* 11.32.
22. Jenkin, 1932, pp. 12–17.
23. X 161 Cornwall Record Office, Truro & Barton DB 1989, p. 179.
24. Under Chairman Col. Bolitho, other members of the original CTMAC included F. Lyde-Caunter; A. Treve Holman; A.K.H. Lenkin; C.V. Paul; W.E. Sevier with J.E. Wickett as Secretary. T&GWU representative W.E. Cavill later invited to join but only when 'reconstruction problem had been nearly completed' (28.12.43). Also later (gently) criticised for not including any broader commercial interests or mining institutes: H. Thomas open letter to *Cornish Post* 06.05.44.
25. X 161, 04.03.42.
26. *West Briton*, 31.05.45.
27. *Cornish Guardian*, 31.05.45.
28. D.W. Parsons, *The Political Economy of British Regional Policy*, London, 1986, p. 101.
29. J.H. Trounson, *The Cornish Mineral Industry: Past Performance and Future Prospects: A Personal View 1937–1951*, Exeter, 1989, p. viii; and Barton, 1989, p. 284.
30. K. Hudson, *The History of English China-clays: Fifty Years of Pioneering and Growth 1916–1966*, Newton Abbott, 1969, pp. 53, 93, 104.
31. J. Murray *et al.*, 1947, p. 286.
32. K. Hudson, 1969, pp. 70 & 97.
33. P. Hennessey, 1992, p. 80; A. Calder, *The People's War*, London, 1969, p. 575; C. Barnett, 1995, pp. 221 & 272.
34. P. Hennessey, 1992, p. 103; P. Addison, 1994, pp. 177–8; S. Fielding *et al.*, 1995, pp. 216–18.
35. R. Saville, in J. Fryth (ed.), 1993, p. 37.
36. IEE, 1989, pp. 65–6.
37. Hennessey, 1992, p. 205.
38. Kelf-Cohen, 1969, p. 66. K.O. Morgan, 1992, p. 34.
39. *CG* 18.01.45, 10.07.47, 10.06.47 & 08.04.48.
40. Cornwall County Council, *Development Plan*, Truro, 1952, p. 192.
41. T. Williams, *A History of the Gas Industry*, Oxford, 1981, p. 98.

42. Williams, 1981, p. 94 & CCC, 1952, p. 190.
43. CCC 1952, p. 190.
44. Kelf-Cohen, 1969, p. 123.
45. Higgans, 1991, p. 62.
46. Morgan, 1992, pp. 469 & 493.
47. Hennessey, 1992, p. 207 & *CG* 19.01.46.
48. Hudson, 1969, pp. 133–4.
49. Board of Trade. *Working Party Reports: The China-clay Industry.* London, 1948, pp. viii & ix.
50. K. Hudson, 1969, p. 94.
51. Board of Trade, 1948, p. 48.
52. Hudson, 1969, pp. 40 & 50.
53. *CG* 09. 09.48, 11.12.47, 23.09.48 & 19.08.48.
54. J. Penderill-Church, *The China-clay Industry and Industrial Relations.* Unpublished but held C.S.L. Redruth, 1980, p. 9.
55. As well as taking and holding Falmouth Penryn/Camborne, Labour's total share of the vote in Cornwall rose from 18.3 per cent in 1945 to 24.2 per cent in 1951. The biggest rise came in North Cornwall, up from just 1.8 per cent in 1945 to reach 16.4 per cent six years later. See F.W.S. Craig, (ed.), *British Parliamentary Election Results 1918–1949 & 1950–1973*, Chichester, 1983.
56. *Cornish Labour Voice*, 03.50 & 11/12.51 held in Courtney Library, Truro.
57. 1950 Election leaflets held C.S.L. Redruth.
58. Morgan, 1992, p. 84.
59. Hayman's Maiden Speech reprinted in *CLV* 04.50 & 1951 Election leaflet.
60. Morgan, 1992, p. 104.
61. *CLV*, 05.50.
62. Fielding *et al.*, 1995, p. 210; & V. Bogdanor, 'The Crisis in Old Labour', in A. Seldon and K. Hickson (eds), *New Labour, Old Labour: The Wilson and Callaghan Governments, 1974–1979*, London, 2004, p. 14.
63. R. Kelf-Cohen, 1969, pp. 287–300.
64. A. Seldon, *Churchill's Indian Summer: The Churchill Government 1951–1955*, London, 1981, p. 195.
65. *The Times*, 03.12.05.
66. D.E. Butler and R. Rose, *The British General Election of 1959*, London, 1960, p. 244.
67. C. Hurry and associates, *A Survey of Public Opinion on Nationalisation*, London, 1959, p. 5 shows their definition of 'marginal seat': one where Conservative majority was J,000 and Labour's 2,000. Cornish results appear on page 25 and p. 7 summarises overall results.
68. Tregidga, in Payton (ed.), 1999, pp. 161 & 179.
69. K. Jeffery, *Retreat from New Jerusalem*, Basingstoke, 1997, pp. 101 & 189.
70. P. Blyton, 'Steel', in A. Pendleton and J. Winterton (eds), *Public Enterprise in Transition: Industrial Relations and Privatised Corporations*, London, 1993, pp. 168 & 181.
71. G. Adams, *Organisation of the British Port Transport Industry*, London, 1973, p. 224.

72. A. Cairncross, 'The Heath Government and the British Economy', in S. Ball and A. Seldon (eds), *The Heath Government 1970–1974: A Reappraisal*, London, 1996, pp. 155–6.
73. M. Holmes, *The Labour Government 1974–1979: Political Aims and Economic Reality*, London, 1985, pp. 37 & 54.
74. *FP* 04.06.76.
75. K.O. Morgan, *Callaghan: A Life*, Oxford, 1997, pp. 527–8.
76. *Western Morning News*, 18.03.77.
77. *FP* 26.11.76 & 04.03.77.
78. *FP* 18.03.77, 19.08.77, 29.07.77.
79. *FP* 04.02.77.
80. Morgan, 1992, p. 384.
81. L. Johnman and H. Murphy, *British Shipbuilding and the State Since 1918: A Political Economy of Decline*, Exeter, 2002, pp. 208–10.
82. Holmes, 1985, pp. 57–9.
83. *FP* 08.10.76.
84. CRO Truro X 900 series, 07/80 & 05/86.
85. *WMN* 15.05.75.
86. S. Ogden, 'Water', in Pendleton and Winterton (eds), 1993, pp. 137 & 145.
87. J. Lawrence, *Report of an Inquiry into an Incident at Lowermoor Water Treatment Works of South West Water Authority on 6 July 1988*, Brixham, 1988, pp. 21–2 & 9.
88. *FP* 22.03.85.
89. Johnman and Murphy, 2002, p. 217.
90. Morgan, 1992, pp. 421–22.
91. See F.W.S Craig, (ed.), *British Parliamentary Election Results 1974–1983*, Chichester, 1984.
92. D. Butler and D. Kavanagh, *The British General Election of 1979*, London, 1980, pp. 340, 161 & 153–6.
93. Pendleton and Winterton (eds), 1993, pp. 9 & 13.
94. M. Caedel, in Gouvrish and O'Day (eds), 1991, pp. 264 & 280.

'GUIZING': ANCIENT TRADITIONS AND MODERN SENISITIVITIES

Merv Davey

INTRODUCTION

'Guizing' is a Cornish dialect expression describing a custom in which revellers disguise themselves in a variety of ways and engage in music, singing, dance and informal theatrical activity. Terms such as *Guizing, Geese Dancing,*[1] *Goosey Dancing*[2] *and Shallal*[3] often appear in descriptions of Cornish folkloric tradition, together with the more widely recognized terms such as 'Mummers' and 'Morris'. Modern folklorists may separate these traditions taxonomically, but the distinction is not so clear in the descriptions of nineteenth-century narrators such as Bottrell.[4] The event known as 'Padstow Mummers' Day' or 'Darkie Day' that takes place in that town during Boxing Day and New Year, involves revellers disguising themselves by dressing up and blacking their faces, and can be considered to be part of a 'guizing' or 'mumming' tradition. However, the guize tradition at Padstow has recently become the subject of debate as to whether or not the activity is inherently racist. This article seeks to inform this debate by considering the origins of the tradition, describing the event as it is today, and considering the principal elements within the 'Padstow Debate'.

MIDWINTER GUIZING AND THE PADSTOW MUMMERS

Compared to May Day—with its world-famous 'Obby Oss'—the Boxing Day and New Year's tradition in Padstow is a relatively modest event, and this would seem to have been the case for much of its history. Prior to the 1990s, press coverage was limited largely to the local *Padstow Echo*. By contrast, the local correspondents for the *Cornish Guardian* have regularly contributed articles about May Day and the Padstow Carol singing, an interest that can be traced back to the newspaper's first edition in 1901.

The New Year edition of *Padstow Echo* in 1967 carried a 'Diary' item thanking Mary Magor, Olive Brunyes and Eunice Williams for 'keeping alive the Padstow Darkies by training the young Padstonians with the Darky Songs which have been traditionally sung here, with also the musical accompaniment'.[5] A letter From Mary Magor in the same edition praised the children involved and describes the event as an 'Old Padstow Custom we were trying to revive before it goes completely out of knowledge'. From her description, it is evident that there were 15 children involved aged between seven and 13 who toured the town, called at the homes of elderly people, entertained them with familiar songs and collected for the Red Cross. The photographs accompanying the article show the children in a variety of dress, from pyjamas to bow ties and top hats, and all with blackened faces.

To trace the event back further, some reliance must be placed on local informants such as John Buckingham,[6] who can recollect the event as far back as the 1940s in his own experience and by inference back to his parent's youth in the early part of the twenthieth-century. He recalls having his face blacked with burnt cork by his mother and being sent to sing for his grandmother. Another local informant, Malcolm McCarthy,[7] recalls other children of his age being taken 'darkying' by Mrs Magor in the 1960s and has a picture of his Great Grandmother blacked up with the mummers in 1936 for the Coronation celebrations. He is of the view that the tradition stems from a mummers' play: 'I believe that the mummers went from house to house performing their play and got fed up with the same old lines and tried out the new at that time Foster music hall songs. This was enjoyed and response probably favourable and the tradition took off in place of the mumming'.

A photograph in the Padstow archive dated circa 1900s has been cited as evidence of the antiquity of Padstow's mummers' day.[8] Malcolm McCarthy has an original of the photograph with the names identifying them as local people on the back. He is able to identify the location as Treator, one of the main places then visited by the 'Obby Oss' on May Day, and points out that the mummers may have followed a similar route. It is, however, possible that this was a photo portrait of local performers for a minstrel variety show, which were popular during this period: the Padstow Archive has posters of 'The Mississippi Minstrels' and other concert parties taking place during the early part of the twentieth century. Certainly, the clothing portrayed in the photograph seems more reminiscent of the top hats and embroidered clothing of Southern Minstrel imagery than guize dancing. From the information we have, it is difficult to be sure that this is a picture of the mummers but it does illustrate the wider contemporary popular culture that might have influenced the Padstow tradition.

Without documentary records, it is difficult to accurately date the origins of the 'Padstow Mummers' but the ubiquity of similar Christmas customs elsewhere in Cornwall provides a wider perspective and takes the tradition further back into antiquity. Jenkin described events during the period between Christmas Day and Twelfth Night in the villages around St Ives and Penzance. The villages were 'Nightly invaded by bands of young people attired in strange grotesque costume. In almost every case the boys are dressed as girls and the girls as boys, some cleverly representing historical or local characters, others merely disguised with blackened faces and Nottingham lace veils . . . but enjoying themselves as much as if they were frolicking under a midsummer sky'.[9] Jenkin's description could equally be applied to a photograph of Padstow May Day revellers circa 1910,[10] providing us with a link to the general phenomena of 'guize dancing'.

Hunt[11] described guize dancing on Plough Monday (first Monday after Twelfth day) in West Penwith: 'Maidens as young men, men for maidens. Thus dressed they visit neighbours . . . dance . . . make jokes . . . and the spirit of drollery and wit kept among the people. Music and dancing, they are kept with liquor then proceed to next house and carry on the same sport.' He went on to explain that 'geese dancing is done in nearly every town and large village. The term applied to all Christmas plays and indeed any kind of sport in which characters were assumed by performers or disguises worn'. This is born out by frequent references to guizing in Cornish local histories[12] and such publications as the *Old Cornwall* journal, together with its general use as a dialect word.[13] Jenkin's quotation from Robert Heath takes us back still further in time. In a

> description of Cornwall during the early part of the last [nineteenth] century the costume of the guise dancer consisted of an antique finery such as would now raise envy in the head of a collector. Male players were to be seen in long waisted, gay coloured coats, resplendent with buttons of brass or tin as large as crown pieces and having long ruffles at their breast and wrists . . . The chief glory of the men, however, lay in their cocked hats which were surmounted with streamers and ribbons.[14]

The significance of the time of year and the occurrence of the festival just after the midwinter solstice and just before Plough Monday, provides some justification for speculation that the origins of the festival may be very old indeed, and possibly pre-Christian. There is no historical evidence at the moment that can take this suggestion much further but it does enter into the meaning and mythology that has grown around the event: it has become 'an ancient tradition'.

The *Old Cornwall* journal provides two examples of 'Darky Songs' still in use for mummers' plays and midwinter guizing in Cornwall as late as the early twentieth century: 'Begone from the Window ' and 'The Derby Ram'. It is important to recognize that the Old Cornwall Society members who contributed to the journal made it clear that 'Darky' was a dialect contraction of 'Darking', and referred to the *activity* of blacking faces and not to either black people or a musical genre. There is no evidence of any significance in the different spelling of 'Darky' and 'Darkie', the latter being used by the local press. The songs are as follows:

BEGONE FROM THE WINDOW[15]

Begone from my window, my love, my Love my Love;
Begone from my window my dear.
For the wind and rain
Have brought him back again
And you'll get no lodging here

Begone from my window, my love, my Love my Love;
Begone from my window my dear.
The wind is in the west
And the cuckoo's in the nest
And you'll get no lodging here

Begone from my window, you rogue, you rogue, you rogue;
Begone from my window you hear.
For my wife I've proved untrue
So I throw her out to you
And you'll get no lodging here

The connection with black faces here is the cuckolding theme, and 'Darky' refers to the guizers who will serenade the guilty parties with a 'Shallal' (an infernal racket made with tins and anything noisy to hand).

DERBY RAM[16]

As I was going to Derby Sir,
Twas on a market day
I saw a fine ram sir,
As ever fed on hay

With my ringle dingle derby,
With my ringle dingle day
With my ringle dingle derby,
With my ringle dingle day

The latter was also known as a 'Darky Song' by John Buckingham,[17] but with 'Derby' being replaced by 'Padstow'; he also remembered variants of 'Old Daddy Fox' being mixed in with the words of the songs when sung.

OLD DADDY FOX[18]

Old Daddy Fox went out one night
When the moon and the stars did shine so bright
He went in to the old farmers yard

Where the geese and the ducks did quack so hard, hard
Where the geese and the ducks did quack so hard.

Old mother wigger wagger jumped out of bed
She down with the window and out with her head
Crying, Rise, Jack, rise, the grey goose is dead

And the fox is gone out of the town , town
And the fox is gone out of the town.

Out jumped the young one's eight, nine, ten
They licked up the goose no plate, knife or fork

And the young one picked all the bones, bones
And the young one picked all the bones

In an information sheet about the Padstow Mummers, made available from the Padstow Archive collection,[19] John Buckingham comments:

It would seem from remarks quoted in the local and national press that there is some confusion about the music used. This is understandable given the noisy nature of the performance and the fact that fragments from a number of songs have 'become one' in the evolution of this exuberant performance of street music . . . Some of the verses come from old folk songs but the majority were part of that body of popular music written for the Minstrel groups by composers such as Stephen Collins Foster (1826–1864). He wrote 'Swannee River', ' Oh Susannah', 'Camptown Races' and 'Uncle Ned, to mention a few of his most famous melodies.

There seems to be a complex process going on here, chaotic even, where celebrative behaviour is passed between generations, shared between communities, borrowed from other calendrical rituals, elaborated on and influenced by the popular customs, dress, music and dance of any given era.

PADSTOW MUMMERS 2005 AND 1983

Systematic collection of data by interviews or questionnaires concerning the attitudes and views of the Padstow Mummers' Day 2005 participants would have been impractical, intrusive and ethically questionable given the background of Police scrutiny that prevailed at the time. In order to gain further insight into the event, therefore, the author accepted an invitation to join the mummers, thus observing the event as a participant. In addition, two volunteers[20] were recruited to observe the event as bystanders and with whom to compare and record experiences. The description that follows draws on the experiences of these two observational routes.

On Boxing Day 2005 the revellers gradually collected together from about 10am in the morning at the Padstow Social Club. Most conversation was informal social exchange but there was some discussion of the concerns expressed about the event by the Police and recognition of the need to use the term 'Mummers' rather than 'Darkie', as well as caution about the type of costume worn. During a previous year someone had apparently turned up wearing a joke shop 'afro' wig, and this was felt by the revellers to be quite wrong and inappropriate. There was also a sense of anger at being misrepresented by people who knew little or nothing of an event that, from the revellers' perspective, involved no more than dressing up, community singing and collecting money for charity, an issue taken up by subsequent correspondents such as Malcolm McCarthy.[21]

Other than a consensus as to which accordionist should lead the music and the route from pub to pub, and some organizing of the collecting tins, there was no evidence of—and apparently no need for—any formal structure to the event. People simply gathered together, started up the music and when there was sufficient momentum, moved off in a roughly grouped procession to the next venue. About 60 people set off initially from the Social Club and the numbers varied during the day as people processed through the town. Stock costume involved blackened faces, top hats and dinner jackets adorned with ribbons, tinsel and a variety of colourful impedimenta. For many people dressing up clearly meant a blacked up face and festive decoration added to what ever they would normally have been wearing that day. Only two people were observed dressed in a way that would be exclusively associated with the southern minstrels: two women wearing brightly coloured headscarves. Conversely, there was certainly evidence of symbolism associated specifically with Cornwall —in the form of black-and-gold rugby shirts, Cornish tartan, and the St Piran's Flag.

The music was driven by a large number of accordions and May Day drums, providing an enveloping sound reminiscent of the Padstow May Day celebrations. The volume level was high and in excess of 80 decibels in the confined area of narrow streets and public houses. This is significant in that it reduces the importance of the words, which, as John Buckingham suggests, become muddled; it also encourages people to join in whether or not they know the words and can sing. A variety of music was used. 'Trelawny'—the Cornish 'national anthem' —certainly featured in the warm up sessions, and for the rest of the day the revellers ranged through a wide repertoire of community songs which included 'She'll becoming round the mountain', 'Scotland the Brave', 'Alabama' and 'Camptown Races', all to the same driving Padstow May Day rhythm.

It is interesting to summarize the general theme of explanations and justifications provided in casual conversation by participants and local traders:

- This is a local tradition that has gone on for a long time
- The custom has merged with other things over the years and any offensive language associated with minstrel songs has been removed
- It's just face painting and dressing up in funny costume
- It is a fertility rite for midwinter
- It is something to do with miners or people black with coal dust from the cargo ships
- A slave ship was wrecked off Padstow and the villagers blacked up to confuse the slavers and help the slaves escape

At a more subjective level, the observation of two 'others' can also offer different insights into the 'Padstow Mummers' tradition . The first is the 'significant other' of post-modernism, and the second is that of the more experiential 'other self' with whom participants engage as part of the tradition.

From the perspective of rural studies, Murdoch and Pratt define the 'significant other' as 'those regarded as in some way illegitimate members of society as a result of a variety of social characteristics such as being gay, a single parent, a traveller, a black person and so on'.[22] Leaving aside for the moment the blackened faces, the observers witnessed no activity or language that they would have perceived as demeaning of any racial or ethnic minority group. There was, however, an impression that by their physical domination of space in the streets, and especially the pubs, the people of Padstow were claiming back their own territory from the 'other': the 'other' being 'tourists' and 'second homers'. But even here the boundaries were by no means clear cut: the ironic question was whether we should add to Murdoch and Pratt's 'significant other' list the middle-class incomers who had settled in Padstow, or whether they were potentially legitimate mummers themselves. As well as being a factor in resistance to outside inter-ference, the mummers' day was also a powerful attraction for all those who wished to participate in the sense of community, continuity, belonging and tradition. But within this complexity, one thing was quite clear: black people were not identified as the 'other'.

The 'experiential other' is the 'other of carnival', a perhaps less tangible category but one that connects firmly to the sense of belonging and tradition. Dressing up in bizarre fashion encourages revellers to step into an alternative persona and enhances the sense of carnival. The relaxation of inhibitions encourages engagement with the music and atmosphere of the event, further supported by the reassur-ance that individual contribution will be balanced out by the overall sound.

Although observed without contemporaneous notes, it is also useful to recall broad details of the same event when visited much earlier, during the Christmas period of 1983. There were no more than 15 or 20 people involved and the costume was less extravagant, with a tendency towards waistcoats rather than dinner jackets, but the same principle of random festive decoration with ribbons and tinsel applied. Some faces were roughly blacked with burnt cork but, unlike 2005, a number of people had taken advantage of grease paint to emulate the BBC's 'Black and White Minstrels' with white circles around the eyes and red lip-stick. As in 2005, the music was driven by May Day style accordions and percussion, and in confined spaces was fairly loud. The repertoire of music used drew largely from what might be termed 'minstrels' music.

THE 'PADSTOW DEBATE'

In January 1998 the *North Cornwall Advertiser* newspaper ran an item on Padstow's Darkie Day which was picked up by the national press and drew the attention of the late Bernie Grant MP (Labour). He actively campaigned to have the festival stopped, making the comment that he thought the days of white people dressing up as black people were long gone. There was considerable local anger at the time that Mr Grant had never attended the event himself and was making assumptions without any real knowledge or evidence. The participants felt strongly that their activities gave no cause for offence and that they should not be subject to outside interference.[23]

Following a complaint, the police attended the event on Boxing Day 2004 and collected video evidence for submission to the Crown Prosecution Service. The Cornwall Council for Racial Equality denied making the complaint but confirmed that concerns had been expressed to the Police previously.[24] This was again picked up by both the local and the national press,[25] which pursued the theme of an ancient custom falling foul of contemporary social mores. In the event the Crown Prosecution Service decided not to proceed with a prosecution, and Devon and Cornwall Police responded with the offer: 'Looking ahead to the 2005–06 celebrations, the police would welcome working with organisers of the celebrations and partners in order to continue the positive steps taken already.'[26]

At one level the 'Padstow debate' is quite simple, and is about whether an offence has been committed within the meaning of the relevant legislation.[27] The response of the Crown Prosecution service to this question in 2005 would seem to be that no prosecution was warranted. On another level it is far more problematical and brings us into the wider debate of what we mean by 'race' and what constitutes a 'racist incident'. Under the Race Relations Act 1976 'racial discrimination' means treating a person less favourably than others on racial grounds—meaning race, colour, nationality or ethnic or national origins. The Stephen Lawrence Inquiry Report[28] defines a racist incident as any incident which is perceived to be racist by the victim or any other person. By these definitions, any observer perceiving the blackened faces of the Padstow mummers as demeaning of black people, and therefore racist, turns the event into a 'racist incident': whatever the intentions of the mummers themselves.

The 'Padstow debate' reached new heights recently when Diane Abbott MP (Labour) picked up Bernie Grant's baton and proceeded

with an Early Day Motion in Parliament at Westminster. The Early
Day Motion declared:

> That this House notes with great relief the decision finally to
> abolish the century-old Cornish festival of Darkie Day where
> locals traditionally black-up with charcoal, wear Afro-wigs
> and perform minstrel songs; is not satisfied however that the
> decision of some locals to go ahead with the event merely
> replacing the word 'nigger' with 'mummer' in the traditional
> songs is sufficient for curbing incitement of racial hatred;
> further notes with concern that the event is still being
> advertised as a tourist attraction by the website Cornish Light;
> and calls on the Government to discourage any repeat of this
> event.[29]

Ms Abbott's Early Day Motion is inaccurate on several counts.
The tradition is more than one hundred years old, the 'afro' wigs are
not part of this tradition, and it is the word 'darkie' (not 'nigger') that
has been replaced with 'mummer'. This replacement was on the advice
of the Police and was made in recognition of the changed meaning and
negative connotations of the term 'darkie' in modern English usage,
compared to Cornish dialect. Furthermore, there is a presumption that
'minstrel' music is integral to the tradition. In fact, it is community
singing that is integral to the tradition, and some of this community
singing may include songs of 'minstrel' origin. In preparation for this
article, a letter was sent to Ms Abbott providing her with the background to the events at Padstow on Boxing day, pointing out that
traditions of this kind take place all over the U.K. and asking how she
would respond to criticism that in selecting Padstow she was guilty of
provincial stereotyping. No reply was received but a copy sent to the
local North Cornwall MP, Dan Rogerson (Liberal Democrat), elicited
the following response: '[I] completely agree with what you have to
say and was pleased to air my displeasure that Ms Abbott chose
to criticise local people without taking the trouble to investigate the
reality. Sadly this issue will be periodically raised by someone in search
of publicity no doubt.'
   The first element of the 'Padstow debate' is, therefore, the accusa-
tion that the festival is either in breach of the Law by inciting racial
hatred or is a racist incident on the basis that it is perceived as such by
a victim or other person. This position is not supported by detailed
research into the intentions and attitudes of the participants, nor into
the history of the event, and—it might be argued—is one driven by
desire for publicity and political interest

Participants are quite unequivocal in their position that 'Padstow Mummers' is not an event that sets out to demean or offend anyone. Malcolm McCarthy[30] comments: 'We as a group are not going out to intimidate or offend anyone. I personally, if I see a coloured person go and speak to them to put them at ease, not that they seem worried, and have never had any problems or complaints.' This is typical of the responses received by the author from other participants during the day and from participants quoted in local press coverage or contributing to the letters columns. The point is made that 'Mummers' must be seen in the context of Padstow, that there is no significant black minority group living in the area, and that efforts are made to explain the custom and reassure any black people—resident or visiting—that it is not intended to be demeaning or to offend.

An important element of the debate is the use of minstrel songs, a *genre* of music represented by the compositions of Stephen Foster, an American music hall performer of the 1830s. There are three issues here; was minstrel music originally conceived within a racist context, are the songs from this *genre* that entered the community singing repertoire racially demeaning today and lastly, is minstrel music an integral to the Padstow mumming tradition or an incidental part of a community singing repertoire?

Cockrell[31] discusses the origins of black-faced minstrels in some detail and challenges the assumption that it was necessarily rooted in racial derogation:

> What I have wanted to do here is, in part, undercut the tired old story that black-faced minstrelsy is about unrelenting hatred of blacks by working class urban white males, for I believe that interpretation to be ahistorical. It ascribes meaning without understanding context, nor even human nature. It does not seek an ethnography of audience. Who were the people in the Bowery Theatre? How did they come to be there, what did they bring with them? For some in that theatre, I do not doubt that hatred and racism formed bedrock. For some, though, probably most, the basic impulse was simply toward entertainment. Most emphatically we must not underestimate this fundamental human need, and dump and bury post-haste the long standing conceit that entertainment is merely cultural detritus.[32]

Cockrell is not without his critics. Christgau,[33] for example, suggests that he is being overly romantic in his view but nevertheless accepts that the southern minstrels as a music *genre* had a variety of influences and interpretations. But even if this musical *genre* was originally conceived within a context that demeaned black people it does not mean that it continues within this context in a different time and a different culture, as Frith[34] show us: 'The problem here is not just the familiar postmodern point that we live in an age of plunder in which musics made in one place for one reason can be immediately appropriated in another place for quite another reason, but also that while music may be shaped by the people who first make it and use it, as experience it has a life of it's own.' As the songs of Foster have entered into the community repertoire, so the words, music and style have been modified by successive generations losing much of their original significance and meaning. Furthermore, it is not possible to enter into, let alone record, the experience of each individual engaging in a community singing event. However, we have seen already seen from the description of Padstow mummers day that the words are negotiable and are likely to play but a small part in the overall experience of a big musical and rhythmic sound.

Although there has clearly been a flirtation with 'minstrel' music by the Padstow mummers, the extent to which this is integral to the nature of the event is, as we have seen, questionable. In 2005 the proportion of clearly identifiable minstrel songs in comparison to 1983 was greatly diminished, without any noticeable impact upon the event. There is some discussion about the date at which minstrel music may have entered into the style and repertoire of community singing employed by the mummers music, and although it is the authors view that this may be as recent as the 1950s and 1960s, some of the participants felt it is much earlier. The fact remains, however, that minstrel music is a relatively recent influence on a much older tradition in Padstow, and an influence that in 2005 had already faded significantly.

A cover story in the magazine *Cornwall Today* in June 1998, entitled 'Welcomed by One and All' responded to Mr Grant's criticism and illustrated what might be described as a wider populist position in the ' Padstow debate'. The story cites examples of two black families with an essentially positive experience of living in Cornwall, before going on to describe Padstow Darkie Day:

> Earlier this year the Campaign for Racial Equality in Cornwall added its voice to a claim by Bernie Grant that the centuries old custom of Darkie Day at Padstow was racist and evil. On Boxing Day and New Years Day each year town's folk 'black up' and perform slave songs for charity. The event is thought to stem from the days when slave ships sheltered

from storms in the camel estuary and the slaves were allowed to come Ashore and sing and dance on the quay. Padstow people were astonished and bemused by the modern day storm, which erupted over what they genuinely believed to be a harmless old custom. 'Racism has never been thought of or meant' declared mayor Alec Rickard and this town's only black resident, Ziggy Holder, added 'As far as I am concerned there is nothing to complain about'.

There appear to be no shipping records to support the slave ship story. It was in evidence on Boxing Day 2005 and regularly appears in newspaper reports,[35] although only as something to be discounted. It was also an explanation for the event noted from Padstow residents who were casual bystanders in 2005. As a myth which has grown up around the tradition, however, it still serves to illustrate the desire of those involved both as participants and audience to justify the event and to demonstrate innocent intentions.

The 'Padstow Debate' has implications for other British traditions, and the issue was pursued in an *English Dance and Song*[36] which considered the implications for English Morris dancing. It seems that forty years ago the only group to black up were the Britannia Coconut Dancers from Bacup, who have since been joined by a number of other Morris sides, especially from the Welsh Border and Molly traditions, apparently encouraged by Cecil Sharp's assertion that Morris dancers from earlier times had blacked their faces. Cecil Sharp and his fellow revivalist were clear that 'the faces were not blackened because the dancers represented Moors, but rather the dancers were thought to represent Moors because their faces were blackened'. The article concludes with comments from a number of contributors, but a Morris dancer by the name of Elaine Bradtke sums up the argument nicely: 'Being a multi-cultural society means tolerating each other's differences, and that includes the customs of the indigenous culture. If something is truly offensive to the general public, its popularity would make it untenable.'

CONCLUSION
In summary, then, the origins of the Padstow mummers can be traced back to the 1800s, with some justification for speculation about much earlier roots. The blackened faces are part of this early tradition and are customary disguise rather than a deliberate depiction of black people. The music/songs used have changed over time and reflect popular culture in terms of community singing. The popularity of minstrel songs within the community singing repertoire in the

mid-twentieth century resulted in these being included in the music for the Padstow Mummers. By 2005 there was much less emphasis on minstrel music, partly in response to concerns about offence which might be taken and but also reflecting the natural evolution of the tradition and popular community singing repertoire.

The 'Padstow debate' polarises between the position that the event is offensive to black people and the position that any offensive interpretation is based on misunderstanding and poor information concerning the background of the event and the attitudes and intentions of the participants. The popular response to the debate reflected in news items and the letters pages of local newspapers presents a 'common sense' position wherein the event is innately innocent and where concerns are expressed about a 'nanny state' and excessive 'political correctness'.

The legal definitions of race and racism, together with evidence to suggest that a significant number of people in Cornwall would describe their ethnicity as specifically 'Cornish',[37] allows for an interesting 'thought experiment' and adds a further dimension to this debate. Suppose a person identifying their ethnicity as Cornish were to complain that the overly enthusiastic brandishing of English Flags in Cornwall during the 'World Cup' summer of 2006 was confrontational, offensive, and therefore racist. It is reasonable to suggest that the reaction of most people would be that this was 'political correctness' out of control and that the intention of the perpetrators was simply to have a good time and to celebrate a football match at the expense of no-one. This, of course, is much the point being made by the supporters of the Padstow Mummers tradition.

The 'Padstow debate' is part of a much wider debate about diversity in modern Britain and what happens when cultural expression in one group is found to be offensive by another. For celebration of diversity to function effectively as a philosophy promoting a healthy society it must be seen to treat all groups equally, and risks being discredited if it appears not to do this. In the Padstow Mummers, we have a tradition which intends no harm or offence, and has modified its language to accommodate changes in word meaning which might result in offence being taken. Any campaign to discourage or ban the event is likely to discredit the ethos of diversity in the mind of many people, and to confirm the view of the mummers that they are misunderstood and misrepresented.

NOTES AND REFERENCES

1. BBC West Region programme, broadcast 5 Jan. 1935, by A.K. Hamilton Jenkin, describes geese dancing and gives instruction on pronouncing s as 'z'. Transcript in Cornwall Centre Library.
2. English Dialect Society, Glossary of words used in Cornwall: Goosey Dance—Burlesque sport on a Christmas eve.
3. A.K. Hamilton Jenkin, *Cornwall And Its People*, London, 1945, p. 249: a band of infernal music with kettles, drums and tea trays.
4. W. Bottrell, *Traditions and Hearthside stories of West Cornwall*, Penzance, 1870, p. 226: The mummers Play of St George and The Turkish Knight is described as a guise dance.
5. *Padstow Echo*, Jan. 1967, p. 30.
6. Interviewed by the author in Feb. 2006 and showed around the Padstow museum and archive. John Buckingham is a local Historian and a trustee of the Padstow archive who has lived in the town all his life and taken a special interest in the Boxing Day/New Years Day traditions of the town.
7. Correspondence with the author in February/March 2006. Malcolm McCarthy belongs to one of the families that lead the event and is a regular participant himself.
8. Photograph Padstow Archive, 'Padstow Minstrels circa 1900'.
9. Jenkin, p. 422. Hamilton Jenkin was a Celtic revivalist and contemporary of Morton Nance, appearing as the Turkish Knight in at least one of his mummer's plays. He refers to Hunt (see below) as well as drawing on oral history through the St Ives and other Old Cornwall Societies.
10. Photograph from Padstow Archive 'May Day Fishermen circa 1910'.
11. Robert Hunt, *Popular Romances of the West of England*, 3rd edition, 1881, p. 392.
12. For example, S.W. Paynter, *Old St Ives, The Reminiscences of William Paynter*, St Ives, 1927, p. 46. Published in 1927, recording memories from 1850.
13. William Sandys, *Specimens of Provincial Dialect*, n.d.
14. Jenkin, 1945, p. 424.
15. *Old Cornwall* Society Magazine, April 1927, pp. 14–15, from singing of Jas Thomas.
16. *Old Cornwall* Society Magazine, Vol. 3, 16, collected by M.H.N. Cuthbert from Joseph Sweet of St Neot and William Pearn of Altarnon in 1934.
17. Interviewed 20 March 2006.
18. St Ives Old Cornwall Society, word sheet from the Old Cornwall Society Festival 1954, Royal Cornwall Museum, Courtney Library.
19. Padstow Archive, Padstow Institute.
20. Ash Fahy and Jowdy Davey. Ash has a professional background in law, little experience of folk traditions but familiar with the multicultural ethos he has grown with in London. Jowdy—my daughter, has a professional arts background and familiar with Cornish traditional music and dance.
21. Malcolm McCarthy, correspondence with the author 6 April 2006.
22. J. Murdoch and A.C. Pratt, 'Strange Ruralities', in P. Cloke and J. Little (eds), *Contested Countryside Cultures*, Routledge, London 1997, p. 53.

23. Delf, Ray. Correspondence and discussion 16 December 2005.
24. Alastair Wreford, *Cornish Guardian*, 3 March 2005.
25. Simon De Bruxelles, *The Times*, 25 February 2005; Richard Savill, *Daily Telgraph*, 25 February 2005; Peter Allen, *Daily Mail*, 25 February 2005; also local press: *Cornish Guardian*, 30 December 2004, 3 March 2005; *Western Morning News*, 15 March 2005.
26. Story from BBC NEWS: http://news.bbc.co.uk Published 3 October 2005.
27. The main body of legislation here is the Public Order Act 1986 with some amendments resulting from the Crime and Disorder Act 1998. Section 17 of the public Order Act defines Racial Hatred as 'hatred against a group of persons defined by reference to colour, race, nationality (including citizenship) or ethnic or national origins'. With regard to public performance section 20 describes as an offence the use of threatening, abusive or insulting words or behaviour with an intention to stir up racial hatred.
28. Available on the Home Office Website www.homeoffice.gov.uk
29. EDM 1317 Cornish Festival of Darkie Day, 9 January 2006.
30. Malcolm McCarthy, correspondence with the author, 6 April 2006.
31. Dale Cockrell, *Demons of Disorder: Early Black Faced Minstrels and Their World*, Cambridge, 1997. Detailed exploration of the European and African American influences on the development of the black-faced minstrel music hall genre and its social context.
32. Cockrell, p. 162.
33. Robert Christou, 'In Search of Jim Crow—Why Modern Minstrelsy Studies Matter', *The Believer*, February 2004, published on website: wwwrobertchristgau.com/xg/music/minstrel-bel.php
34. Simon Frith, 'Music and Identity', in Hall and du Gay (eds), *Cultural Identity*, London, 1996, p. 109.
35. Simon De Bruxelles, *The Times* 25 February 2005; Richard Savill, *The Telegraph* 25 February 2005; Peter Allen, *Daily Mail* 25 February 2005, also local press: *Cornish Guardian* 30 December 2004, 3 March 2005, *Western Morning News* 15 March 2005.
36. Derek Schofield, *English Dance and Song—the Magazine of the English Folk Dance and Song Society*, Summer 2005, page 12 and front cover.
37. Philipa Aldous and Malcolm Williams, 'A Question of Ethnic Identity', in Philip Payton (ed.), *Cornish Studies: Eleven*, Exeter, 2002, p. 217; in a survey of school children in Cornwall 29.2 per cent self-defined as 'Cornish'.

NOTES ON CONTRIBUTORS

Graham Busby is Senior Lecturer in Tourism Management at the Plymouth Business School, University of Plymouth. A native of Cornwall, he is interested in the development of Cornish tourism and has undertaken empirical research at the Daphne du Maurier Festival and with regard to visitors to the Cornish church heritage.

Terry Chapman was recently awarded the degree of Doctor of Philosophy for his thesis on 'The National Dock Labour Scheme in Cornwall', researched and written at the Institute of Cornish Studies, University of Exeter. A former Royal Navy officer, he continues in retirement to examine post-war UK national policies in the local Cornish context.

Merv Davey is a mature part-time postgraduate student at the Institute of Cornish Studies, University of Exeter. He has had a life-long interest in Cornish song and dance, and is author of *Hengan*—a book widely recognized as the classic introduction to traditional Cornish music.

Bernard Deacon is Senior Lecturer in Cornish Studies at the Institute of Cornish Studies, University of Exeter (Cornwall Campus), where he is Programme Director for the degree of Master of Arts in Cornish Studies. He is the author of numerous publications, including *Mebyon Kernow and Cornish Nationalism* (2003) (with Dick Cole and Garry Tregidga) and *The Cornish Family* (2004).

Gemma Goodman is a postgraduate student at the University of Warwick. Her research interest is in the relationship between literature and anthropology, with a particular reference to 'insider' and 'outsider' constructions of Cornwall.

Patrick Laviolette is Post-Doctoral Fellow in the Department of Anthropology and the Bartlett School of Graduate Studies, University College London. He is interested in how cultural perceptions of Cornwall's landscapes act as metaphors of 'difference' and social distinction. Other research interests include the embodiment of extreme sports, recycled art, housing co-operatives, hitch-hiking, fairy-lore, and the domestication of assistive technology.

Jim Lewis was born in Liskeard, Cornwall, and spent a life-time in banking. In 1989 he returned to Cornwall to manage Lloyds Bank in Newquay. He is a specialist on eighteenth- and nineteenth-century Cornish economic and mining history, and among his publications is *A Richly Yielding Piece of Ground: A History of Fowey Consols Mine from 1813 to 1867* (1997).

Ronald Perry is former Head of Management at Cornwall College at Pool, between Camborne and Redruth, now one of the Combined Universities in Cornwall partnership institutions. He has written extensively on the economic history of Cornwall, especially in the Edwardian era, and has made a major contribution to our under-standing of the socio-economic condition of modern Cornwall.

Matthew Spriggs is Professor of Archaeology and Director of the Centre for Archaeological Research at the Australian National University in Canberra. Descended from the Cornish Spriggs, who are now sadly extinct in Cornwall, he has long had an interest in the social history of the Cornish language, as well as in Southeast Asian and Pacific archaeology.

Charles Thurlow lives in St Austell, where he is owner and director of the publishing firm 'Cornish Hillside'. A well-known publishing house in Cornwall, 'Cornish Hillside' has been responsible for the publication of a string of Cornish titles, many on mining themes, including the reappearance of several Cornish 'classics'.

Nicholas J.A. Williams is Associate Professor of Irish and Celtic at University College Dublin. He has written extensively on the Celtic languages, including Cornish, of which he is acknowledged as a leading international specialist, and he is co-editor with Graham Thomas of *Bewnans Ke/The Life of St Kea: A Critical Edition with Translation* (University of Exeter Press, forthcoming, 2007).

Briar Wood is Senior Lecturer in English and Creative Writing at London Metropolitan University. Her teaching interests encompass Postcolonial Theory and Feminism and Women's Writing, and her research activities include Comparative Literatures and Women's Writing. Her Cornish ancestors emigrated to New Zealand from Penzance in 1874.